THE GREATEST THREAT

IRAQ,

WEAPONS OF MASS DESTRUCTION,

AND THE CRISIS OF GLOBAL SECURITY

RICHARD BUTLER

 PublicAffairs NEW YORK

Published in the United States by PublicAffairs™,
a member of the Perseus Books Group.

PublicAffairs books are available at special discounts for bulk
purchases in the U.S. by corporations, institutions, and other
organizations. For more information, please contact the Special
Markets Department at The Perseus Books Group, 11 Cambridge
Center, Cambridge MA 02142, or call (617) 252–5298.

Book design by Jenny Dossin.

Library of Congress Cataloging-in-Publication Data
Butler, Richard, 1942–
    The greatest threat : Iraq, weapons of mass destruction, and
the growing crisis of global security / by Richard Butler
        p.   cm.
    Includes index
    ISBN 1-58648-039-1 (pb)
        1. United Nations. Special Commission on Iraq.
2. Iraq—Military policy.   3. Weapons of mass destruction—
Iraq.   4. Arms control—Verification—Iraq.   5. Security,
International.   6. World politics—1989–   I. Title.

DS79.755.B88 2000
327.1'745'09567—DC21

                                                    00-029098

10 9 8 7 6 5 4 3 2 1

To Barbara, my beloved wife

CONTENTS

The only thing necessary for the triumph
of evil is for good men to do nothing.
—EDMUND BURKE

PREFACE TO THE NEW EDITION

The Greatest Threat is a record of the incomplete attempt by the United Nations Security Council to disarm Saddam Hussein of his weapons of mass destruction in the aftermath of the 1991 Persian Gulf War. The last action by the Security Council was taken in December 1999, when it established the successor arms control organization, UNMOVIC, to the one I headed, UNSCOM. As of this writing, the new UNMOVIC inspectors have yet to visit Iraq.

Much has happened in the past two years but nothing has been done to restore control over Saddam's weapons. Indeed, supported by his lucrative and growing black market oil exports, the crumbling of sanctions, and with assistance from a variety of countries—including permanent members of the Security Council who knowingly broke the law they made—Saddam is back in the business of developing nuclear weapons. (Iraqi defectors say he already has them.) He has also extended the range of his missiles and manufactured chemical and biological weapons.

The subtitle of this book includes the notion of "the crisis of global security." That crisis is upon us now. The authority of the Security Council has been thwarted by the dictator of Iraq who is now posturing to lead an Arab intervention in Israel, presumably with his weapons of mass destruction.

The United States had led the resistance to Saddam starting with the Gulf War, yet the Clinton administration took no serious action after December 1999 to restore arms control in Iraq. The new administration of President George W. Bush is now in search of an Iraq policy. Its task has been made all the more difficult by the events of the last two years, proving that postponement of a solution to a serious problem only makes it harder to solve.

Saddam's propaganda on the impact of sanctions on ordinary Iraqi's has been brilliantly successful. As it draws attention away from the brutal reality that he is responsible for their imposition and retention, his regime and military both profit from the food and medicines supplied under the UN arrangements for the Iraqi people and restrict its availability.

Saddam now has an extensive, worldwide constituency—including in western countries—for the unconditional removal of sanctions. Many argue that the relative danger Iraq poses is no worse than other countries seeking weapons of mass destruction or other situations of equal or greater political concern in the Balkans, in Africa, between India and Pakistan, and between Israel and Palestine. While there are other lamentable situations in the world, justifying inaction on a wretched situation by pointing to other serious concerns is deplorable

To these practical realities must be added the growing unease that is developing about the uses to which the sole superpower, the United States, will put its unprecedented reach and strength. This too is an important element of the environment in which the new administration must find its Iraq policy.

For that policy to be effective, if should be founded on a few fundamental principles: the spread of weapons of mass destruction must be contained; Saddam's regime, which according to the UN human rights rapporteur has the worst human rights record since Hitler's Nazi Germany, is not one which should be given any comfort, especially from permanent members of the Security Council; and a stop has to be put to members of the Security Council acting outside the Council to undermine its authority and decisions.

The United States would make a difference if it elevated such principles to the level of major priorities, both in its Iraq policy and in its relations with other concerned countries. Only by taking such a principled stand will its policy have a chance of success and, also, answer the charges of arrogance or of unilateral abuse of its great power. In practical terms, the U.S. would insist on the restoration of international arms control in Iraq, target sanctions directly at military exports to Iraq, and make stronger efforts to alleviate the oppression of the Iraqi people by Saddam. The Iraqi people need and deserve a government prepared to act in their interest and efforts to bring such a government into existence should be supported.

Iraq would be able to defeat such policies only if the U.S. is unable to restore consensus first in the Security Council and then amongst the countries most affected by Saddam's military and political aspirations. Iraq would not be able to persist in its actions, which continue to threaten the world, directly and through terrorist surrogates, if such a consensus is rebuilt.

Beyond this, it remains necessary to establish a reliable means of enforcing key arms control obligations against rogue states. This too, should be a major objective of the Bush administration, more important than attempting to build a defensive shield against the likes of Saddam. Such prevention would be more effective than the proposed cure, the reliability of which is uncertain and the consequences of which may be to foster a new arms race amongst nuclear weapon states. Saddam's shadow over our history would then truly lengthen.

RICHARD BUTLER
MARCH 2001

ACKNOWLEDGMENTS

VERY MANY PEOPLE deserve thanks and recognition for the part they have played in this book and, far beyond that, over the years in their work in arms control and disarmament and for the help and friendship they have given me. Some of them are named in the text that follows but, of necessity, not all. I thank them all and hope they will stay the course and stay well.

At this point, my deepest gratitude goes to the men and women of United Nations Special Commission, all of them. Their work for UNSCOM and the sacrifices they made were unique. That they were treated wrongly in the end was a product of flawed politics. History will do them justice. It was the greatest privilege of my professional life to have worked with them. And I will never forget their friendship and solidarity.

This book was prepared at the Council on Foreign Relations, New York, the place I went to as Diplomat in Residence when my time at UNSCOM ended. The president of the Council, Les Gelb, offered me that place, for which I was and remain deeply grateful. Les and the organization he and its chairman, Pete Peterson, brilliantly lead deserve its recognition as the premier institution for the study of international relations and security issues, certainly in the English-speaking world.

The Council on Foreign Relations houses the journal *Foreign Affairs*, also a product which has no equal. I am indebted to its editor, James Hoge, for his advice, assistance, and comments on my manuscript.

My writing project and my place at the Council has been directly supported by the generosity of: Joseph H. Flom, Yue-Sai Kan, Stephen M. Kellen, The Albert Kunstadter Family Foundation, Mr. and Mrs.

Leonard A. Lauder, Ronald Lauder, Nina Rosenwald, Paul and Daisy Soros, Donald and Barbara Tober, Stanley A. Weiss, Ezra Zilkha, and Mortimer B. Zuckerman. I thank them for their faith in me and this project. I hope its result will not disappoint them. Their support was crucial.

Also, at the Council and as a consequence of the financial support to which I have just referred, I was provided with a research assistant, Leonardo Arriola, a recent master's graduate from the Woodrow Wilson School at Princeton University. Leo worked tirelessly with me in the research and preparation of the manuscript. He is a fine product of the United States and his Mexican family, gifted with intelligence, civility, and humor. I am certain we will all hear much more of him in the future.

Writing a book, in contrast to the speeches and documents that were the stuff of my career as a diplomat, was a new task for me and not easy. The way was smoothed through the assistance of the remarkable Karl Weber, whose clear sight of language and ideas is extraordinary. He was generously provided to me by my publisher, PublicAffairs, the head of which, Peter Osnos, and senior editor Geoff Shandler, played their part in preparing this book at the highest levels of their craft.

Something of a leap of faith was required from others in their agreement to support this book, and key among those who made that leap were my literary agent Amanda Urban of International Creative Management and Lord Weidenfeld of Weidenfeld and Nicolson, London.

Among those who read my drafts and whose critical judgment made a difference were: Dr. Rachel Bronson, Olin Fellow for National Security Studies, Council on Foreign Relations, New York, whose extensive consideration of the draft was immensely helpful; Jacqueline Shire, a former officer of the U.S. State Department and UNSCOM; and the remarkable A. M. Rosenthal, whose distinguished career at the *New York Times* spanned fifty-five years and who is widely regarded as having shaped the modern form of the newspaper during the fifteen years in which he was its managing editor. Former Deputy Executive Chairman of UNSCOM, Charles Duelfer, also offered useful comments.

Early and hard work in physically preparing the original drafts was done by Fiona Gosschalk, a young Australian woman who had given wonderful assistance to my wife and me when I was Australian ambassador to the United Nations.

My family's resettlement from official to private life in New York was generously facilitated by Mr. Lewis Rudin. We thank him.

I am grateful for the protection given me by the security officers of the United Nations, led by their chief, Mike McCann. Two of those officers, in particular, were close to me and deserve my special thanks and recognition: Dennis Grimm and Moataz Mohamed Khalil.

I thank the members of my family, especially my wife and children, for their loving support and forbearance during the UNSCOM period. My father was always very worried about my safety while I was in Iraq. In that sense he probably came to share the Russian view, although for his own reasons, that it was best that I stop doing it. My mother, who in 1983 cried when I was made Australian Ambassador for Disarmament, explaining that her tears were not because I'd been made an ambassador, but because it was *for disarmament*; she had no fears for my safety in Iraq because she was then deep into Alzheimer's disease. She is now at peace.

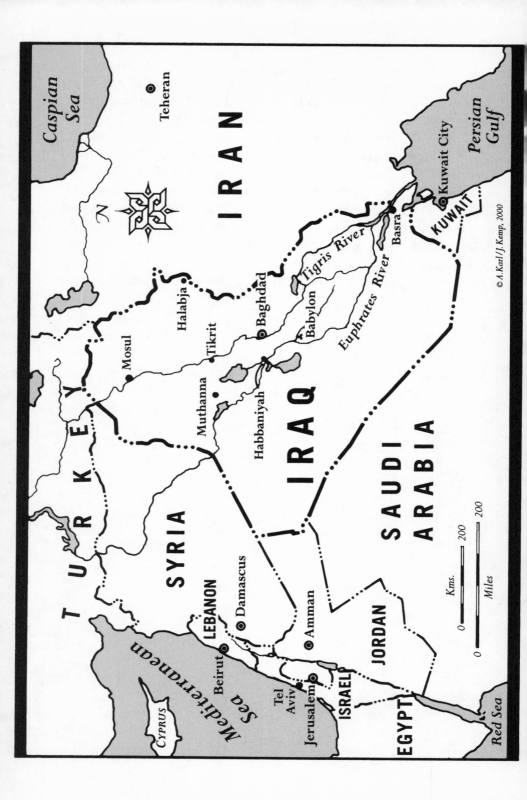

© A.Karl / J.Kemp, 2000

INTRODUCTION

THE GREATEST THREAT to life on earth is weapons of mass destruction—nuclear, chemical, biological.

These weapons do not exist in nature. They have been made by man, generally as the result of sophisticated research and complex, costly processes. Ironically, they are the product of some of the highest science, knowledge that should be applied to saving life rather than ending it.

The community of nations has recognized this threat; indeed, perhaps its most important achievement in the second half of the twentieth century was the weaving of a tapestry of treaties designed to contain and then eliminate it. This work was never easy, and its implementation has been challenged repeatedly. The most determined and diabolical of such challenges has been that mounted by the dictator of Iraq—Saddam Hussein.

For almost two decades, he has sought to acquire these weapons and the means of their delivery. In most cases, he has been successful and even took the further step of actually using them. This included their use against the people of Iraq. He shares with Adolf Hitler the infamy of having used chemicals for genocidal purposes.

Ten years ago, in response to this challenge to law and civilization, the community of nations isolated Iraq and imposed upon it stringent requirements for the removal of its weapons of mass destruction. That effort produced some good results, but it was opposed, root and branch, by Saddam. Every step in disarmament, every discovery and destruction of weapons and the means to make them, was achieved in the face of Iraqi concealment, deception, lying, and threats. The result is that, notwithstanding the massive amount of time and resources that were devoted to this job, it is not known, accurately, what capability for making and using weapons of mass destruction Saddam retains.

This lamentable fact is mirrored in the politics that has enabled Saddam to succeed in his defiance of international law.

Three permanent members of the Security Council of the United Nations—the lawmaker and enforcer in this field—have decided to end any serious effort to disarm Saddam, to oblige him to conform with the law. Russia, France, and China have done this because they prefer to pursue their own national interests rather than to carry out their international responsibility.

Also, in 1998, at a key moment of extreme defiance by Saddam, the secretary-general of the United Nations, in many respects the guardian of the law, sought to solve the crisis through diplomatic means substantially disconnected from the matters of substance—weapons of mass destruction and the authority of international law.

In addition, during my time at UNSCOM, members of the Security Council increasingly sought to shift political responsibility to me for their failure to enforce their own law. They asked me to make judgments about the threat posed by Iraq, an issue well beyond my mandate and one that they alone could settle. When I pointed out that they were asking me the wrong question, they resented it. When I gave them the facts as I knew them and for which I was competent and responsible, if they didn't like these facts, they joined Iraq in charging that UNSCOM, not Iraq, was the problem.

Nowhere in my mandate was it stated that I should decide on or recommend military action. But in November 1998, the Security Council instructed me to produce a factual report on Iraqi compliance against a background where, if my report showed Iraq was not in compliance, there was likely to be military action by the United States and Britain. My job was to report on the disarmament facts. I did so and military action followed, in December 1998.

It could be argued that I should have deciphered the political code: report negatively on Iraq's conduct and there will be war; if you don't want that, don't report negatively; this is not about facts, it's about politics.

I "read" the code, thought long and hard about it, and decided to report the facts because to do otherwise would have involved revising the record of the preceding seven years of work on disarming Iraq; and what was at issue was truly serious—weapons that remained unaccounted for.

At one stage in discussing the problems surrounding my December 1998 report, I explained to Secretary-General Annan that among my concerns was a situation in which we came to terms with the political demands to declare Iraq disarmed only to see, say a year later, the launch of a prohibited Iraqi missile. This would be a disaster as such and for the UN. We must stick to the facts. He seemed to agree.

The important aspect of this shabby passage of events is what it has revealed about the state of high international politics today. In addition to setting the record straight, this book suggests a way in which those politics may be changed in order to address the unique threat to humanity posed by weapons of mass destruction.

Saddam seized the opportunity these political machinations presented. He cut and ran, returning to the business at hand: building up a terrifying arsenal of weapons of mass destruction.While the full nature and scope of his current programs cannot be known *precisely* because of the absence of inspections and monitoring, it would be foolish in the extreme not to assume that he is developing long-range missile capability, at work again on building nuclear weapons, and adding to the chemical and biological warfare weapons he concealed during the UNSCOM inspection period. This reflects his track record, capabilities and intentions, and the scattered evidence that continues to emerge outside Iraq.

The failure to complete the task of disarming Saddam and the politics on which it has rested—including the failure of the Security Council to maintain its own authority—constitutes a serious crisis in global security.

I've often been asked the question—"Why?" Why does Saddam want these weapons? Why has he so callously traded off the welfare of the Iraqi people for his possession of weapons of mass destruction? What purpose do they serve? A complete answer could come only from the mind of Saddam Hussein. But a possible answer to these questions can be constructed by reference to standard tools of political analysis and Saddam's own statements.

Saddam's fundamental goal is to retain his own power and position. This hardly makes him unique, but it does explain a great deal about the system of terror and patronage he runs in Iraq and the extraordinary wall of security he has built around himself. His weapons support this goal, to which he is ferociously attached.

The question is often posed about whether weapons of mass destruction are necessary for this purpose. Couldn't it be achieved through conventional weapons? Of course it could, but clearly Saddam doesn't think so. The evidence for this is plain—he has used weapons of mass destruction on his internal enemies.

There is also the issue of his psychology, his evident need to be seen as invincible. Devastating weapons in his hands serve that image, one that he cultivates assiduously, for example, by comparing himself especially to the all-powerful, terrifying leaders of ancient Iraq and, most preposterously, to the biblical ruler of Babylon, Nebuchadnezzar.

Conventional analysis rightly points out that any leader will be greatly concerned about the security of the state he leads. The weapons and armies maintained by that leader will be determined in good measure by the nature of the threat he assesses the state faces from outside. This threat assessment itself may or may not be rational.

Saddam's statements indicate that he sees Iraq as threatened on virtually all sides, particularly by Iran and Israel. He has sought weapons of mass destruction to deal with that threat. He has used them against Iran, and, to some extent, Israel. In addition to seizing Kuwait, he has also attacked Saudi Arabia, Bahrain, and Turkey. Every thoughtful leader in the region assumes he may do so again.

The irrational aspect of his international actions and the associated use of weapons lies principally in his repeated inversion of reality: The Iraqi invasion of Kuwait was "Kuwaiti aggression," and, of course, Iraq won the Gulf War, "the mother of all battles." What I've just described as "irrational" might be considered mere propaganda. More important, however, is that these inversions reveal Saddam's worldview and way of thinking. He sees victory where there was defeat; he sees unity where there is division.

On several occasions during the recurrent crises since 1997, when he has been threatened and indeed attacked by Western forces, Saddam has made appeals for Arab solidarity with Iraq. His speeches have a revealing common theme: The posited existence of a united Arab nation; leadership in each of the other Arab states that is failing the Arab people (he recently referred to such leaders as President Mubarak of Egypt and King Fahd of Saudi Arabia as "dwarfs on Arab thrones"); and his willingness, ability, and strength to lead the Arab nation against what he claims are its Jewish and Western enemies.

Clearly, weapons of mass destruction are central to Saddam's claim to be fit and able to lead the Arab world. It is very important to recognize that this strident, bellicose appeal is addressed particularly to the underprivileged masses, not the many educated, worldly, sophisticated Arab citizens. In my experience, educated Arabs typically think Saddam is a deeply dangerous man who has done incalculable damage to the image and reputation of Arabs and Muslims. They have good reason to think this.

Missile, bomber, artillery shell, even crop duster: All are means of delivery for the chemical weapons built and, in some cases, used by Saddam. But these are not the only ways to kill with chemical weapons. As the 1996 terrorist attack in the Tokyo subway showed, it can be done at a ridiculously simple level of technology. On that occasion, the terrorists used a chemical weapon, a nerve agent called sarin, or GB. They simply set plastic bags filled with sarin into the corner of one subway station, opened the bags, and let air currents do the rest. Because the subway's tubes are filled with constantly rushing air, the system produces a powerful, deadly means of dispersal. The air-conditioning ducts in a large public building would be another effective way to disseminate chemical weapons.

Given Saddam's track record on chemical weapons and their use and his attitude toward the West, particularly the United States, I am going to assume that he might take a decision to support such a terrorist attack. Why, and in particular when, is not fathomable. But let's play out a scenario:

A hit squad from somewhere in the Middle East travels to New York City carrying a one-liter bottle filled with one of the several chemical weapons agents we have long known Saddam Hussein to be developing. Using a simple sprayer (like one that a gardener or house painter might own), they diffuse the contents into the air over Times Square on a Saturday night or into the main concourse at Grand Central Station at 5:30 P.M. on a weekday evening. Hundreds, maybe thousands of people die agonizing deaths as a result. Because of their own handling of the substance and the strategic concern to maintain ambiguity over the source of the attack, the terrorists may have to be prepared to die themselves.

Obviously, the world would erupt in almost unprecedented horror and outrage. A search for the perpetrators would be launched. Identifying them, dead or alive, on the ground in New York may prove difficult, but even if their identities became known quickly, it may not be clear whom they represented or, above all, who provided them the deadly weapon. Answering this question beyond a reasonable doubt might not be easy.

Most Americans (and American allies around the world) would be loath to punish any single nation or people through military strikes or other assaults without specific proof. And assembling such proof might take years, as the ongoing struggle to affix responsibility for the explosion of Pan Am flight 103 over Lockerbie, Scotland, and the 1996 attack on the Khobar Towers complex in Saudi Arabia suggests. Under these circumstances, it's quite possible that Saddam could get away with the act. Sadly, on the question whether there is a defense against such an event, the answer seems to be probably not.

Even if the crime could be clearly traced to Saddam—if, for example, Saddam were to boastfully acknowledge his responsibility in a public statement or simply say he supported it—it's not clear exactly how the U.S. government and world community could and should respond. Of course, the sense of anger and the demand for retaliation would be overwhelming, and the media would feed these reactions. (Imagine the televised scenes from hospital emergency rooms overwhelmed by victims, the weeping relatives, and then the shots of anti-American demonstrators in Baghdad dancing with glee in the streets.) The president, Congress, and the U.S. military would be pressured from all directions to hit back at Iraq—and hard.

But what would be the purpose of an American attack? Would it be simple revenge? If so, would it be fair to slaughter innocent Iraqi civilians, the most likely victims of U.S. bombing raids? Would the purpose be deterrence of future terrorism? In that case, if those actually perpetrating the crimes are not the ones who suffer, it's unclear how effective the deterrence would really be. Would the purpose be removal from power of Saddam? If so, who would take his place as the head of the Iraqi government? Whose support would he enjoy? How could we know the new strongman would be better than the old one?

The answers to these questions would be far from obvious, yet they are essential to determine the nature of the appropriate response. Would the United States be prepared to land American soldiers on the ground to go to war against Iraq? What level of U.S. casualties would be acceptable for such a mission. A hundred? A thousand? Ten thousand? What would we ask our allies to do? What could we expect from the other Arab nations? (President George Bush barely managed to hold together the Gulf War coalition against Saddam; an invasion aimed at overthrowing Saddam's government would find little support among other Mideast regimes.) Would Russia simply stand on the sidelines? What would happen to Israel if the Mideast erupted?

Merely to list these questions makes it clear that the decisions involved would be intensely difficult. Clearly, it would be unacceptable for Saddam Hussein to use chemical or biological weapons to kill thousands or tens of thousands of innocent people and to do so with impunity. Yet it would probably be equally unacceptable in the eyes of the world community to see the United States respond by killing tens of thousands of Iraqi civilians in return.

Such a terrorist action would bring us to a virtually unmanageable place, a situation in which angry Americans are baying for blood; the more sober heads at the Pentagon and the White House are trying desperately to figure out how to keep the situation from exploding; and leaders of dozens of other countries—from Russia, China, and France to Syria, Iran, North Korea, and maybe even Cuba—maneuvering to exploit the crisis to their own advantage. It's likely that all of the choices facing the U.S. president (and, for that matter, world leaders at the UN and NATO) would be horrendous, not readily promising peace and justice but, more likely, more death and terror.

The only real solution to the dilemma posed by weapons of mass destruction is to ensure that no such dilemma should ever be faced—that the world act now to prevent any attack with a chemical, biological, or indeed, a portable nuclear weapon, not only by Saddam Hussein but by other states, terrorist movements, "armies of liberation," lone lunatics—anyone with the motivation to launch such an attack. The only reliable means of prevention we know is offered by the treaties, conventions, and global organizations directed against the manufacture of such weapons and to their ultimate elimination. But the effectiveness and possibly the very existence of these restraints is now being undermined by Saddam Hussein.

That is why I've written this book. The story of the last two climactic years of the struggle to disarm Iraq in accordance with the UN mandate is interesting, I hope, with its share of strange encounters, amazing characters, and ironic twists. But the story of the demise of the United Nations Special Commission (UNSCOM), the unique body charged with the disarmament of Iraq, and the apparent victory by Saddam Hussein over attempts by the world community to take away his weapons is far more important than it is colorful. The failure of the world community to deal effectively with Saddam Hussein—a man determined at all costs to obtain, stockpile, and, if possible, make use of weapons of mass destruction in pursuit of his personal and political goals—is a profound one, constituting a crisis in the management of global security.

This book tells the story of these events, including the destruction of UNSCOM. These events have consequences going far beyond the business of dealing with a dictatorship addicted to truly hideous weapons. Saddam's possession of weapons of mass destruction is disastrous. As long as he has such weapons, the likelihood that they will be used remains high. The human destruction thus caused could be massive. The terror would be electric. The political and military consequences would be incalculable.

This is the greatest threat, but it would also constitute the most profound historical failure because it would have come from weapons declared by civilization to be inadmissible, deployed by or under the aegis of a person widely known to have repeatedly committed crimes against humanity. What more complete failure of human will is imaginable?

The greatest threat is already at work in a more deeply embedded way. Iraq's successful violation of the treaties against weapons of mass destruction has shaken those agreements and the faith held by nations in them. None of the treaties is perfect. Criminality and insanity are a part of human life and can lead to attempts to cheat on agreements and break solemn promises. What is crucial is that such cheating be detected and then stopped. The treaties offer mechanisms for such detection.

Saddam's cheating has been detected, but it has not been stopped. Nations that could take action have chosen not to. The implication of this for the maintenance of the strictures against weapons of mass destruction, built so painstakingly over almost half a century, are dire. If Saddam finally gets away with it, the whole structure could well collapse.

The end of the Cold War held the prospect that the tapestry of treaties controlling weapons of mass destruction would be strengthened greatly, through cooperation among former adversaries, and their ultimate purpose achieved—a world free of these weapons. It is a bitter irony that the current response to Saddam Hussein has revealed that the real contours of the post–Cold War world are not so different from those of that deeply dangerous period. The perennial conflict between power and interests on the one hand and principle and law on the other is increasingly being resolved in favor of the former. Because weapons of mass destruction are vastly different from other sources of danger— they literally threaten all life—they must be made an area of exception to that perennial conflict.

At the end of World War II, with its global devastation, its fifty million dead, and its death camps, a meeting at San Francisco produced the Charter of the United Nations "to save succeeding generations from the scourge of war." What took place at San Francisco was remarkable and new. But it was an instance of historical change authored by catastrophe. Hindsight showed that the appeasement of Hitler was a grave and avoidable error: On many occasions, as Hitler was building his power, his ambitions were clearly visible.

The 1945 UN Charter took no account of weapons of mass destruction, mainly because what has become their modern dimension did not then exist. As this changed, however, treaties governing weapons of mass destruction were written, beginning a few years after San Francisco and continuing ever since.

The rational human response to the greatest threat, essential to avoid change being driven by catastrophe, is for the key agreement— made possible by the end of the Cold War—to be reached now. The permanent members of the Security Council must solemnly commit to jointly enforcing the obligations set forth in the global nuclear, chemical, and biological weapons treaties, including with respect to their own weapons—which they have promised to eliminate through appropriate negotiations. This would mean that they must act whenever a credible report of any violation of those treaties is made. There must be no veto, no Cold War client statism. A judgment about the character of regimes must be made. Outdated Cold War dictums—"The enemy of my enemy is my friend," "He may be a bastard, but he's our bastard"—are not appropriate when weapons of mass destruction are at issue.

Unambiguous action by the Great Powers to make an exception of weapons of mass destruction would be applauded and supported by the community of nations. When their resolve becomes clear to all, only on the rarest occasions will the Great Powers need to use force. Such a principled commitment would represent a beacon to all humanity and it would enhance the security of all.

The greatest threat leaves no alternative. On weapons of mass destruction, power must serve principle and life itself. The phrase "mass destruction" means what it says: These are weapons that can decimate cities, infect countries, poison millions. They are hideous, utterly contrary to civilization. Saddam Hussein is not simply a wicked dictator, and he is not unique by any stretch. But his stance on weapons of mass destruction and the failure of the community of nations to deal with him means that he holds a lit match, and with each passing day he brings it closer to the fuse. If we do not stop him before the fuse ignites, then the results will be truly cataclysmic. Perhaps only then, in brief moments before the end, will we realize how great was our failure.

1

A GLIMPSE OF TERROR

S OMETIMES IT IS THE SIDESHOW, not the main act, that is most revealing. Such a moment occurred late one evening in Baghdad in March 1998, almost a year after I had begun the job of leading UNSCOM—the UN effort to remove Saddam Hussein's weapons of mass destruction. Yet another day of inconclusive talks between the government of Iraq and UNSCOM representatives was coming to a close. I was feeling tired, a bit tense, and increasingly frustrated with Iraq's relentless efforts to defeat our mission.

All our meetings had been hostile in tone, but this session had been among the most heated. Deputy Prime Minister Tariq Aziz, whom Saddam had appointed to lead the anti-UNSCOM effort, had evidently decided to step up the level of combat in his dealings with UNSCOM and in particular with me. He'd spent the evening hurling insults and insinuations across the table, accusing me of wanting to prolong the disarmament process, of capriciously shifting UNSCOM's demands, of seeking to indefinitely extend the UN sanctions against Iraq in a deliberate effort to harm the Iraqi people. Evidently, he hoped to provoke an angry response from me, to be captured on tape by one of the five video cameras silently recording the action around the huge, dim conference room. Footage of an outburst by the man whom the state-controlled Iraqi media had dubbed "Mad Dog Butler" would be useful propaganda.

It was tempting to fight back, to try to break out, but there was nowhere to go. I refused to rise to the bait.

The hemmed-in atmosphere in the conference room was no help. Located on the seventh floor of the grim concrete-block structure that housed the offices of the Iraqi Foreign Ministry, the room was a huge

space, some 10,000 square feet, inadequately lit by strip lights and dominated by a large, open-centered rectangular table covered in green baize.
Along the Iraqi side of the table sat ten men in olive uniforms decorated with
a variety of insignia I never quite learned to decipher—combinations of
oak leaves, eagles, seven-pointed stars, and crossed scimitars. Tariq Aziz
sat at the center of his frontline. Behind the ten at the table were twenty-
five or thirty supporters in ranks of chairs that vanished backward into
the increasing gloom of the outer edges of the conference room, a mixture of men in military garb and business suits and a single woman, the
notorious Dr. Rihab Rashida Taha, once dubbed by a Western tabloid
"Dr. Germ" because of her role in directing Iraq's program of biological
warfare. This half-lit room, through which the periodically moving
video cameras floated with their red indicator lights, had no decorations
other than an Iraqi flag beside the inevitable grandiose portrait of Saddam Hussein in military uniform.

Across the table from Aziz and his entourage, the UNSCOM party
numbered about a dozen. I sat directly opposite Aziz with my deputy, the
determined, if somewhat taut Charles Duelfer, at my right side. Duelfer
was provided to UNSCOM by the U.S. State Department. There were
also policy officers—Gustavo Zlauvinen from Argentina, Eric Fournier
from France, and Nikita Zhukov from Russia. These men were there to
provide advice and counsel to me. They were all professionals, but the
Russian and French officers clearly had the responsibility of seeking to
influence my decisions toward the Russian and French viewpoints,
which by this time had begun to distinctly favor Iraq. So the challenge I
faced did not originate solely from the other side of the table.

Also in attendance were my legal adviser, John Scott, a Briton, and
leaders representing each aspect of UNSCOM's tripartite mission:
Nikita Smidovitch, a Russian, head of missile disarmament; the German
Dr. Horst Reeps, who ran the chemical weapons group; and Dr.
Gabrielle Kraatz-Wadsack, another German, who led our biological
weapons work. Three commissioners, members of UNSCOM's twenty-
one-person advisory body representing sixteen nations, were also present as observers.

In Baghdad, it was typical for us to meet with the Iraqis twice a day: in
the morning and then, after a break during the period of the extreme
afternoon heat, at an evening session starting around eight o'clock. On
this particular occasion, little of substance was discussed. The more we

pressed for answers to our questions about the nature, extent, and purposes of the Iraqi weapons-manufacturing programs, the more Tariq Aziz spat out his abuse. In fact, Reeps and Smidovitch, both longtime staff members, had commented to me, during a break, that the level of hostility on the part of Iraq was now greater than they'd seen at any time during the commission's seven-year history.

The hostility wasn't merely unpleasant. A veiled threat of physical violence was always signaled, if only subliminally. This was not simply because of Saddam's well-known propensity to use violence as a way of seizing and consolidating power, but because of actual attempts to intimidate and harm us. Two months before, an Iraqi rocket-propelled grenade had been fired into UNSCOM headquarters—fortunately killing no one. We'd stepped up our security precautions as a result, but the undercurrent of anxiety among our staff in Baghdad had heightened thereafter.

When it became obvious that the evening's discussions were proving fruitless, we agreed to call a halt. Clearly, Iraq was going to give us nothing of the materials and evidence we had asked for. For our part, we were in no mood to be sucked into a theatrical confrontation. It was time for me to return to New York, to report Iraq's continued intransigence to the Security Council, and to plan future surprise inspections in the hope of uncovering the evidence of what we knew to be their programs for making and retaining weapons of mass destruction.

I rose, along with the rest of the UNSCOM team, and prepared for the usual phony, polite, formal leave-taking. Stepping around to the Iraqi side of the conference table, I extended my hand to Aziz. He then began the unexpected sideshow. Rather than shake my hand, Aziz signaled to a group of figures barely discernable in a dark corner of the room. Two uniformed men strode up into the light, pulling between them a third man. He was a slight fellow dressed in the typical garb of an Iraqi farmer: an open-necked shirt, rough cotton trousers, and a pair of much-worn sandals. He had the gnarled skin and dark complexion of one long exposed to the harsh Mideast sun, and he wore the black moustache affected by nearly all Iraqi men in imitation of Saddam Hussein. But what struck me most forcibly was his obvious, intense fear. He was hunched as though to shield his body from expected blows, he was trembling all over, and when he glanced at me, I saw in his eyes the look of terror.

The men in uniform held this man firmly and thrust him toward me. Aziz declared, "Mr. Butler, I want to show you something important. You have accused us of testing biological weapons on human beings. It's an outrageous lie. In particular, you have shown a photograph of the forearm of a person on which there were sores. You said the sores were caused by the testing of weapons. You asked for an explanation. Well, here's your explanation! This man is the man in your photograph. Look at his arm!" Aziz yanked up the left sleeve of the farmer's shirt, exposing an unmarked forearm. "So much for your claims!"

I felt deep pity for the farmer. *Aziz has had his thugs grab you off the street and drag you up here for this charade,* I thought. *God only knows what you think is happening or fear what will be done to you if the foreigner doesn't like what he sees on your arm, or if in some other unknown way you fail this test.* He must have known how cheap a life like his had become in Saddam's Iraq.

As evidence of anything real, the charade was ludicrous. We'd heard from Iraqi defectors that inmates at the Abu Ghraib prison outside Baghdad had indeed been used as subjects of biological weapons testing. The photograph we'd obtained was consistent with such reports. Our efforts to inspect the prison and study inmate files that might prove or disprove these allegations had been illegally rebuffed. Aziz's answer to this was to present a randomly selected man and, incredibly, insist that his was the forearm shown in our photo. It was horrible and a travesty.

Such behavior was typical of Iraq's treatment of UNSCOM: a mixture of bluster, brazenly inept lies, and thinly veiled threats of violence. Under the circumstances, I decided not to argue with Aziz; why further frighten his poor victim? I simply said, "I see what you're seeking to demonstrate. Good night."

THIS EPISODE has haunted me, mainly because of its cynical cruelty, but also because it encapsulated some central truths about the regime of Saddam Hussein, the nature and importance of the struggle by the world community to deprive him of weapons of mass destruction; and why the loss of control over the spread of such weapons poses the greatest threat to world peace and security, to life on earth.

First, the regime of Saddam Hussein. Its brutal and tyrannical nature has been documented elsewhere in detail for almost two decades. The political currency of his regime is homicide, frequently threatened and often delivered. But there was something particularly chilling about the relatively minor display of this fact we saw that night: It evidently did not trouble Aziz or his henchmen that we saw it firsthand. Far more important was that they act out their lie about their biological weapons program, no matter how cruelly or implausibly.

The incident also illustrated the callousness of the regime toward its own people—a quality we witnessed daily in our dealings with Iraq, something that gives the lie to Saddam's public protestations that his primary goal is to lift the awful burden of international sanctions from the backs of the Iraqi people. Because the United Nations has tied the removal of those weapons to the removal of the sanctions on 22 million Iraqis, he could achieve sanctions relief at any time by giving up his weapons. He has resolutely refused to do that, thus trading off the welfare of the Iraqi people—of which that night's victim was a small but perfect example—for his own power and weapons.

The intimidating aspect of that night's charade, directed at UNSCOM, was also clearly not lost on Aziz. His actions that night, coded through their handling of one of their own, sent a calculated message to us: *This is how we deal with those who oppose us.*

We'd discussed with Tariq Aziz the photo of the scarified forearm because we believed it represented evidence that the Iraqi government had not only developed chemical and biological weapons—facts already established—but also tested them on living humans in violation of every code of human rights. Iraqi defectors we'd interviewed had told us that Iraq tested biological agents on Iranian soldiers taken prisoner during the Iran-Iraq War of the 1980s, as well as on the Abu Ghraib inmates during 1994 and 1995. To this day, the full facts are obscure. But when we sent an inspection team early in 1998 to the prison to search for the documentary evidence, all the inmate files were there except those covering the two crucial years. And when Iraq realized what we were looking for, it abruptly terminated the whole inspection.

This is Saddam Hussein's regime: cruel, lying, intimidating, and determined to retain weapons of mass destruction—weapons capable of killing thousands, even millions, at a single blow.

In fact, while Tariq Aziz was stage-managing his hideous charade that night, developments in the UNSCOM search for Iraq's weapons of mass destruction capabilities were coming to a head. A smoking gun we'd long sought was about to fall into our hands. I learned of its existence, two months later, in June 1998, at the start of my next visit to Baghdad.

A s USUAL, I arrived in Iraq by way of the Habbaniyah air base, accompanied by several key UNSCOM staff members and technical experts. We disembarked into the painful glare of a Baghdad summer's day and were greeted by the Iraqi government protocol people and an Iraqi TV crew wanting to ask me about our visit. The latter never involved anything remotely like a Western-style news conference. Journalists working for the Iraqi media mainly make statements rather than ask questions. These would include "questions" like, "When do you plan to stop murdering Iraqi babies through your cruel sanctions?"

As I addressed such questions and then chatted with my Iraqi government handlers, two of our technical experts—Horst Reeps and Igor Mitrokhin—were drawn aside by Tim Blades, one of our chemical experts then in Baghdad. Blades appeared agitated. He'd met us at the airport because it was the earliest moment at which he could present us with a newly completed laboratory report. Reeps read it immediately. The look on his face made plain that its contents were very serious.

When our luggage had been loaded into the cars and we were ready for the ninety-minute ride into Baghdad, Reeps and Blades approached me. "There's something you must see *now*," Reeps said, handing me a thin sheaf of papers. It contained the results of an analysis recently conducted in a Maryland laboratory, one of thirty such laboratories in the world registered under the Chemical Weapons Convention (the treaty banning chemical weapons) as a source of verification of chemical weapons data. At UNSCOM's request, the laboratory had analyzed a collection of metal fragments, remnants of missile warheads deliberately destroyed by explosion by Iraq and buried in a pit at a place called Nibai, forty kilometers outside Baghdad. The question we'd posed was: What sorts of weapons agents, if any, had been loaded into these warheads before their destruction?

It hadn't been easy arranging these tests. The warheads had been unilaterally and secretly destroyed by Iraq, not under international supervision as required by the UN resolutions. The intent, obviously, was to conceal the number of warheads destroyed as well as their nature and content. The only way UNSCOM could verify the truth of Iraq's claims to have destroyed a particular number of warheads was by literally digging up and piecing together thousands of metal fragments from the extensive pits at Nibai—a task just as arduous, time-consuming, and frustrating as it sounds. And as difficult as assembling those fragments was, finding out the nature of the original warheads could be even more difficult.

After months of work, we managed to recover a horde of metal pieces, apparently parts of destroyed missile warheads. We took these bits away in plastic bags and stored them in a locked shed near Baghdad, securely labeled and with their contents carefully recorded on video, with the ultimate objective of having them analyzed by a competent laboratory.

Immediately, Iraq started arguing about who really owned the metal pieces and about whether they could be taken out of the country. This was the first sign that Iraq was concerned—that something significant might be revealed when we analyzed these fragments. Of course, the Security Council resolutions under which UNSCOM was charged with disarming Iraq gave us every right to examine relevant evidence for signs of weapons of mass destruction. After a difficult standoff we won our point. We had the pieces sealed in environmentally safe containers and flew them in our own plane to Bahrain, from where they were then sent via secure transport to the laboratory in Maryland.

Now the results of the analysis were ready. The chemists had swabbed each of the pieces of metal to remove and collect the surface residues for analysis. As one might expect, they found a spectrum of substances on the metal surfaces, ranging from ordinary dirt to chemicals of various kinds. But there were also clear traces of a chemical called EMPA, short for ethyl methyl-phosphoric acid. It was this finding that had caused Horst Reeps to blanch. EMPA is a degradation product of one and only one known compound in the universe—the chemical VX, one of the most toxic substances ever made.

As it turned out, VX was not the only chemical weapons agent or the only nerve agent made by Iraq. Essentially, Iraq made virtually all of the prohibited agents and used some of them both in and outside Iraq. But VX was and is the most devastating of them. It can be sprayed as a liquid or scattered into the atmosphere as an aerosol. A missile warhead of the type Iraq has made and used can hold some 140 liters of VX, which could be dispersed by a burster tube, which breaks opens the warhead on impact, creating a lethal aerosol that would quickly spread through the atmosphere of a city. A single such warhead would contain enough of the chemical to kill *up to 1 million people*. (A single droplet of VX on the skin constitutes a lethal dose.) And the missile targets within a modest 600-mile range from Iraq include such populous, politically and culturally important cities as Damascus, Tehran, Amman, Tel Aviv, and Jerusalem. This is one of the reasons why the Security Council imposed a range limit of 150 kilometers on Iraqi missiles (a limit Iraq is now breaching).

I read the laboratory report carefully, and the scientists on the UNSCOM staff confirmed its significance to me.

Initially, Iraq had denied having ever manufactured, let alone deployed, VX. But this was not true. The Muthanna State Establishment had once been a busy, powerful laboratory and factory for the development and manufacture of advanced chemical and biological weapons. It had been largely destroyed by Coalition bombing during the Gulf War, and later UNSCOM had smashed the remaining scientific equipment found there and built thick-walled concrete bunkers in which the leftover chemicals were safely sealed. When I'd visited Muthanna, 100 miles northwest of Baghdad, I'd seen a vast area of destruction, four square miles, surrounded by high barbed-wire fences and sensitive machines constantly monitoring the desert air for traces of deadly substances. It was *under* one of the destroyed buildings at Muthanna that we'd found documents proving that Iraq had been making VX. We also found traces of VX in soil samples gathered nearby.

Confronted with this evidence, the Iraqis then admitted having manufactured VX but claimed that the quantity produced amounted to no more than 200 liters. Subsequent probing by UNSCOM showed they'd made at least 3,900 liters (about 3.9 metric tons). So Iraq's initial complete lie had been replaced by a false statement on quantity.

We also discovered that they were using the so-called choline method for manufacturing VX, which from a scientific and technical standpoint is the more sophisticated of two possible methods. Clearly, production of VX was no small experiment or minor sideline for the Iraqi arms makers but rather a major effort.

It is important to record, in this context, that under the UN resolutions that created UNSCOM and imposed sanctions on Iraq, Saddam's regime was required to provide us with full, final, and complete declarations of their weapons inventories and weapons-manufacturing capabilities. Our first job in Iraq was to verify those declarations and, after that, to "destroy, remove, or render harmless" any prohibited items. We were never supposed to play the role of detectives. But the lies we were being fed forced us into such a role.

Having been obliged to admit that they'd manufactured VX, and then sought unsuccessfully to lie about the quantity involved, Iraq then reached for its third lie on VX: They'd never "weaponized" the chemical—that is, deployed it in missile warheads or other means of delivery. So when I read the June 1998 report about the warhead fragments from Nibai, it was clear that we had a major problem on our hands. Iraqi VX had been weaponized and, perhaps, used in warfare as well. That was serious indeed.

The first decision I faced was how to manage this discovery. I chose to handle it in a low-key fashion. Rather than make any public statement about our findings or report them immediately to the UN Security Council, I decided to start the process by asking the Iraqis for an explanation. Thus, the next morning, in my first meeting with Tariq Aziz, I quietly informed him that we'd received certain laboratory findings related to the Iraqi deployment of VX. We needed more information about this subject, I said, and in any case we were still waiting to learn how much VX had been produced—a fact that now carried greater importance in light of the current information.

"We don't want to jump to conclusions," I assured Aziz, "so perhaps our chemical experts from both sides should withdraw into another room to discuss the findings." Aziz agreed, and the chemical experts accordingly adjourned to a smaller committee room.

When we later reconvened in the larger room, the Iraqis gave us their response. Predictably, Tariq Aziz denied everything. "You claim to have found the chemical VX in missile fragments from Iraq. But this can't possibly be true! As we've told you many times, we *never* put VX into any missile warhead or any other weapon. This so-called laboratory report is a fabrication cooked up by you or your friends to slander and harm Iraq. It's no surprise that these findings were produced in an American laboratory—what else would you expect? We demand new tests before we'll even discuss the issue further."

This response was unsurprising, and I was ready with a reply. I said our chemical experts had already prepared letters to the Swiss and the French governments, describing the problem and asking for further examinations of the missile fragments in a French defense laboratory and in an independent, government-funded laboratory in Switzerland. Both establishments had impeccable reputations for scientific objectivity and were also registered under the Chemical Weapons Convention.

I told Aziz, "We have no objection to further analysis. Would you consider laboratories in France and Switzerland acceptable? Good. But let me make it clear that I utterly reject your suggestion that these first results have been falsified because they were done in the United States. *The results are valid.*"

"In deference to your wishes," I continued, "we'll have the French and Swiss scientists comment on the methodology used by the American chemists. And they'll also perform their own tests on different metal samples. But even if the French and Swiss laboratories find no traces of EMPA—and I hope that will be the case—Iraq will still need to explain why the missile fragments already tested contained EMPA. No future test results can wipe away that question."

"Furthermore," I said, "I remind you that you have never adequately declared how much VX you made. That's really the more important question. Weaponizing this chemical is one issue, but of fundamental significance is that you tell us how much of the stuff you made! Give us the documents—show us the throughput of raw materials—*let us verify the truth.*"

It wasn't the first time, or the last, that I made such a plea. As was most often the case, the plea went unanswered.

After wrangling over whether more missile fragments could be sent out of the country, we went forward with additional testing. The Swiss laboratory reported finding no EMPA on the shards it examined. The French laboratory reported ambiguous findings: It discovered traces of MPA, a different chemical closely related to EMPA and associated with other chemical weapons, as well as traces of other substances possibly consistent with EMPA but possibly also consistent with a detergent that might have been used to wash the samples. (There were questions about the French laboratory work. The results had taken uncommonly long to arrive, even allowing for the usual extended August holidays of the French, and we'd been hearing whispered reports through our own scientists that political pressure had been brought to bear by the French government on the laboratory—denied by French diplomats.)

However, when we held a meeting in New York with representatives from all three laboratories as well as our own chemistry staff, all agreed that the procedures that had been followed by the Maryland laboratory were impeccable and their findings unimpeachable. Iraq still had to explain those findings.

It is not known whether Iraq ever used VX in warfare. It's possible—though generally considered unlikely—that Iraq used VX during the Iran-Iraq War. A more plausible alternative is that Iraq used VX on its own citizens. Dr. Christine Gosden at Liverpool University in the United Kingdom has long studied Saddam Hussein's attack in 1988 on Kurds in the northern Iraqi village area of Halabja. Gosden has evidence that nerve agents—including VX, she firmly believes—were among the chemical cocktail used against these northern areas. The overall size of Iraq's VX production remains unknown to this day.

2

PEACE AS A CAREER

THIS BOOK HAS AT ITS CORE in chapters three through twelve the account of my dealings with Iraq in 1997 and 1998. It is fair for any reader to ask at the outset, how did Butler get the job? Did he have the appropriate background and knowledge? It is also essential, if one is to gain an understanding of the somewhat arcane world of UNSCOM and Iraq, to know something of arms control and disarmament and the role it has come to play in international relations and in attempts to maintain global security. This chapter seeks to provide that information.

My passage toward a life in arms control had seemingly incongruous origins. I grew up in the eastern part of Sydney, Australia, in a place called Bondi, an aboriginal word for "booming waves." Appropriately named, Bondi is a one-mile stretch of golden sand on the Pacific Ocean just five miles from downtown Sydney; it is also the most famous beach in Australia, a country of endless beaches. As a town, Bondi is what Brooklyn is to New York—a working-class, polyglot community that is also home to a free-spirited surfing community. It is quintessentially Australian.

I was the second of three sons in a proud working-class family. My father, who worked with his hands as a landscape gardener, volunteered in World War II when the Japanese threatened Australia. Out of fear that the Japanese would soon begin bombing Australian coastal cities, my mother went inland to a little place some of her relatives had in the bush—the rural part of Australia. That's where I was born, in 1942.

After the war and my father's return, my parents, my older brother, and I went to live in a tiny flat in Bondi, directly overlooking the northern end of the beach. Half of my schoolmates were refugees, mostly

Ashkenazi Jews, from Hitler's Europe. In talking and playing with them, I was introduced to the world beyond Australia, a world I realized was filled with armed conflict, political problems, and real beastliness by humans against one another. I became very interested in those things.

At high school, my earlier exposure to refugees from Hitler's war was added to by the arrival of refugee kids from the Soviet invasion of Hungary. This again increased my interest in international relations. After finishing high school, I entered the University of Sydney, where I majored in politics and economics. When I graduated in 1964, I became a policy assistant at the Australian Atomic Energy Commission (AAEC) in the department of international relations. Eager to learn more about my new job, particularly nuclear weapons, I went to the AAEC's library but couldn't find much relevant material about the control of nuclear weapons. In fact, just five authors were then listed in the catalog; I decided to become the sixth. I went back to the University of Sydney and sought permission to work part-time on a master's degree in the Department of Political Science.

While continuing this graduate work, and after a nine-month stint in the prime minister's office in Canberra (the Australian capital), to which I'd transferred, I decided to try a career in diplomacy. Accordingly, I approached the Department of External Affairs (now called the Department of Foreign Affairs and Trade, the equivalent of the U.S. State Department).

In 1965, I was one of 800 graduate applicants who responded to a recruitment notice for professional diplomats, published in the newspapers. After a series of examinations and interviews, I was among fourteen recruits selected.

My first overseas posting was to the Australian embassy at Vienna. I was sent there, specifically, to serve as an Australian representative to the International Atomic Energy Agency (IAEA), the UN agency created following President Eisenhower's "Atoms for Peace" speech, given at the United Nations in December 1953. While in Vienna, I saw another of the Cold War's infamous events—the Warsaw Pact invasion of Czechoslovakia. By chance I was visiting Prague at the time. Even as a relatively junior representative of the IAEA, I found that I could fix a lot of important problems, make deals, and manage to get votes in the Board of Governors to come out the way we (the Australians) wanted. Above all, my time in Vienna became the beginning of a lifelong involvement in

what might be called the "atomic circle," the world's nuclear cogno-
scenti who all know each other—including some of those five authors
whose names I'd previously seen in the AAEC library and whom I then
got a chance to meet.

When I returned from Vienna, the department assigned me to the
Africa/Middle East section, selected specifically because of its extreme
distance from what I'd done for the preceding three years. The idea, I
was told, was to "bring me down to earth . . . to re-Australianize" me.
Fortunately, within a year I found a mentor who'd support my desire for
a new overseas posting—Sir Laurence McIntyre—who was about to
become Australian ambassador to the UN. By mid-1970, I was in New
York as one of eight diplomats in the Australian mission to the UN.

My first assignment in the mission was aid to developing countries—
not much arms control. During this period the newly formed nation of
Bangladesh went through its terrible flood disasters, and I was very
involved with the rescue efforts, working literally day and night to help
keep that beleaguered land afloat.

At the beginning of 1973, I returned to Australia. A few months earlier, Gough Whitlam's Labor Party government had been elected—a
watershed event in contemporary Australian political history. It was similar to John F. Kennedy's election in the United States—the arrival of a
young, bright, charismatic, liberal-minded leader promising great
change for a country that was much in need of a shake-up.

While back in Canberra, I made many approaches to Whitlam's office
(both directly and through my friends there) about the possibility of a
job. I was always treated politely but never got an offer. So in 1975 I
accepted a proposal from the department to go to Singapore as deputy
high commissioner. (The Australian embassy in Singapore is called the
Australian High Commission, a terminological requirement because
Singapore is a fellow-member of the Commonwealth of Nations.)

The Singapore posting coincided with the aftermath of the Vietnam
War, which led to my first serious conflict with a fellow diplomat from
the United States. I was a member of the allied intelligence community
in Singapore, which met to share information and ideas about the
unfolding political, military, and economic situation throughout the
region. The American member of this group wanted me to send alarmist
reports to my government about what he asserted was the southward
thrust of communism from Vietnam through Malaysia. I resented the

pressure he exerted on me. It came to a head one day in a shouting match in which he demanded my loyalty. I remember telling him, "I remind you that when the Vietcong were pouring over the walls of Saigon, the CIA station chief at the embassy was still sending messages back to Washington declaring that everything was hunky-dory. You may be willing to participate in such bullshit, but I'm not." Our relationship never recovered, and I'm sure my ideological unreliability was reported to Washington. This was not my only showdown with the United States, and while I've sometimes been accused of being too tractable to the Americans, over the years I've been skeptical of hard-line U.S. positions.

I HAD BEEN in Singapore for only some six months when a political crisis occurred in Australia, leading to the dismissal of the Whitlam government. Then in January 1976, only two months after the dismissal, Tungku Abdel Rahman, Malaysia's most distinguished and important prime minister of the postwar period, died. (I remember seeing images on TV of rows of Islamic clerics sitting on rugs and chanting prayers as soon as he died.) A massive funeral service was held in Kuala Lumpur, attended by dignitaries from the world over.

Gough Whitlam, then Leader of the Opposition, came to Singapore after the funeral—looking the worse for wear following his great political defeat. I had the opportunity to get to know him, and a few weeks later I got a message from Whitlam's office saying that his chief of staff had resigned. Would I like the job? I promptly left my foreign service career behind.

Within two years, I was managing a national election campaign. (Back in my university days, I'd been elected president of the Economics Society and a student representative on the board of directors of the University Union. That had been my sole preparation for a real electoral process.) Australian elections are a blood sport played with take-no-prisoners intensity. In 1977, we hit the road, and for several weeks the polls looked promising. But our hopes were dashed in the last two weeks of the campaign. We lost.

I learned much about politics from Gough Whitlam—negotiation, framing an argument, the need for factual precision—skills I was still applying at UNSCOM twenty years later. I particularly remember how Gough would bang on the table and declare, "Richard, I didn't ask for your *opinion*. I asked for the facts! When we have them, and only then, we can discuss what we think about them!"

This fact-based approach was engraved in my mind by Whitlam. It was still there when I was in Baghdad, twenty years later. The Iraqis hated it.

ANDREW PEACOCK, the new foreign minister following the 1977 elections and, most recently, Australian ambassador to the United States, was, of course, a conservative, but a relatively liberal one. He didn't think it appropriate to punish me for having worked for the opposition. He called me to his office and said, "Richard, you've had a fabulous experience. Gough Whitlam is a great man, and you've learned a lot. I want you to put it to work for Australia in an overseas posting." So I was sent to be deputy chief of mission in Bonn, where I spent three years.

This was a welcome posting, especially since, alongside my routine embassy work, it enabled me to get back into the nuclear weapons issues, which were highly contentious in Europe at that time. Debate was raging about the deployment of theater nuclear forces in Europe, including U.S. Pershing missiles. I also had a new level of exposure to those who were managing nuclear weapons and the Cold War through my work at the Australian military mission in Berlin. After three years in Bonn I returned to Canberra, where I finally went back to work in the nuclear disarmament area, focusing for two years on Australian uranium policy and arms control. I also was elected head of the Foreign Service Association—the diplomats' "union." At the end of 1982, I was promoted and sent to Paris as the minister and deputy permanent representative of Australia to the Organization for Economic Cooperation and Development (OECD).

In 1983 the political situation in Australia changed again. Bob Hawke, a former labor union head, was elected prime minister. He made Bill Hayden, his predecessor as Labor Party leader, foreign minister.

Soon thereafter, Hayden came to Paris for an OECD ministerial meeting. He and I were walking together by the River Seine when he said to me, "Richard, I'm deeply concerned about the standstill in progress on nuclear disarmament that we've had since Reagan became president." Remember the atmosphere of those days. Reagan wouldn't even speak to the Russians during 1981 and 1982; he was talking about the "evil empire" and vowing an arms buildup against their perceived threat. As a result, the world was as worried about nuclear war as it had ever been; the film *The Day After* was released, scientist Carl Sagan and others were writing and speaking about "nuclear winter," and so on.

Hayden said, "Richard, you're an expert on nuclear matters. What can we Australians do about it?" I said, speaking largely theoretically, that if we wanted to make an impact we would have to devote new and specific resources to the task. Hayden subsequently came up with the idea of creating an entirely new diplomatic position, called Australian Ambassador for Disarmament, with a cabinet-level mandate to do whatever he could to move the world toward disarmament. But we didn't discuss who ought to be appointed to this role.

Hayden went back to Australia and, in June 1983, gave the annual Evatt memorial lecture in Adelaide—named after the Australian who famously helped shaped the UN charter. In that speech, he announced this new post—and named me to it.

FOR FIVE YEARS in Geneva, I led the Australian delegation to the Conference on Disarmament—the single multilateral negotiating body for disarmament agreements—then comprising forty countries. I also worked on such related matters as the Seabed Treaty, the Nuclear Nonproliferation Treaty, and the Chemical Weapons Convention (CWC).

I so vigorously pursued agreement in the Conference on Disarmament that it should establish a negotiation committee for a Comprehensive Nuclear Test Ban Treaty (CTBT) that I became known there as "Mr. CTBT." (My secretary, Sue Badham, once took me into the filing room and pointed to the CTBT files, on which my reports and cables on that subject alone were lodged. They occupied half the room!) Unfortunately, political will on the part of the United States and to some extent Britain and France was lacking. So when I left Geneva at the end of 1988, we hadn't yet closed the CTBT deal.

On the chemical weapons front there was more substantial progress. The 1925 Geneva protocol against chemical weapons was clearly inadequate to modern purposes. So the need for a chemical weapons convention had been agreed upon, and a committee to negotiate one had been formed. While I was in Geneva, Australia was given the job of chairing this negotiating committee. (We held this job for most of my five years in Geneva, handing it off toward the end to Sweden, indeed, to Rolf Ekeus, who was to be my predecessor as executive chairman of UNSCOM.) This gave us the responsibility and the opportunity to shape the basic structure of the "rolling text" of the convention. We also completed a crucial first step toward the CWC by defining the chemicals that were at issue—the key precursors, thirty-five in all.

During the period prior to the agreement of a CWC, it was realized that like-minded countries could agree not to provide these chemicals to countries where they might be misused. Accordingly, an informal export regime was created. It met for the first time at the Australian embassy in Paris and included about twenty countries—NATO countries, the nuclear suppliers group, and most of the other major chemical-producing countries, including the USSR. This so-called Australia Group still exists today, meeting at the Australian embassy in Paris and now including some forty nations. Its existence is not based on any treaty but rather on informal memos of understanding among the member nations. Formal chemical weapons negotiations didn't conclude while I was in Geneva. That happened two years later. Today the Organization for Prevention of Chemical Weapons is up and running with headquarters in The Hague—conducting inspections and otherwise monitoring compliance with the CWC.

BETWEEN 1983 AND 1988, while I was in Geneva, Iran and Iraq were at war. We began to hear reports that chemical weapons had been used in this war—in particular by Iraq. Iran was recruiting teenage boys as soldiers and telling them that if they died in battle they would be martyrs who'd go straight to heaven. These boys were then deployed in massive numbers as human waves of troops, rushing at the Iraqi forces in the marshes of southern Iraq. It appeared Iraq might be overwhelmed by these human waves—hence, apparently, their resort to chemical weapons.

In public, Saddam Hussein always evaded the question of whether Iraq had used chemical weapons, but one of his generals was less politic. He said, with stunning frankness and cold brutality, "What do you expect? When you've got an insect problem, you use insecticide."

This caused outrage in the Conference on Disarmament. Since World War I, nearly seventy years, no nation on earth had used chemical weapons (unless Hitler's use of Zyklon B in the Nazi death camps may be so described). Now it seemed these evil weapons, which had once traumatized a generation of European soldiers (and those from Australia, New Zealand, and Canada), had reappeared in one of the world's most volatile political regions. Something had to be done. So during a period in 1985 while I held the presidency of the conference (which rotates among the member nations monthly, like the presidency of the UN Security Council), I summoned the representatives of Iraq and Iran to separate meetings. I told each, on behalf of the Conference on Disarmament, that their nation must stop any use of chemical weapons.

The Iranian representative with whom I met was Foreign Minister Ali Akhbar Velyahti, who happened to be in Geneva at the time. He'd been foreign minister ever since Ayatollah Khomeini had come to power. A sophisticated, soft-spoken diplomat, he took courteous note of my concerns while giving no ground. He said the Iraqis were completely at fault and would admit nothing more.

By contrast, the Iraqi ambassador shocked me by the ice-cold ruthlessness of his demeanor. He offered no explanation, defense, or apology; instead, he reacted scornfully, making it clear that Iraq claimed the right to use any weapons it chose regardless of international attitudes. This was my first direct encounter with the regime of Saddam Hussein. It had an atmosphere about it that would later become very familiar to me.

The Conference on Disarmament also launched an independent effort to investigate the facts on the ground in the Middle East. We asked member states to volunteer an expert to visit the battle area to see whether chemical weapons had been used, and Australia offered the services of Dr. Peter Dunn, a senior scientist at the Australian Defense Labs in Melbourne. Dunn—a generous, decent man and a fine scientist— traveled to Geneva, met with me, then went to Iraq and traveled across the desert toward the battle lines. There he found an unexploded artillery shell that he opened; it was filled with an orange-brown liquid. He drained a sample into the nearest available container, which happened to be a Coke bottle, and brought it back for laboratory analysis.

Dunn called on me in Geneva and was literally trembling, hand and lip, when he arrived. The brownish substance had turned out to be mustard—not the kind you put on a hot dog. The mustard in this instance was the same toxic chemical used in World War I. Had he spilled a drop of the chemical on himself, he'd have been gravely harmed. (Technically known as a "blister agent," mustard produces wounds resembling burns and blisters on the skin, then severe damage to the eyes, the respiratory system, and other internal organs.) But personal safety was least of Dunn's concerns. Dunn trembled because it was so deeply shocking to him that he held in his hand the first evidence of the use of chemical weapons in over half a century.

Dunn's father had served in World War I and, like millions of others, was innately fearful of the word "Gas!" that the soldiers would shout out in warning to one another as the awful smell of mustard or chlorine spread across the battlefield—a fear inscribed in the Australian historic consciousness. Now Dunn himself had been exposed to the first reappearance of this crime on the world landscape.

When Dunn's report on the use of mustard in the Iran-Iraq War was given to the Conference on Disarmament, Iraq was denounced by many governments, and a further impetus was given to the negotiation of a Chemical Weapons Convention. A dozen years later, as head of UNSCOM, I would be confronted with fresh Iraqi defiance of human decency and world opinion concerning the use of mustard agents in war.

B OB HAWKE'S GOVERNMENT had been elected in 1983. But from the start it was under political pressure, leading to an early election after some eighteen months in office, which Hawke would have preferred to avoid. The election was called for the fall of 1984, and Hawke's Labor slate won. However, prior to the election, I was caught up, almost accidentally, in a bit of political intrigue involving the United States.

I was in New York for the UN General Assembly meeting when I received a tip from a very reliable Washington contact. Apparently, the Reagan administration had told Hawke that if he won reelection they'd expect him to drop Hayden as foreign minister and get rid of me as Ambassador for Disarmament. There was, of course, an underlying message implied: a threat that the United States might express support for the opposition if Hawke didn't agree to these terms. Though I'd gotten on well with Ken Adelman, head of the U.S. Arms Control and Disarmament Agency, and the several U.S. representatives to the Conference on Disarmament in Geneva, it was apparent that the pressure I was exerting on the disarmament front wasn't finding favor at the White House.

I considered this information political dynamite, and I pondered what to do with it. Ultimately, I decided to refer it to Hayden in a private message. As I'd hoped he would, Hayden confronted Hawke about the story, who dissembled in remarkable fashion. Shortly afterward, a message arrived in New York, through diplomatic channels, from Hayden. It reported a denial by Hawke that there'd been any such communication with the United States and expressed outrage that anyone would think he'd countenance such a demand. Dick Woolcott, the Australian ambassador to the UN, and I both saw this message. But then, even more extraordinary, an hour later another message came through on instructions from the prime minister: "Destroy all copies of the message and expunge its number from the system."

I've been sending and receiving secure messages for decades. This was the only instance I saw of an attempt to pretend that a message sent had, in fact, never existed. I burned my personal copy of the message in front of Woolcott, holding it aloft and setting it aflame with a Zippo. "You're my witness," I told him with a chuckle.

Despite Hawke's denial, it was later confirmed to me that the information I received from my Washington contact was basically correct. And years later, of course, the Iraqi government would claim that I was a puppet of the Americans. How little they knew.

With Hawke safely re-elected in 1984, I repeatedly toured Australia during the next two years to speak about the uranium issue—that is, the question of whether and how the vast Australian reserves of uranium ought to be exploited. Our government's position was that we should sell uranium only to countries that were willing to sign an agreement that the uranium would never be used for military purposes.

I was sometimes asked why, as a staunch disarmament advocate, I didn't support the "leave-it-in-the-ground" position advocated by disarmament activists. After all, it seemed to hold out the promise that military (and other) uses of nuclear power might be eliminated at the source. I did not support this approach because I considered it fundamentally illusory. It would work only if *all* the world's uranium-producing countries held to it—which would never be the case. Countries like Japan and France needed uranium to generate electricity, a fact that would not change in the foreseeable future. So the only result of a leave-it-in-the-ground stance by Australia would be that France would buy uranium from, for example, the Ivory Coast or Chad with no safeguards whatsoever. Such an uncontrolled uranium trade would be the worst outcome for nuclear nonproliferation. An attempt at absolute prohibition on uranium, I believed, would be about as successful as the prohibition of liquor. Eventually, most Australians agreed.

In 1962, President John F. Kennedy predicted that within two decades at least thirty nations would possess nuclear weapons arsenals. In fact, the number of "official" nuclear states today remains what it was when Kennedy spoke—five (the United States, Russia, China, France, and the United Kingdom). Unofficially, Israel has now acknowledged that it is nuclear-armed, and two others—India and Pakistan—have a nuclear explosive capability, probably soon to be weaponized, for example, by loading bombs into missile warheads. The fact that the globe is not bristling with the nuclear weapons to the extent that Kennedy (and most experts at the time) feared is a testament to the effectiveness of the Nuclear Non-Proliferation Treaty (NPT) of 1968.

Under the terms of that treaty, a review conference to evaluate its performance was to be held once every five years, starting in 1970. Those meetings were duly held, and in 1985 the fourth such review conference was scheduled for Geneva. As Ambassador for Disarmament, I led the Australian delegation, in partnership with a more senior official from Canberra.

The two-week meeting was held under very difficult political circumstances. The NPT establishes two categories of states: those with nuclear weapons (the so-called nuclear weapons states), and those without. (The five recognized nuclear weapons states also happen to be the same as the five permanent members of the UN Security Council.) The two-tiered system established by the NPT is a pragmatic one. The NPT states that those with nuclear weapons must negotiate in good faith to get rid of them; those without must never acquire them. And it further enjoins the Haves never to transfer nuclear weapons to the Have-Nots or to station such weapons in their territory. Given these overall provisions, this treaty enshrines the norm that no state should have nuclear weapons, but the fact that the treaty has two categories strikes many as inherently discriminatory. But today the NPT has more adherents than any comparable treaty in history—187 countries. The brake it has put on the spread of nuclear weapons has shown that nonproliferation is a viable idea worth defending.

However, as the scheduled 1985 review approached, the NPT appeared to be in trouble. At the previous conference, in 1980, the member nations had failed to reach agreement on a final document stating their conclusions. (All the treaty adherents attend each conference, and decisions are made by consensus.) This was a grave failure. It opened up the possibility that another unsatisfactory review might call into question the viability of the treaty.

The heart of the problem was that the nuclear weapons states had refused to end weapons testing, a step that almost all the other countries—and the NPT—had demanded. Further, Article VI of the treaty pledges the nuclear weapons states to negotiate, in good faith, for the elimination of their weapons. Progress on this, too, had stalled, and leaders of many nations believed that although the Have-Nots were keeping their part of the NPT bargain the Haves were not.

Never the less, as the conference devolved into working groups focusing on various aspects of the treaty, some progress occurred. The elements of a final document that might attract a consensus seemed to be coming together. But toward the end of the conference, two member states, Iran and Iraq, began to quarrel bitterly, seemingly over everything. They were, of course, in the midst of their protracted conflict. Each feared that these provisions might somehow advantage the other side.

During the last evening of the conference, we were still wrangling over language that would satisfy everyone. The several hundred delegates were gathered in a large amphitheater. It was an unwieldy, almost unmanageable process. We adjourned for dinner and returned to the conference hall at 9:00 or 9:30 P.M., but as we resumed discussions on the floor of the hall, in the lobby, and in smaller rooms elsewhere in the building, it became clear that failure was proving unavoidable.

At one point, the German ambassador, a brilliant and robust man (and a friend of mine) named Henning Wegener, went to speak to both the Iranians and the Iraqis, hoping to knock their heads together and force an agreement. They rejected his advances. Finally, Wegener came over to me on the floor of the conference and said, "These people are dreadful. I can't get anywhere with them. Maybe you should have a talk with them—see if you can come up with something."

As the night wore on, I'd taken off my suit jacket. I had on a pale-pink shirt and a dark-blue tie. (I mention these details because they've been referred to in subsequent accounts, and in the ultraconservative world of international diplomacy, anything other than a starched white shirt was viewed as frivolous.) At 3:00 A.M., with the conference hall almost emptied except for the Iranians and the Iraqis huddling in opposite corners like boxers in a ring, I started shuttling back and forth across the floor between them. After an hour of this—wheedling on one side, cajoling on the other—I finally got both countries to agree to a form of words that each could live with. Literally every word, every comma had to be hammered out separately. The result was scribbled by me in pencil on a little slip of paper. The president of the conference read them out and they were adopted.

This so-called Pink Shirt Night won me a measure of renown in the diplomatic community for my role in helping to save a treaty that might otherwise have collapsed. In fact, in 1988, when I was awarded the Order of Australia, "for services to international peace and disarmament," the documentation made particular reference to actions I had taken "one night in Geneva" to rescue the Nuclear Non-Proliferation Treaty.

FROM 1989 TO 1991, I served in Bangkok as Australian ambassador to Thailand. I was in charge of Australia's fifth largest embassy and a staff of 350 people—a virtual microcosm of the Australian government, with departments dealing with the military, drugs, immigration, finance, trade, politics, and so on.

Shortly after I arrived in Bangkok, Australian Foreign Minister Gareth Evans made a detailed proposal for a peace settlement in Cambodia. That country, a neighbor of Thailand, had been in continual internal war since the time of the genocidal regime of Pol Pot, some fifteen years earlier. Evans's proposal was published in a small book, *Cambodia: An Australian Peace Proposal*, to which I had made a contribution.

Early in 1990, Evans instructed me to work in Thailand with leaders of the Khmer political factions, including the Khmer Rouge, to try to gain acceptance of the Australian approach. This work came to absorb the substantial portion of my next two years in Thailand. The culmination of this effort was agreement on a settlement based on the Australian plan. Consequently, in July 1991, I was named Australian ambassador to Cambodia and traveled to Phnom Penh to present my credentials to Prince Sihanouk.

Cambodia was, of course, half a world away from Iraq, but the same can't be said of the leaders of the Khmer Rouge I met in 1990 and those in Iraq I met seven years later. On my first visit to Baghdad I was struck by the same iciness, pervasive brutality, and dogmatism that I had felt when I had first dealt with the Khmer Rouge leaders, Khieu Sampan and Son Sen (also known as the "butcher of Phnom Penh").

At the end of 1991, I was named Australian ambassador to the UN in New York—the assignment I'd wanted for as long as I'd been in public service. For the next five years—1992 to 1997—I would hold the UN ambassadorship. This led to several other challenging roles.

I led the Australian delegation to the Conference on Population and Development. It brought me back into UN economic development work—the themes I'd focused on in my first UN posting. It was a huge conference, including thousands of delegates drawn from all countries, held in an ultramodern, efficient conference center outside Cairo.

Reaching an agreement on policies and programs was difficult, especially because of conflicts over such topics as contraception, abortion, homosexuality, and the rights of women. The Holy See (Vatican) was able to participate because it is a state, and this was a conference of all states. The Holy See tended to side with the Islamic world. (In fact, a wicked cartoon at the time, much circulated at the conference, showed the pope in bed with the ayatollah.) A diverse range of groups, with interests and goals on one side or the other of the contentious issues at stake, actively sought to turn up the heat. For example, a film showing the act of genital mutilation being performed on a young girl in Cairo was shown during the conference by some nongovernmental women's rights groups—almost impossibly painful to watch.

Despite the pressures and ideological hostilities on all sides, it was hoped that a Declaration of Cairo could be crafted to state some general principles about the rights of men and women and the needs of the family. I was one of fifteen persons from as many countries selected to be part of a smaller group charged with drafting such a declaration.

Crunch time came at midnight. The Egyptian representative in this small group took the floor—a junior minister in Hosni Mubarak's government. Speaking in a low voice, she riveted our attention: a classic example of the old principle that *not* shouting is sometimes the most emphatic way to talk—saying, "I appeal to you around this table for understanding. We *must* have this paragraph, in this form, or everything else we've agreed upon will collapse. There will be no Declaration of Cairo, and there will probably be no final program of action of the conference as a whole. All the work we've done on funding, programs, and other agreements will be lost."

I spoke up and supported her. The Vatican representative expressed misgivings, and others in the room shuffled their papers and their feet, but in ten minutes we voted to approve the declaration as written. Next day, in the plenary (whole-conference) session, the program of action and the Declaration of Cairo were adopted, with much jubilation.

I was subsequently elected by the UN General Assembly to be vice chairman of the Conference on Social Development in Copenhagen. It focused on poverty, employment, and social inclusion/exclusion. I ran one of the two main negotiating groups charged with producing the final documents recording our conclusions. The group met for some eight days and nights, and this work was one of the most strenuous things I've ever done. I barely ate the whole time; I'd start the morning with cereal and coffee, then work straight through till midnight subsisting on water and more coffee. There were always side meetings through the luncheon hour, meaning no meals and an increasing sense of exhaustion.

The whole process was one of bitter and tough negotiations with disagreements on a host of issues, divided along North/South, developed/undeveloped lines. But eventually we settled our disputes and crafted a declaration on social development that was widely applauded.

In 1994, I'd been elected president of the UN Economic and Social Council (ECOSOC), one of the principal organs established in the UN Charter. ECOSOC is made up of fifty-four member nations, elected by the General Assembly. Their decisions are translated into specific policy implementations by such UN organs as the World Health Organization and the United Nations Children's Fund.

ECOSOC, I found, was badly in need of reform. It had a vast, unwieldy agenda leading to paper decisions that caused little to happen. I decided to try to modernize and rationalize the system and, on the whole, succeeded, changing ECOSOC's decisionmaking processes in ways that still prevail.

My time as UN ambassador included one more very public and rather contentious role, having to do with the commemoration of the fiftieth anniversary of the UN in 1995. Ten years earlier, for the fortieth anniversary, because of the Cold War and other tensions, there had been no consensus on how to mark the occasion, and the entire project was shelved. There was obviously a risk that the fiftieth anniversary commemorative efforts might end the same way. I was elected chair of the preparatory committee, which made me the political representative of the community of nations on this issue.

For two and a half years I chaired a series of assembly-wide meetings on the impending anniversary, where the decisionmaking rule was consensus—never an easy thing to achieve. It took eighteen months of intensive work to develop the text of the anniversary declaration.

Most of the details had been agreed upon when the Arab countries, led by Syria, withheld consensus based on one sentence they insisted on including, concerning the right of any state to use military force to resist aggression. Article 51 of the UN Charter recognizes "the inherent right of individual or collective self-defense," but the Syrians choose rather to focus on Article 2, which refers to "territorial integrity" and "political independence" instead. Based on this focus, they came up with a sentence for the Anniversary Declaration, the wording of which implied the *right* of the Arab nations to expel Israel, by force, from the Golan Heights! And it was clear to all that this was the implication and the intent.

On the final Saturday before the opening of the fiftieth anniversary session of the UN, there was an emergency meeting at the Lebanese mission to the UN, attended by most of the foreign ministers of the Arab states, who were already assembling in New York. I was summoned to this meeting. The Arab foreign ministers immediately put the arm on me to give the Syrians what they wanted—because, after all, it was only "fair" and "just." The meeting lasted all day, with no result.

The preparatory committee continued to talk all day Monday at the UN itself. It adjourned without a result. From the chair, I said to the assembled representatives, "I'll come back at six o'clock, and we'll either settle this or not." Leaving the conference room, I took a seat in a corner of the UN lobby, where I invited Mohammed Alsharaf, the foreign minister of Syria, to join me.

I'd already decided on my strategy. Turning to the foreign minister, I handed him a slip of paper and said, "This is the language I've developed for the crucial sentence of the declaration. I can give you no more. I believe it's fair. You may interpret it any way you wish; in fact, you may say on the floor of the conference that you propose to interpret it a certain way. Others may interpret it differently, and say so. But I cannot change the wording of this sentence without running the risk that others will claim that it distorts the UN Charter and is therefore unacceptable. I beg you to cooperate. I don't believe you want Syria to be the country that blocks consensus."

Alsharaf replied, "Were your proposed wording to be rejected, we would not be alone in rejecting it."

"I know that," I replied, "but it's already well known that Syria is leading the rejection effort. Surely Syria does not want to be in the position of being the nation that prevented the UN from properly recognizing its fiftieth anniversary."

Acerbically, he responded, "We don't want to be in the position of having our territory taken from us, either. You must understand: For us, this is a matter of the deepest principle and importance, and I can't deviate from the different language that we've insisted upon."

We fell silent. The impasse appeared as complete as ever. I looked at my watch—it was almost five minutes to six. I said, "Mr. Minister, I'll tell you what I intend to do. First, I'm going to visit the men's room— because I need to. I'll then return to the conference room, where I'll gavel the meeting back to order and say, 'I've conducted exhaustive consultations with the concerned members, and I believe we have the text of a declaration.' I'll read it aloud, including the sentence I've just shown you. I think it's fair, and I think it's the best we can do. I'll then put it forward for adoption by the committee, and if I hear no objection, it will be adopted. Any delegation that wishes to explain its position *afterward* may do so."

I did exactly as I'd said. I gaveled the meeting to order, and the room filled up with representatives of the member nations, including the foreign minister of Syria. I read aloud the proposed wording and asked the committee to adopt it. I then asked, "Do I hear any objection?" After four or five seconds of silence, I announced, "I hear none, and the declaration is adopted."

Syria then took the floor. The foreign minister complained about the sentence and said that Syria wanted the complaint noted. I assured them it would be. But in any case we had a declaration for the UN's fiftieth anniversary.

Later, Alsharaf came over to me. To my profound surprise, he gave me a bear hug and said, "You're a good man, Butler. I respect you."

In retrospect, the fiftieth anniversary declaration—over which so much sweat and toil were spent, especially by my personal assistant, Narelle Grieve—is evidently not a masterpiece of statesmanlike eloquence but only an average read that adds little or nothing to the principles or policies of the international community. In fact, neither Narelle nor I can remember any delegate or diplomat referring to it subsequently.

In 1995, the usual quinquennial conference on review of the Nuclear Non-Proliferation Treaty was scheduled. The 1990 conference had occurred with no particular incident; I was serving in Thailand at the time and so was not involved. The 1995 conference was to be held in New York. It had a special, additional significance: according to the treaty, at the twenty-fifth anniversary conference, an extension of the treaty was also to be discussed. Since the nuclear weapons states were still widely perceived as not having kept their side of the bargain (i.e., by negotiating in good faith toward eliminating their own stores of weapons), trouble at the conference was, again, anticipated.

I was chosen to lead the Australian delegation to the conference. Early on there was trouble. First, we in the so-called Western Group attended a meeting summoned by the British ambassador, whose stance appeared to be to tell all the Western nonnuclear states how to behave—in effect, demanding that we follow the guidance of the United Kingdom, the United States, and France. In particular, they asked us to sign a pledge to vote for an indefinite extension of the treaty if the issue was forced to a vote.

I clashed with the ambassador, calling his approach heavy-handed. I urged him to talk more with the nonaligned countries in an effort to create consensus, rather than threatening a vote simply because we in the West had the numbers to win a majority. And I refused to sign his pledge, calling it insulting and premature.

My stance caused a bit of a stir. Over the next two weeks, many messages passed among London, Washington, and Canberra debating the question, "Is Butler out of control?" To their credit, the Canberra leadership backed me fully, and to the end Australia never signed the foolish pledge.

Complex and tortuous negotiations followed. Australia had developed the idea of negotiating two separate documents—one on indefinite extension of the treaty, the other on future actions. We passed these to the South Africans because, then, no nation in the world had more prestige or respect than Nelson Mandela's South Africa. The apartheid regime had created an atomic bomb and tested it (in secret). Mandela voluntarily disassembled and destroyed it. No other country has taken such action. The South Africans agreed with our ideas and were happy to take over promotion of them. They soon became the basic working principles of the conference.

Toward the end of the conference, it was obvious that it would be necessary to push very hard to forge an agreement, as a highly excited atmosphere filled with accusations of double-standardism on the part of the nuclear weapons states had developed.

Recalling my past efforts in Geneva, a number of key players suggested to me that I should get the leading parties together, informally, to try to narrow the gaps, so I hosted a dinner at my New York apartment at One Beekman Place near UN headquarters. Fifteen people attended: Jayantha Dhanapala, the president of the conference; the representatives of the five nuclear powers; the South Africans; the Canadians; and the representatives of the key nonaligned nations, including Indonesia and Iran. (The Iranians, in particular, were making a lot of trouble at the conference.)

After dinner, we adjourned to my sitting room with coffee; we sat in a circle of chairs till 2:00 A.M., arguing, debating, and gradually hammering out solutions to the issues that divided us. The agreement we crafted included several central principles. Consensus, rather than voting, would remain the basis for decisionmaking within the conference; the treaty would be extended indefinitely; and a firm commitment would be made by the nuclear weapons states to "principles and objectives for the future in nuclear disarmament." All of this, we agreed, would be put before the conference as a package, to be voted up or down in its entirety.

The group of us sold the idea the next day to our own capitals and then to our friends and allies at the conference. The following day it was adopted by the plenary session. So the Nuclear Non-Proliferation Treaty was extended, indefinitely.

S HORTLY AFTER I'd left Geneva in 1988, a committee to negotiate a nuclear test ban treaty was established there, and by early in 1996 its members had agreed on the text of a treaty. It was a much more complex document than we'd previously anticipated, including verification mechanisms, establishment of a treaty organization in Vienna, and other provisions. It also included a paragraph requiring forty-four states—which it named—to sign the treaty before it could take effect. The list included the nuclear weapons states, the uranium-mining states (such as Australia), and states thought to be threshold or clandestine nuclear weapons states, such as Israel, India, and Pakistan.

As the negotiations in the conference neared their end, India announced that it was not prepared to allow the treaty to be transmitted to the General Assembly in New York, where it would be brought into existence and opened for signature. Under the rule of consensus, any single state could block the treaty's progress in this way.

India's action was a cause of much concern and discussion among the world's capitals. Canberra expressed interest in leading a circumventing action, and I was asked to manage it. I devised the following approach: I'd submit to the UN General Assembly the text of a resolution saying, "Attached to this draft resolution is the text of a treaty banning all nuclear tests. It is identical to the text of a treaty recently negotiated in Geneva. I propose that the resolution be adopted by the membership of the UN and the annexed treaty text be opened for signature." In this way, I'd technically evade India's refusal to release the Geneva text, while "smuggling" its substance before the UN.

To pave the way for this maneuver, I conducted five weeks of negotiations involving every member state of the UN. The Australian mission divided all the nations by groups and invited them to visit our offices, where we asked for their support for the treaty. This process was repeated four or five times for each group, as the consultations continued. In this way, a broadly supportive consensus was built.

In August 1996, a special meeting of the General Assembly was called. I was the first speaker, rising on the procedural ground that I wanted to introduce my draft resolution. I did so.

I was immediately followed by the Indian ambassador, Prakash Shah, who thoroughly denounced our parliamentary gambit as a "transparent hijacking." He went on to say that the treaty was bad, that it could have been made better if it had been negotiated further, and that this act of circumventing the normal procedure set a dangerous precedent. Only on the last page of his speech did Shah come to the real heart of the matter: "By the way," he said, "India reserves the right to conduct nuclear tests of its own in the future." This desire was, of course, India's true motivation all along.

The General Assembly debate went on for a day or so (U.S. Secretary of State Madeleine Albright endorsed the treaty), and in the end the treaty was adopted by a 158–3 vote. (The three negative votes were cast by India, Libya, and Bhutan.) A week later, the text of the treaty was formally opened for signature in a room adjacent to the General Assembly chamber, and the first person to sign it was Bill Clinton, representing the United States. He was followed by the representatives of the other four nuclear weapons states—and then by the foreign minister of Australia, in recognition of our special role in bringing the treaty to fruition.

Soon thereafter, work began on building the prescribed Comprehensive Test-Ban Organization in Vienna. Some sixty countries have now signed the test-ban treaty and are complying with its provisions. However, India and Pakistan have meanwhile conducted nuclear tests. Then, in late 1999 the U.S. Senate refused to ratify the treaty, apparently motivated largely by partisan, domestic political concerns.

Many of the arguments advanced in the Senate against the treaty misrepresented it. Time was not allowed for debate, the Senate leadership apparently being more concerned to hand President Clinton a defeat in the wake of its failed impeachment than to sort out the facts on the treaty and how the United States might seek to amend it to take care of its concerns.

The cost has been horrendous. India and Pakistan were likely to join the treaty if the United States ratified it. This hope was dashed, and world leaders expressed deep concern about what they saw as a serious failure of U.S. leadership.

T OWARD THE END of 1995, the Australian government, under the leadership of Labor Prime Minister Paul Keating (who had replaced Bob Hawke), decided to take a major initiative in nuclear disarmament. This was the formation of the Canberra Commission on the Elimination of Nuclear Weapons.

The commission, which the prime minister asked me to chair, brought together seventeen experts from around the world in the field of nuclear arms control, with the mandate of drawing up a safe and practical plan for the elimination of all nuclear weapons. Over the course of a year, the commission met four times—twice in Australia, once in New York, and once in Austria. It included people who'd managed nuclear weapons systems, such as former U.S. Defense Secretary Robert McNamara, Michael Lord Carver of the United Kingdom, and Michel Rocard, former French prime minister, as well as disarmament activists and experts such as 1995 Nobel Prize recipient Joseph Rotblat.

As chairman, I ran the meetings, controlled the draft report, and wrote key sections of it. Issued in August 1996, the report is still widely viewed as the best and most practical plan for nuclear disarmament ever created. It was presented to the UN General Assembly and the Conference on Disarmament.

Halfway through our work, Keating and the Labor Party lost the Australian national elections, and the Conservatives returned to power, making John Howard prime minister. During the election campaign, the Conservatives denounced the Canberra Commission, calling it a Labor "stunt."

Shortly afterward, Alexander Downer, the new foreign minister, visited New York. I gave a dinner in his honor to which I invited a very influential group. At the appropriate time I made a toast to the new Australian foreign minister. In his reply, he said, "I toast the permanent representative of Australia, who of course will not be permanent much longer." There was polite laughter. Over coffee two of my guests said they had found his remarks tasteless and not funny.

Events shortly afterward provided the government with the perfect excuse for Downer to act on his implied threat. But the loss of my UN ambassadorship would prove to be only the beginning of a long, surprising journey that would take me to a place I had never been and, indeed, never expected to go: Iraq.

3

TO DISARM SADDAM

I N 1945 following their victory in World War II, the Allies
supervised the establishment of the United Nations. The UN
Charter contains a number of unique and fundamental prin-
ciples of international law. One of these is that no state should invade or seek
to absorb any other state. Forty years later, in violation of this principle,
Iraq invaded Kuwait, seeking to turn it into its nineteenth province. It
was the first time in the UN period that a UN member state had sought,
forcibly, to absorb another.

The international reaction was unambiguous but measured. The
nations of the world condemned the invasion strongly, and demanded
that Iraq withdraw. Under U.S. leadership a plan evolved for forcibly
ejecting the Iraqi invaders, if necessary. Over a period of six months, the
administration of President George Bush gradually assembled a coalition of nations willing to use military force to liberate Kuwait. In the
end, the Coalition included twenty-nine countries, including, notably,
Saudi Arabia, Egypt, and other Arab countries. At the same time, political
legitimation of the potential military action was obtained through the
passage of a series of resolutions by the UN Security Council.

The involvement of the UN was no mere fig leaf for a power play on
the part of the United States or any other member of the coalition. The
Gulf War, as it came to be called, was a legitimate expression of the
ideals of the UN and of the proper operation of the UN's mechanism for
establishing and enforcing international law. The founders of the UN
made the Security Council's decisions binding on all states, and Chapter
VII of the UN Charter gives the Security Council the ability to enforce
its decisions by military force, if needed. Accordingly, when the Security

Council demanded that Iraq withdraw from Kuwait, this was law Iraq was bound to obey.

The process of building support for military action, if necessary, extended throughout the latter months of 1990. Simultaneously, there was a series of repeated demands for withdrawal from Kuwait by the Security Council and the imposition of sanctions on Iraq. Finally, in January 1991, with Iraq having failed to comply with the UN's demands, the decision was made to apply the force needed to expel the invaders from Kuwait.

When the Coalition offensive began in January 1991, I was in Bangkok, preoccupied with the negotiations for settlement of the Cambodian conflict. Yet even there, distant from the battle zone, I was directly affected by the crisis in the Gulf.

Just before the outbreak of war, Iraq sent hit squads around the world to attack diplomats and government officials of Coalition nations. Western intelligence agencies and their collaborators around the world picked this up, and as ambassador I'd seen reports about this in Bangkok. Nonetheless, I went about my business normally, that is, until one night when the issue hit home forcibly.

I was at a black-tie dinner party when I was called to return to the embassy immediately, which, of course, I did. I went into my office, where I was handed urgent papers from a collectivity of intelligence organizations. They revealed that an Iraqi terrorist group had assembled in Bangkok with rocket-propelled grenade launchers and an array of other weapons, with which they planned to attack the U.S., Israeli, and Australian embassies.

The U.S. and Israeli embassies were obvious targets. But why was Australia third on the Iraqi hit list? Not only were we important supporters of the United States and members of the Coalition, but Australia maintains a big, modern embassy complex—a well-known landmark in Bangkok, a highly visible and inviting target for terrorists.

I decided to ask the Thai government to provide us with protection— a big step, but a necessary one under the circumstances. We usually hired local security companies to handle routine perimeter guard duty, but in an emergency like this we needed more. And so I asked the host country to provide military guard, something that was in line with diplomatic practice. The call to the Bangkok authorities was made, and soon I found myself, at 1:00 A.M., still dressed in black tie, watching canvas-covered Thai army trucks rolling into the embassy courtyard to disgorge forty to fifty steel-helmeted Thai soldiers.

These soldier-protectors settled in for a month, remaining throughout the Gulf War (we even had to set up a basement kitchen for them). I compared notes with my colleague, the U.S. ambassador, who had also requested Thai military support, despite the fact that the Americans had a U.S. Marine Corps contingent on hand, as is true at U.S. embassies around the world. Later, there were some arrests of Iraqis in Thailand, and caches of arms were found. So the terrorist threat was real, not imaginary. It was the first time I had an occasion personally to experience the willingness of Saddam Hussein to employ violence even at a great distance from Iraq.

T HE STORY OF the Gulf War has been told elsewhere, in detail. The Coalition forces, led by U.S. General Norman Schwarzkopf, drove Saddam Hussein's army from Kuwait with remarkable ease and swiftness, suffering few casualties while inflicting grievous damage on the Iraqi military.

Kuwait, however, suffered terribly during and after the six-month Iraqi occupation. Ten years later there are still signs everywhere in Kuwait of the occupation and the destruction the Iraqis wrought. During 1998, I visited the emir of Kuwait in his palace—an imposing, gracious marble structure that is opened to the general public every weekend. I learned that it had to be completely rebuilt after the war— the Iraqis had destroyed it in an act of simple vandalism.

I also passed an ice-skating rink while driving around Kuwait City. "Isn't that extraordinary," I remarked to my guide, "an ice-skating rink here in the desert!"

"Yes," he replied, "people here love to ice-skate." But he went on to say that during the Iraqi occupation this same rink had been pressed into service as a morgue. People who'd lost family members came to the rink because that's where the Iraqi authorities would lay out their bodies—on the ice.

The invading Iraqis also stole masses of Kuwaiti property—autos, computer equipment, TVs—in fact, almost anything movable. Years later, when I was head of UNSCOM, we discovered in Iraq scientific equipment of Kuwaiti origin that had been stolen from physics and chemistry labs—spectrometers, balances, and so on. I decided—much to the chagrin of the Iraqi officials—to repatriate these items to Kuwait, where they were received with gratitude.

None of Saddam's fellow Arabs would have participated in the Coalition if there had been any doubt as to its legitimacy. As it happened, Saudi Arabia provided major bases for the troops, the Egyptian navy sent ships, and Bahrain participated through the U.S. naval base there. What Saddam had done was so wrong that these nations, normally cautious about the U.S. role in the Middle East because of its patronage of Israel, were willing to support the U.S.-led coalition against him.

Saddam's actions in the 1990–1991 period also extended to violations of the international laws concerning weapons of mass destruction. We know, for example, that Saddam deployed chemical weapons to Iraqi forces in the field, although we don't know to what level the authority to use those weapons was devolved—division, battalion, brigade, or platoon.

U.S. intelligence efforts uncovered the fact that chemical weapons were being readied for use against the Coalition, and a prompt diplomatic response by the United States may have helped prevent their use. Shortly before the start of the war, U.S. Secretary of State James Baker and Tariq Aziz, then Saddam's foreign minister, met in Geneva. Baker told Aziz that the United States knew about the deployment of chemical weapons, and he warned Aziz that any use of such weapons would be met with "the most terrible response." Baker was intentionally ambiguous allowing the Iraqis to interpret his statement as: If you use chemical weapons, we will respond with nuclear weapons.

Years later, in conversation with me, Tariq Aziz cited Baker's prewar threat of "the most terrible response" as an example of U.S. attempts to "bully" Iraq, for which he expressed scorn. He had taken Baker's threat as meaning nuclear retaliation, even though, in my view, it is very hard to believe the United States would in fact have crossed the nuclear threshold in response to a chemical attack, and to this day Baker has declined to clarify what he meant.

A COUPLE OF SPECIFIC STORYLINES in the Gulf War itself deserve comment in the light of later history. One is the use of SCUD ballistic missiles by Iraq. During the fighting, Iraq fired SCUDs at several neighbor nations—one at Bahrain, five or six at Saudi Arabia, and thirty-nine at Israel. The SCUDs fired at Israel—mainly at Tel Aviv—killed no one, but they certainly frightened people and provoked televised scenes of rejoicing in the streets of Baghdad. One missile with a 140-liter cement warhead was fired at the Israeli nuclear research and development plant located at Dimona. It missed.

The SCUD attacks on Israel were Saddam's attempt to get Israel into the war. Saddam reasoned—no doubt correctly—that in a war between Iraq on one side and the United States and Israel on the other, the other Arab nations would choose, at worst, to be neutral and leave the Coalition. Thus, a major U.S. policy objective was to keep Israel out of the war.

It succeeded—but barely. The Likud government of Yitzhak Shamir in Israel was under enormous political pressure to respond to the Iraqi attacks. Two or three more SCUDs might have forced the Shamir government to act. In fact, there have been reports that Israeli air force jets were fueled, armed (perhaps even with nuclear weapons), and ready to go—and that only last-minute intervention by George Bush and James Baker prevented an Israeli assault on Iraq.

A continuing controversy from the Gulf War involves its abrupt conclusion. With the Iraqi army in flight, why, many people ask, did the Coalition forces not drive to Baghdad and get rid of Saddam altogether? Had they done so, the issue of disarming or containing him would have ceased to trouble the world.

U.S. General Henry Shelton, the current chairman of the Joint Chiefs of Staff, led a group of forces that actually followed the Iraqi army up the western side of Iraq before halting. I later asked General Shelton why (in the words of some critics), we'd "left the job half-done." He gave me two reasons, one lesser reason, the other greater.

The lesser reason, he said, was military principle. "The army of a democracy," Shelton remarked, "doesn't shoot teenaged soldiers in the back. If they'd stood and fought, even for ten minutes, we would have engaged them. But we weren't going to mow them down as they ran away."

But the greater reason was geopolitical in nature. The mandate of Operation Desert Storm was to eject Iraq from Kuwait, not to change the government in Baghdad. If the military leaders of the ground forces had tried to do the latter, the Coalition would have collapsed, just as it would have if Israel had entered the war.

The Arab Coalition partners were willing to stop Saddam from invading a neighbor. After all, once Saddam invaded Kuwait, the obvious question was "Who's next?" (Actually, we know the answer: Saudi Arabia. It was later discovered that Saddam already had produced car license plates that contained the phrase "Iraqi Saudi." Having claimed Kuwait as Iraq's nineteenth province, he was planning to annex Saudi Arabia, or at least its northeastern portion, as number twenty.) But by the same token, the Arabs couldn't tolerate a Western-led coup in an Arab nation. If they had, the question would again have been "Who's next?"—meaning which other Arab nation might be next to have its leadership overthrown by the West?

So Desert Storm—unavoidably, in my view—left Saddam Hussein in power.

It also left behind an economically, socially, and physically damaged Kuwait. Thousands of Kuwaiti people had disappeared, many of whom are still missing—people whose existence Iraq refuses even to acknowledge. And the fleeing Iraqi forces torched over 200 oil wells in a stunning act of vindictiveness and vandalism, causing ecological destruction at an extraordinary level. The resulting fires had to be put out, one by one, at tremendous risk by daredevil firefighters like Red Adair. When I first flew into Kuwait six years later, the stains where the fires had been—black pockmarks on the skin of the desert—were still clearly visible, as were the pools of oil on the desert surface, testifying to Iraq's eco-warfare.

In January 1991, at the conclusion of the Coalition's lightning offensive, the UN Security Council approved a series of measures that were, in effect, cease-fire resolutions. No formal peace treaty has ever been signed between the warring parties, which means that to this day the issue of Iraq's invasion of Kuwait remains unconcluded in international law.

The most important cease-fire resolution was Resolution 687. It specified Iraq's weapons of mass destruction—nuclear, chemical, biological, and missiles with a range greater than 150 kilometers—and required that they be "destroyed, removed, or rendered harmless."

Resolution 687 also set up the UN Special Commission—UNSCOM—as an organ of the Security Council to conduct the actual disarmament work and establish a monitoring system designed to ensure that Iraq did not reconstitute weapons of mass destruction in the future. The Security Council made completion of the disarmament work a prerequisite to the lifting of the economic sanctions imposed on Iraq in 1990.

Disarmament was not the only condition of the cease-fire; compensation to Kuwait for the damage and destruction it suffered in the invasion and the return of all missing persons were also required. In the ensuing decade, substantial compensation has been paid, though not the full amount envisioned; and the return of missing persons hasn't happened.

As an organization, UNSCOM had certain crucial characteristics that must be understood if the story of its successes and failures is to be properly appreciated.

First, it was an organ of the Security Council and, as such, was unprecedented. Ad hoc peacekeeping forces have been put together by the Security Council, but never a permanent organ charged with carrying out operational fieldwork in the name of the Security Council. In fact, never before had there been such a disarmament body. At the end of World Wars I and II, disarmament decisions were made, but no international organization was created to move into a country and take away its weapons. After World War II, Allied occupying forces in Germany and Japan enforced disarmament.

Make no mistake: UNSCOM's mandate was a serious one, and the requirements placed on Iraq were heavy. Shortly after I joined UNSCOM, I met with John Scott, my legal adviser—a skilled international lawyer from Britain who'd been around the UN for over twenty years and had been attached to UNSCOM from its beginning. I asked John to list Iraq's obligations under the Security Council resolutions: "Don't embellish or explain—just list the key points from the resolutions themselves in simple, unadorned form. I'll ask for interpretation if I need it." The list turned out to be twenty-eight pages long.

Iraq was required to be divested of every element of a program for creating or maintaining weapons of mass destruction—every weapon, every plan or document, every factory or piece of equipment. In pursuit of this goal, UNSCOM and its personnel had the right to do anything, go anywhere, break down any door. Some of the specific requirements in the UN resolutions were extraordinary. For example, Iraq was obliged to make it a crime under Iraqi law for anyone to be involved in making weapons of mass destruction. Iraq never passed such a law (no surprise, since those who would pass it were themselves already in violation of it).

Some degree of professional judgment would inevitably be involved in enforcing some of these requirements. For example, much of the equipment used in making weapons of mass destruction is potentially dual-purpose; the same fermenter used to make anthrax could be rinsed out and used to make beer, and the same equipment used to make the nerve agents sarin and tabun could be used to make aspirin tablets. UNSCOM had the legal right to destroy all such equipment. But how and to what extent to exercise that right would be a matter of judgment—and controversy.

On my watch, we did order the destruction of a good quantity of this kind of dual-purpose equipment in the chemical area. In fact, Tariq Aziz implored me three times to let some equipment remain intact—allegedly for peaceful uses. UNSCOM experts advised me against complying, pointing out that the equipment had been used for chemical weapons purposes and could be again. We destroyed it—smashed glass tubing, filled heavy machinery with concrete, buried machine and material. Would carrying out these obligations in full—to the letter of the UN resolutions—have destroyed Iraq's chemical industry? Far from it. But it would have seriously impeded their program for creating weapons of mass destruction as intended.

In giving UNSCOM such far-reaching rights and powers, the Security Council had in mind a four-step system for disarming Iraq.

First, Iraq would declare honestly all of its illegal weapons and the means to make them. "Full, final, and complete disclosure statements" were required within fifteen days of adoption of the resolution. It now seems remarkable, but at the time the Security Council honestly believed that the entire disarmament job would be completed within a year—hence the demand for declarations within fifteen days.

Second, UNSCOM and IAEA would verify the accuracy of the declarations. It was anticipated that this process would take several months. Suppose, for example, that Iraq had said, "We made 100,000 artillery shells filled with mustard, and here's where they were made, where they were stored, and how they were deployed." UNSCOM's job would then be to check out this story—to study the facilities where mustard was manufactured, to look at the shells, to read the army records concerning deployment and use of the shells, and so on.

Third, whenever the first two steps of this process revealed the existence of prohibited weapons and materials, these would be "destroyed, removed, or rendered harmless" under the direct supervision of UNSCOM staff.

Finally, where facilities used in creating weapons of mass destruction had potentially benign purposes—the manufacture of pesticides, medicines, and so on—there would be a fourth step: monitoring. UNSCOM staffers would be charged with studying operations at the dual-use facilities, looking at the raw materials that came in the laboratory or factory door, counting the products that came out, and examining the production process in between.

Naturally, detailed scientific knowledge is essential for this process. Some of the thirty-five key precursor substances useful in making chemical weapons are no good for making anything other than chemical weapons, while others can be used for benign purposes. For example, DDT and some chemical weapons are almost the same and contain overlapping lists of precursors. For UNSCOM to do its work effectively, highly expert technicians would be required on the ground in Iraq, and they would need free access to all the relevant Iraqi sites.

T HESE DISARMAMENT requirements would mean little without an enforcement mechanism. The postwar UN resolutions also specified that, until Iraq complied fully with the UN demands, international sanctions on trade, travel, financial exchange, imports, and exports—including oil exports—would remain in full effect. These had the potential to severely hamper, if not cripple, the Iraqi economy and were, in some measure, intended to do so. The UN wanted Saddam to pay a heavy price every day he failed to act to relinquish his illegal weapons.

All of the steps taken by the UN in the wake of the Gulf War were consistent with international law and precedent. This certainly includes the economic sanctions, whose effects in Iraq have been the subject of both honest controversy and a continual barrage of propaganda from the Iraqi regime and its apologists.

First, the legal background. Chapters VI and VII of the UN Charter spell out the powers of the Security Council in the exercise of its exclusive responsibility for "the maintenance of international peace and security." Chapter VI specifically discusses the peaceful resolution of disputes, wisely acknowledging that disputes will inevitably arise, but arguing that it's always preferable for them to be settled peacefully. Ways to seek peaceful settlement are listed and described, including such alternatives as negotiation, discussion, mediation, adjudication by the International Court of Justice, and intervention by the good offices of the secretary-general. Furthermore, a history and repertoire of diplomatic practice has built up over the years, which includes a role for special representatives of the secretary-general to go on his behalf to mediate in world trouble spots. Thus, under Chapter VI, the world community has many ways of seeking peaceful settlement to disagreements among nations.

Chapter VII turns to the question of enforcing the decisions and resolutions of the Security Council. When mediation, adjudication, and other means of peaceful settlement don't work, two options exist. First, in Article 41, the Charter lists "soft," nonmilitary means of enforcement, which include "complete or partial interruption of economic relations and of rail, sea, air, postal, telegraphic, radio, and other means of communication, and the severance of diplomatic relations"—in a word, sanctions.

When Iraq invaded Kuwait, one of the first reactions of the international community was UN Resolution 661, which imposed sanctions on Iraq, in particular an oil embargo. The resolution provided that no one should buy oil from Iraq, and it froze all Iraqi funds in banks around the world. These sanctions, imposed prior to the Gulf War, ultimately helped define my job as head of UNSCOM. If I'd ever been able to report that all the required disarmament actions had been taken by Iraq, and if the Security Council had accepted my report to that effect, then the oil embargo and the financial sanctions would have ended automatically.

In the months between the invasion of Kuwait and the start of the Gulf War, additional sanctions were imposed on Iraq, including restrictions on communications, trade, travel, and other activities. However, humanitarian imports were excepted—in particular, food and medicines. All of this had some impact on Iraq, but obviously not enough. It was apparently more important to Saddam to hold on to Kuwait than to have the sanctions lifted.

Consequently, the Security Council moved on to the military enforcement options outlined in Article 42 of the Charter. This article authorizes the UN, either directly or through its member states, to deploy air, land, and sea forces to exercise enforcement powers. The twenty-nine-nation Coalition acted in accordance with this article.

Once Iraq had been expelled from Kuwait, Resolution 687 specifi-cally continued the prewar sanctions, and it linked the oil and financial sanctions, which were considered the heaviest, to the disarmament requirements. Therefore, disarmament was given special weight in the postwar UN rulings.

Almost a decade after the sanctions were first imposed, it is clear that their main impact has been on ordinary Iraqi people. The members of the Iraqi power structure have been scarcely affected, either in terms of the quality of their lives as individuals or in terms of their retention of control over the economy, the military, and the nation.

This isn't the outcome anyone anticipated or hoped for: Where Sad-dam and his policies were the target, it is average Iraqi men, women, and children who have suffered the brunt of sanctions. Understandably, it's a cause of dismay and controversy around the world—feelings the Iraqi propagandists delight in exploiting to sow confusion among their ene-mies. As I'll explain, I harbor doubts about the efficacy of sanctions. But many of the facts of the Iraqi case aren't widely known or understood.

First, it's important to recognize that, from the beginning of sanc-tions, Iraq was permitted to pump a certain amount of oil to raise money for approved purposes. The entire Security Council, meeting as the 661 Committee, had to approve Iraqi applications for these approved pur-poses. These included the importing of humanitarian goods (basically, food and medicines), the payment of Kuwaiti reparations, and the de-fraying of UNSCOM's expenses. This program, known as Oil for Food, was permitted to grow over time. In theory, then, through the 661 Committee, the UN controlled the amount of oil Iraq pumped. The amount allowed was reviewed every three months and steadily increased over time.

Yet even this fairly porous restriction has not been imposed without difficulty. Iraq refused even to implement the Oil for Food program for two years, viewing it (correctly) as an attempt to control their behavior. And once they did implement it, Iraq often listed eye-catching items for "humanitarian" use, including potential weapons materials. Because the executive chairman of UNSCOM was consulted on their requests, I had occasion to review the documents. One list included a huge amount of condoms. Another requested spraying devices that could easily be used for disseminating chemical or biological weapons. The first of these two items, although curious in its magnitude, was easy to approve; I refused the latter.

There is also mounting evidence that food and medicines purchased through Oil for Food have been hoarded by the Iraqi army. For example, when searching for illegal weapons, UNSCOM inspectors came across military warehouses filled with medicines. Furthermore, Iraq has developed a black market oil industry of growing scope. This oil flows from Iraq across the border to Turkey, or in vessels that sail from the port at Basra through Iranian waters (protected thanks to bribes paid to Iran) and then dash across the Gulf to the oil emirates, past the patrols of the U.S. Navy. This oil ends up in markets all around the world, earning huge markups for everyone involved. As a result of these illicit exports, the Iraqi military and leadership are awash with money.

During my time in Iraq, I could plainly see the real-life effects of the black market. On my first visit there, in 1996, I was impressed with the pervasive sense of poverty and stagnation. The cities were filled with neighborhoods made up of the typical "shop houses" of the developing world, each with a shop front downstairs and basic sleeping quarters upstairs. Most of the shop windows were devoid of merchandise. Otherwise, the cityscape was dominated by junkyards piled high with worn-out tires and spare auto parts—axles, gear boxes, radiators. Most of the houses and cars were in an advanced state of disrepair; I'd guess that 35–40 percent of the cars in Baghdad had cracked windshields, including the old Mercedes provided to me by the Iraqi government.

However, all of this decrepitude was set against the backdrop Saddam had constructed in past years, prior to the war and to the imposition of sanctions: a Baghdad of modern concrete overpasses and freeways, vast mosques and huge public buildings, and fascistic monuments to Saddam and his vision of an Iraqi empire. One enormous sculpture—depicting giant hands holding crossed scimitars—stays with me today because it was so typical of the bombastic and bellicose Iraqi public style created by Saddam. Sprinkled among the decrepit old cars were a few brand-new Mercedes and Volvos—owned by the leadership. And behind high walls in a particular district of Baghdad could be seen glimpses of the utterly sumptuous houses and palaces owned by the cronies of Saddam.

Almost two years later, in 1998, when I made my last visit to Iraq there were many signs of the gradual improvement of the economy. I now saw new auto tires, fresh from the factories, many still encased in factory wrap, piled up in roadside warehouses. There were new cars on the streets, food on display in the markets, more lights glowing at night, and brightly decorated storefronts with goods in the windows.

Nevertheless, much of the city's infrastructure was still in bad condition. And the presence of the military was pervasive. Armed soldiers were everywhere. So were tanks, jeeps, and other military vehicles, painted in camouflage colors, mostly of Russian origin, all dirty but in operating condition. At the airport, I saw lots of MiG and Sukhoi fighters and the big Mi-18 helicopters. We would sometimes fly over an aircraft graveyard with heavy Soviet bombers up on blocks, with parts missing, even entire tail sections—probably being cannibalized to equip other planes.

The growth of economic activity that I could observe through these superficial changes over the eighteen months of my direct involvement within Iraq couldn't all have been coming from the Oil for Food program; that was simply not possible. The growing black market in oil clearly made the difference.

On the last morning of one visit to Baghdad around the middle of my tenure, I visited the house of the Russian ambassador for breakfast. This was a tradition begun by my predecessor, Rolf Ekeus. I followed it until, frankly, I got tired of having to be gracious while being lied to (or flattered—hard to tell the difference!) for forty-five minutes. On this occasion, the Iraqis for some reason changed my security escort. Suddenly, while I remained in my old Mercedes with the cracked windshield, the escorts before and behind me were driving absolutely brand-new Volvos—of a model not yet available in the United States. Such imports were forbidden under the sanctions.

G IVEN ALL THIS, many have declared the sanctions against Iraq—indeed, sanctions in general—as misguided and immoral. But the truth is more complicated. The UN Charter is wise to recognize the need for a nonmilitary means of encouraging compliance with international law, and because sanctions seek to avoid loss of life (unlike military attacks), they are a relatively humane method of coercion.

There's also a moral dimension to the notion of sanctions. If the citizens of the United States, Australia, or any other nation have condemned a state for invading another state (as Iraq did), or for imposing a racist system like apartheid on their own citizens (as South Africa formerly did), sanctions make moral sense: After all, how can we trade with a pariah nation—making money from those we condemn morally? Of course, like many moral strictures, this cuts both ways. The states that impose sanctions pay a price, too, because we must desist from making profits where we could.

As an embodiment of international moral condemnation and political pressure, then, sanctions make sense. But on the most practical level, do sanctions work? The evidence is discouraging.

Our experience for ten years with Iraq (and, previously, for twenty-five years with South Africa) suggests that when sanctions are leveled against a nation with resolute and immoral leaders, those leaders will act to minimize the impact on themselves both politically and personally. Thus, the people responsible for the immoral policies rarely suffer the consequences. In Iraq today, the army remains well fed because the leaders need a well-fed army to stay in power. And the leaders remain well fed because they pay a lot of attention to their own personal comfort—a characteristic of many despotic regimes. For example, the East German communist leadership lived in opulence amid public squalor, while after the fall of Nicolae Ceausescu in Romania his massive indulgence in all manner of useless objects was discovered. Then there was Imelda Marcos's shoe collection! Does anyone think that her notorious horde of footwear would have been smaller if the Philippines had faced sanctions for her husband's corrupt rule?

Furthermore, experience suggests that the longer sanctions go on, the more counterproductive they become. Over time, the leaders dig in to ensure their own position, and they create black markets to soften the worst effects of the sanctions. They also use sanctions for propaganda purposes to enlist the support of ordinary people: "See how our enemies fear and hate us? If not for our beloved leader's protection, they would surely destroy you." The leadership can also camouflage their own mismanagement, blaming scarcity and inefficiencies on sanctions. Also, it seems to be a fact that the stature of the sorts of regimes to which sanctions are applied is proportional to the size of their enemy. That is, the more forces allied against them, the more important they feel.

In fact, it could even be argued that eventually sanctions can help to *prop up* an embattled, tyrannical regime. Before the Gulf War, Iraq didn't have a particularly fair distribution of wealth. History suggests that any general improvement in the standard of living of the Iraqi people is likely to produce a rising interest in getting rid of Saddam. Middle-class incomes and lifestyles tend to generate greater interest in democracy. For this reason, among others, Saddam is not keen to alleviate sanctions, whatever his propaganda may claim.

And here is a prediction: If and when sanctions are finally lifted, the economic benefits of renewed trade will take a long, long time to flow to the ordinary citizens of Iraq. Saddam will say, "We must rebuild our nation first" and call for renewed sacrifice on the part of his people. Rebuilding the nation will, of course, start with rebuilding the military and its weapons.

So sanctions are of questionable efficacy—at least when the national leaders are able to evade their worst effects. Cuba's Fidel Castro has ridden out decades of a U.S.-led trade embargo. The South African trade sanctions lasted twenty-five years and didn't really work to undermine apartheid; in fact, the sense of embattlement they produced encouraged white Afrikaners to dig in and helped produce some of the worst excesses now being investigated by the Truth and Reconciliation Commission. Change came only when key South African bank accounts around the world were shut down through U.S. legislation passed over the objections of President Reagan and later implemented by the nations of the British Commonwealth. So getting the money of the leaders is much more effective than conventional trade sanctions, which often merely keep foods or goods away from the ordinary people.

Iraqi bank accounts abroad have been frozen under the current sanctions. But Saddam personally has ridden out the freeze quite comfortably; in fact, *Fortune* magazine recently listed him as the sixth richest man in the world. Evidently, the Iraqi leaders did a better job of shielding their money than did the South African leaders.

During our disarmament meetings, Tariq Aziz would often lecture me about the immorality of sanctions, saying, "Your insistence on pursuing us about our weapons is a deception. All you are really trying to do is to find an excuse to continue sanctions, so you can oppress and harm the Iraqi people." He became very aggressive about this topic. But his claims to be concerned for the well-being of the ordinary Iraqi citizen rang hollow—often comically so.

Once, to illustrate the hardship that sanctions were causing, Aziz cited the fact that he was no longer able to travel to international meetings in his private plane; instead, he had to suffer the indignity of driving across the border to Amman to board a commercial airliner. He'd then fly the Concorde from Paris to New York. Once in New York, he'd take a suite of rooms at the Carlyle Hotel for himself and his entourage, hire several stretch limousines, and dine nightly in expensive restaurants, at which he was photographed. Aziz's posturing as one of the "victims" of UN sanctions was more than ridiculous—it was outrageous.

So, over the long haul, sanctions have proven a relatively ineffective weapon against Saddam and his flouting of international law, and they've provided a propaganda opportunity he hasn't hesitated to milk. It seems clear that if Saddam is to be brought to comply with the disarmament regime demanded by the UN, more forceful steps will be necessary.

T HE ISSUE OF sanctions has been somewhat muddied by a controversy over remarks made by U.S. Secretary of State Madeleine Albright in March 1997. She gave Saddam a propaganda weapon by saying that the United States, even if Iraq did comply with the disarmament regime, would not favor the lifting of sanctions until Saddam had gone. Some commentators have described this as a major mistake because it supposedly removed any incentive for Iraq to cooperate with UNSCOM. A few have even written as though Saddam is *justified* in refusing to cooperate with arms inspectors because of Albright's comments.

I agree that Albright shouldn't have made this statement, but I don't consider it a blunder. Albright's main point was that the Clinton administration considered the removal of Saddam from the leadership of Iraq as an elemental change needed for both disarmament and the welfare of the Iraqi people—a contention that is beyond dispute. But, this remains basically unrelated to the question of UN sanctions. In fact, shortly after she made this statement, UN Secretary-General Kofi Annan privately reproached Albright for it, reminding her that no UN resolution named Saddam's removal as an objective. That would scarcely be possible for a UN resolution, because the UN is not in the business of interfering in any nation's self-governance.

In any case, the UN resolutions make it clear that it is not up to the United States to decide whether or not sanctions are to be lifted. As I've noted, some of the sanctions—those related to the exporting of oil and the financial restrictions on Iraq—are specifically tied to disarmament, and paragraph 22 of Resolution 687 clearly states that once the Security Council is satisfied that Iraq has complied with the disarmament requirements, then these sanctions are to lapse automatically. No specific decision or vote on sanctions by the Security Council is required. Paragraph 22, as you will see, became central to UNSCOM's work. The other sanctions—travel and communications sanctions, for example—are described in various other UN resolutions and are tied to other conditions, such as reparations to Kuwait; and sanctions decisions do kick in where these are concerned.

Furthermore, it's absurd to imagine that Iraq's failure to cooperate with UNSCOM was *in fact* due to any misstatement by Albright—as opposed to what Iraqi propagandists might claim. Iraq failed to cooperate with the UN from the start, years before most of the world had heard of Madeleine Albright.

Administration spokespersons clarified Albright's statement later, making clear that "of course the United States would obey the law and the letter of the UN resolutions." I consulted on this with Bill Richardson, then U.S. ambassador to the UN, before my penultimate visit to Iraq in June 1998 and got his permission to say to Tariq Aziz, "I have consulted with the U.S. government on this matter at the cabinet level, and I am absolutely satisfied that once the disarmament work is completed, there will be no impediment to the lifting of sanctions." This statement should have cleared up the issue, but Iraq has never given up its propagandist use of the original statement, demonstrating again that the goal of its policy is to keep its weapons, not to have sanctions lifted.

ANY DISCUSSION OF the sanctions on Iraq must return eventually to one central fact: The sanctions persist simply because, from day one, Iraq has refused to cooperate with the plan for disarmament laid out in the binding UN resolutions.

First, they did not make the required arms declarations within fifteen days, as demanded, aside from a few pages handwritten in Arabic that listed some items as allegedly destroyed. A full six months later, in August 1991, the Security Council was forced to demand a response from Iraq—at which time a series of purportedly "full, final, and complete" declarations were provided by Iraq. Of course, they were nothing of the kind. Fully seven years later, in my role as executive chairman of UNSCOM, I had to report that after 2,500 days—never mind fifteen!—Iraq's declarations were still not full, final, or complete.

To be more specific: In the chemical and missile areas, by the time of my last biannual report to the Security Council, in October 1998, the declarations had improved and were *almost* full, final, and complete. But the biological weapons declarations still weren't worth the paper they were written on. "This is nonsense," I told the Iraqis. It wasn't simply a personal opinion; international experts that UNSCOM had consulted four times had called the Iraqi statements "incredible" and impossible to use as anything like a basis for a verifiable full, final, and complete declaration.

The Iraqi evasion of the UN disarmament requirements was a determined policy throughout the life of UNSCOM. Iraqi leaders had no difficulty sitting across from me and spontaneously changing a reported fact or figure—for example, six previously reported warheads could suddenly become fifteen, or vice versa—with no explanation or apology about a previous lie.

To justify the absence of required data or documents, they offered stories that were the equivalent of "the dog ate my homework." One actual example: "The wicked girlfriend of one of our workers tore up documents in anger." Another: "A wandering psychopath cut some wires to the chemical-plant monitoring camera. It seems he hadn't received his medicine—because of the UN sanctions." Why of course!

The fact that UNSCOM's verification and monitoring efforts were continually hampered forced the arms inspectors to become more investigative than had ever been intended. Rather than verifying the data Saddam's people provided, it became a question of digging, probing, questioning, challenging, and cross-examining a system designed to obscure, confuse, and deceive. As I repeatedly said to Tariq Aziz, "*Your* actions have forced us to become forensic to a degree never intended—yet this is what you complain about!"

The unilateral destruction of materials by Iraq was a second major problem with which both Rolf Ekeus and I had to grapple. The Security Council resolutions specify that all destruction of illegal weapons must be conducted under international supervision. Iraq ignored this requirement. Beginning in 1991, Iraq destroyed significant quantities of prohibited weapons in total secrecy. Missiles were cut up, chemical weapons and warheads were exploded, and the shattered fragments were buried in pits in the desert. Tariq Aziz privately confirmed that this decision to act unilaterally was designed specifically to hide the real size and scope of their weapons program. "In that pit, we destroyed ten missile warheads," they'd tell the UNSCOM inspectors. "That was all of them." So we had to dig up the pit to check that it was ten—and then we had to investigate whether ten was, in fact, the total quantity at issue.

The third problem was concealment of weapons and weapon-making systems. This began in earnest in 1991 with a high-level committee meeting among the leaders in Baghdad on how to deceive UNSCOM. (We know of its existence from documents discovered years later.) Saddam gave Tariq Aziz responsibility for concealing Iraq's weapons. Thus, the Iraqi missile arsenal, for example, was divided into two parts—the declared part and the hidden part. Those destroyed were only from the declared portion. Ever since, Tariq Aziz's primary job has been to run Iraq's anti-UNSCOM industry, which I estimate became the third largest government industry in Iraq after oil and the military.

All these efforts at deception—the false declarations, the unilateral destruction, the concealment of weapons and weapons making—forced the staff of UNSCOM to become detectives. The arms inspections had to become intrusive, even, at times, aggressively so. And the proposed one-year disarmament process dragged on for seven years—after which it was still not completed.

All this time, the UN-imposed sanctions remained in place. Iraqi propaganda blames the world community for this. Yet the fact is that Saddam had the power to end the sanctions at any time, simply by obeying the law. One of the wickedest things I've ever seen is how Saddam was prepared to trade off the welfare of 22 million Iraqi citizens in order to conceal his program for weapons of mass destruction.

In response to Iraq's anti-UNSCOM efforts, Rolf Ekeus decided to create a special capability within UNSCOM to pursue the truth—the Concealment Unit. It had a specialized staff of six individuals who used technical means to try to break the Iraqi wall of deceit, including U-2 aerial photos, intensive analysis of Iraqi statements and documents, interviews with Iraqi citizens, and interviews with defectors. As I'll explain, the members of the Concealment Unit, small as it was, became a source of significant controversy, and managing it was one of the larger challenges of my job.

ROLF EKEUS HAS BEEN quoted as calling UNSCOM's work "the equivalent of war in arms control"—a kind of twist on the classic dictum of Carl von Clausewitz that war was diplomacy continued by other means. Sadly, this strikes me as an accurate summary of the situation. Certainly Iraq viewed it this way. Nikita Smidovitch, chief of UNSCOM's missile section, and one of the cleverest and most thoughtful people I've met, used to put it this way: "You must realize," he'd say, "that as far as Iraq is concerned, they are at war with UNSCOM."

Even stranger, perhaps, Iraq asserts—and, I think, believes—that they *won* the Gulf War. As I mentioned earlier, this reflects something fundamental about Saddam Hussein's mind-set. This belief is not merely a propagandist's boast or a Goebbels-like Big Lie but rather a reflection of a unique definition of "victory." Victory, in these terms, is when you are certain that the enemy has *not* achieved *all* of his objectives. Thus, although the "evil Coalition" did drive Iraq out of Kuwait and destroy a good portion of Iraq's army and military capability, it did *not* remove Saddam from power, eliminate his arsenal of weapons, or turn Iraq into a vassal state—the Coalition's real objectives, in the Iraqi view. Saddam has publicly crowed about the fact that Bush is now gone, Gorbachev is gone, and Thatcher is gone—while Saddam is still in his palace in Baghdad, having outlasted them all.

So, for Iraq, the battle with UNSCOM was simply the last battle of the Gulf War. And for Iraq to cement its "victory" in that war, they had to defeat UNSCOM and, in the last phase, Richard Butler personally. In fact, one of Iraq's explicit foreign policy objectives became my removal from UNSCOM. This is no paranoid fantasy on my part. The removal of Butler was the ninth item on Iraq's list of nine demands presented to the Security Council in November 1998 in its attempt to forestall the Clinton bombing.

This Iraqi definition of "victory" strikes most Westerners as ludicrous, and it is clearly self-serving; but it's also a logical view for a revolutionary, guerrilla, or insurgent movement. It considers victory to be any situation in which "we remain alive to fight another day." After all (so the true believer reasons), so long as we survive, the ultimate, inevitable demise of the evil system against which we battle grows closer every day, *because it is inevitable.*

This was the mind-set of the adversary I took on when I agreed to become executive chairman of UNSCOM in 1997. Understanding this goes a long way toward explaining the nature of the war of attrition Iraq is still waging against the UN and the security of the world community—sadly, with growing success.

4

THE SUMMONS

I N 1995, my involvement with UNSCOM, Iraq, and the
attempted disarmament of Saddam Hussein remained in the
future. I was still serving as Australia's ambassador to the UN,
the post I'd held since 1992, and was deeply involved in international
diplomacy and politics on several fronts.

The constitution and workings of the United Nations are inadequately known and often obscure. Because these matters are central to
the story that follows, I'll explain them briefly here.

The secretary-general, the chief administrative officer of the UN, is
appointed by the General Assembly on recommendation of the Security
Council. Any one of the five permanent members of the Security Council—
that is, the United States, the United Kingdom, France, China, and Russia—can veto a nomination. So the secretary-general is, in this very real
sense, a product of the Security Council. Although he is responsible to
the UN membership as a whole, he relies on the council for fundamental
political support.

The Security Council comprises fifteen members—the permanent
five and ten elected members. The presidency of the council changes
hands every month, rotating among all fifteen member nations alpha-
betically (in English). So during the month when a particular president
is in place, he may push hard, within some limits, to promote a cause his
nation favors. As it happens, because of the spelling of their formal titles,
the United Kingdom and the United States hold the presidency during
successive months, creating a sixty-day window during which joint
Anglo-American initiatives can be promoted—a frequent occurrence,
since these two countries think very much alike.

The ten elected members of the Security Council are elected by the General Assembly for two-year terms. They may not seek election for a successive term. A seat on the council is both prestigious and powerful, and nations have been known to jockey for electoral support as much as eight years in advance of a particular election. By informal agreement rather than charter provision, Security Council memberships are distributed (and have been since the UN's earliest days) among several regional groups: Asia (including most of the Arab nations), Africa, Latin America, Eastern Europe, and the so-called WEOG nations (Western Europe and Others Group, including Canada, Australia, and New Zealand). Israel is the only member state that is not a member of any of these electoral groups and hence has never served on the Security Council. This is a purely political situation and a very contentious one.

The UN's group-by-group electoral system is designed to ensure that every region of the world is adequately represented on the Security Council. Under this system, each nation in the WEOG group normally serves a term on the council every ten to twelve years. During 1995, it so happened that Australia decided to seek a seat on the Security Council as part of this customary rotation. We formally announced our candidacy early in 1995, hoping to be elected in December 1996 and to serve in the council during the 1997–1998 term. As the process of lobbying for support among the member states began, we felt confident about our chances of winning the seat. However, a number of complications arose.

First, the election turned into a very competitive one, beginning within WEOG itself. When there are more candidates for the Security Council than there are places, the election is vigorously contested. In this case, three candidates emerged for two council seats allocated to WEOG: Sweden, Portugal, and Australia. The members of WEOG worked long and hard to resolve this conflict before the election, but none of the candidates was willing to withdraw. So it fell to the General Assembly to elect two of the three candidates, and for two years prior to the election all three nations lobbied hard for votes.

Each of the three candidate nations had reason to feel its claim to a seat on the council was a fair one. Sweden had run for a seat two years earlier and, to its surprise and deep chagrin, lost out to New Zealand in a complicated election. The Swedes are accustomed—justifiably, for the most part—to think of themselves as "good guys" in the family of nations: peace-loving, generous, progressive, responsible. The idea that some other nations might not like them—might actually prefer to vote for a different candidate in an election such as that in 1994—felt like a shocking affront. To right this wrong, Sweden decided to run again immediately. So for the 1996 election, Sweden was determined to hang in at all costs.

For quite different reasons, Portugal was equally determined. It had recently emerged from decades of dictatorial rule under Antonio Salazar and then Marcello Caetano to become one of the world's newest democracies. This successful transition to a new Portugal produced a wave of powerfully positive international feeling toward it. Furthermore, the former Portugese colonies, let by Brazil, were strong supporters of a Portuguese candidacy—somewhat ironically, given the fact that Portugal had managed the process of decolonization so poorly (in Angola, for example, and then especially in East Timor, as the subsequent twenty-five-year dispute and the 1999 upheaval there demonstrates).

One of Portugal's strongest arguments was the fact that it had served on the Security Council only once in almost two decades, from 1978 to 1980. During the long years of Salazar's rule and Lisbon's refusal to liberate its colonies, Portugal could not have been elected UN dogcatcher (had there been such a post), let alone Security Council member. By contrast, Australia had served on the council four times previously, Sweden three times.

Thus, Australia faced two strong adversaries in its quest for the Security Council seat. Another complication involved my own visibility in the UN.

As I've explained, during my term as Australian ambassador, I'd served in several significant roles within the UN, including president of ECOSOC and chair of the UN's fiftieth-anniversary committee. This is unusual: The great majority of UN ambassadors never serve in any single position like those I'd held. My prominence raised hackles among some UN delegates, who felt I seemed to be everywhere, doing everything. My high profile was in good measure a matter of chance events; for example, I'd been named president of ECOSOC only when the agreed-upon Western candidate had to withdraw at the last minute. Many people around the UN knew and understood this, but our opponents spun my prominence against me.

Furthermore, 1995 had been an event-packed year for me, in ways not always to the advantage of Australia's candidacy. In forging and passing the UN's Anniversary Declaration, I'd had to knock a lot of diplomatic heads together, making a number of countries unhappy with my forcefulness. The indefinite extension of the Nuclear Non-Proliferation Treaty had been negotiated in my Beekman Place apartment. And then there was the passage of the Test-Ban Treaty, which also required some tough measures. All of these high-energy, high-visibility activities on the part of the Australian ambassador to the UN served as a distraction from the Security Council election. They also, clearly, alienated some nations whose votes we might otherwise have won. The Indians, for example, who were also running as a candidate from Asia in the same election, were unforgiving of what I had done on the Test-Ban Treaty and so worked against our election.

The upshot was this: When the Security Council election was held in the General Assembly in November 1996, Sweden came in first among the WEOG candidates, Portugal second, and Australia third, although only Sweden had obtained the required two-thirds of the vote. A second ballot was therefore required and, in that ballot, Portugal beat Australia and crossed the two-thirds threshold. It won the second seat.

When I'd visited Canberra nine months earlier to confer with Alexander Downer, the newly selected minister for foreign affairs, he'd warned me that he'd have difficulty keeping me on as UN ambassador because of my former Labor affiliation. It had been a long time since I'd been involved in partisan politics, and I resented the implication that I couldn't do a good job for my country because of my past party ties, especially given my substantive achievements at the UN. I told Downer so. A bit embarrassed, he backed off slightly, saying, in effect, "Get Australia elected to the Security Council, and we'll give you another year in New York. But no more."

When we lost the Security Council election, it was a bitter blow to Australian national pride, and this was fulsomely expressed in the Australian media. All of us who'd participated in the vote-getting effort were shaken; one of my senior political advisers, a superb young woman named Caroline Millar, was tearful in the General Assembly hall. She had worked tirelessly on our election and felt our defeat personally. I felt I'd let her down.

Back in Australia, the editorialists, columnists, and party loyalists mounted an intense debate about what the defeat meant and, above all, who was to blame. In truth, I considered this a petulant overreaction, encouraged, for political reasons, by partisan commentators. After all, in any contest there must be winners and losers. Why should Australia be exempt from an occasional loss? A bit irritated, I made these points in a televised interview but, apparently, changed few minds in the process. As the furor continued, a public hanging seemed increasingly necessary— and I was the one being fitted for the noose.

The Conservatives who held power in Canberra had always been uncomfortable with me—after all, I wasn't one of them. Now they had no reason to be even civil to me. My career representing Australia in New York was over.

My future prospects as a career diplomat seemed cloudy at best. I was told that I was being considered for another ambassadorship—specifi- cally, for a post in "an important European nation"—but Prime Minister John Howard intervened and scotched the notion. Then my name was discussed for the job of director-general of the International Atomic Energy Agency in Vienna, which was about to become vacant. But sup- port for such a post from one's home government is essential. Prime Minister Howard emphatically refused to give that. I asked why. Was I not qualified? My question was dismissed—it was about political col- oration, not ability.

AROUND THIS SAME TIME, the UN Security Council had been considering the nomination of a new secretary-general. The incumbent, Boutros Boutros-Ghali of Egypt, was approaching the end of his first five-year term and was seeking the customary second term in office. Madeleine Albright, as U.S. ambassador to the UN, made clear that the United States would veto this. The Americans put forth the name of Kofi Annan, a UN official from Ghana. Though vetoed by France in the first round of voting (as payback for the American ouster of Boutros-Ghali, a French favorite), Annan was eventually approved.

Because the Security Council had endorsed his nomination, approval of Annan by the General Assembly—though a necessary formality—was expected to be automatic. Not all member states appreciated this domi- nance of the world body by the Security Council, especially by the per- manent five. Ismail Razali of Malaysia was president of the General Assembly at the time Annan's candidacy was formally introduced to that body. For the occasion, Razali took the podium in traditional Malay dress, including his full knightly regalia, and after Annan was elected (by acclamation), Razali somewhat sardonically announced, "I have arranged immediately after this election for the secretary-general–designate to be present in the Indonesian lounge [a caucus room adjacent to the General Assembly Chamber], so that those of you here who have not yet met the man—of which I assume there is no small number—may have an opportunity to do so." Laughter ensued. It was Razali's small protest against the way the permanent five had hand-picked Annan and imposed him on the rest of the UN. And, indeed, we all did file out to greet Annan in the Indonesian lounge—many for the first time. This was not my situation, since I knew Kofi reasonably well.

As I shook the new secretary-general's hand, I said, "God bless you, Kofi Annan." He replied, quickly, "May God help me." As I later came to know, Annan is a religious or at least a spiritual man.

By early 1997, I'd seen Kofi Annan installed as the new secretary-general, but my own future was still in doubt. I visited Sydney, where I met with several headhunters about university or private-sector jobs. They all said much the same thing: "You've had a fine career, Mr. Butler, but frankly we wouldn't know what the hell to do with you." They explained to me their view that Australia was too provincial a place for a person who had "trod the world stage." That view, if accurate then, is no longer true, but only those few years ago it seemed to prevail, at least for a diplomat without portfolio and a peacemaker with no mandate to make peace.

My circumstances changed shortly afterward, on a Saturday in March 1997, when my wife and I were asked to lunch with Kofi Annan and his wife, Nane, at the Waldorf-Astoria Hotel in New York. At that time, the secretary-general's official residence in Sutton Place was being redecorated, and so for six weeks or so the Annans had a suite at the Waldorf. It so happens that the Waldorf Towers is also where the U.S. ambassador to the UN has his official residence—a grand apartment on the forty-second floor of the hotel tower. I've always found it a little surprising that the United States, when making its extraordinarily generous gift of some of the most valuable real estate in the world for the headquarters of the newly formed UN, made no provision for an official residence for the U.S. ambassador.

At any rate, Barbara and I joined Kofi and Nane for lunch at the Waldorf. Also present at the luncheon was Gareth Evans, the former foreign minister of Australia and a good friend of Annan; and, Nane's parents, who were visiting from Sweden, he a judge of the European Court of

Human Rights, she a member of the famous Wallenberg family. (Nane's uncle was Raoul Wallenberg, the great Swedish diplomat and heroic opponent of the Nazi Holocaust.)

Just before we had sat down, Annan drew me aside. He quietly said, "Richard, Rolf Ekeus has told me he wants to finish up his work as executive chairman of UNSCOM. I told him, 'Rolf, I won't let you go unless you first find me a good successor.' He recommended you, and I like the idea."

I knew Rolf Ekeus well from our time together in Geneva and had subsequently followed his career, especially his service to the effort to disarm Iraq. Rolf is a fine man, an outstanding diplomat highly regarded throughout the world, and, incidentally, a skillful jazz pianist. Like me, Rolf had devoted much of his life to arms control. He'd been a member of the Canberra Commission on the Elimination of Nuclear Weapons, and we'd served five years together in Geneva while we served as Ambassadors for Disarmament for our respective countries. Rolf had then served as Swedish ambassador to the Organization for Security and Cooperation in Europe in Vienna before being named executive chairman of UNSCOM in 1991. Now Rolf had been offered what would probably be the final job of his diplomatic career—the position of Swedish ambassador to the United States.

Kofi Annan asked me whether I would take over Rolf's job as head of UNSCOM by July 1—a little less than four months away. "Let me know soon," he urged, "so I can speak with the members of the Security Council as to whether this would be an acceptable appointment." I told Annan I'd talk with my wife and get back to him soon. We then commenced with lunch.

Later, Barbara and I talked at length about this new opportunity. We both had mixed feelings. Head of UNSCOM was certainly an appropriate job for me. Having spent years learning about weapons of mass destruction and crafting treaties and procedures for controlling and limiting them, I found it exciting to consider taking on the challenge of physically eliminating them from one of the world's most troubled and important regions. But the job would clearly be a difficult and dangerous one. Saddam Hussein and his regime had a long-established reputation for ruthlessness and dishonesty, and it was well known that Rolf Ekeus had found himself in a real battle as he tried to enforce the UN's disarmament mandates. Was the job feasible, or was this really an impossible assignment? I didn't know enough to judge.

I spoke to Rolf Ekeus about it. He was very positive in recommending the post to me. "This is a fabulous job," he declared. "The last five and a half years have been among the most interesting times of my life. The details of the work are absolutely engrossing, and you'll find you have tremendous flexibility and freedom of action. You'll fly everywhere in your own plane, and you'll get to meet all the important heads of state, from President Clinton to King Hussein in Jordan. In fact, I leave UNSCOM with a heavy heart. The truth is that my wife Kim has had enough of all the travel and the risks involved. The U.S. ambassadorship will be my last job, and it's a great honor to have been offered the post. I really can't say no to such an assignment. But being the head of UNSCOM has been unique. I'm sure you'll like the job."

In short, he sold it to me.

Knowing Saddam's murderous reputation, I asked Ekeus about how great he believed the personal danger really was. He played it down: "Oh, there were some vaguely hostile gestures and rumors, but no real danger." As I learned subsequently, this had been an understatement. In fact, Ekeus's life and the lives of his children had been threatened, and this had been a factor, at least from his wife's point of view, for wanting to leave the post.

Some people have said that the UNSCOM chairmanship, when it was passed to me, was a poisoned chalice and that Rolf knew it. The first part of this proposition proved true; the latter treats shabbily a man who deserves the gratitude of the world.

These are retrospective observations. At the time, my sense of the difficulty and danger of the assignment was far less vivid than it would later become. I knew that disarming Saddam would be an enormous challenge, but I considered it an important and necessary task from which I wasn't inclined to shrink. What I did not and could not know was how extraordinarily politicized the job would become; it would be squeezed between the great powers; the style and approach of any Executive Chairman would be deeply irrelevant given Iraq's determination to have UNSCOM destroyed.

With Barbara's consent, I made up my mind to accept Kofi Annan's offer.

I MADE AN APPOINTMENT to visit Kofi Annan in his office on the thirty-eighth floor of the UN Secretariat building. After the usual pleasantries, I explained my decision in terms I'd planned in advance.

"Mr. Secretary-General, I've decided to accept the post of executive chairman of UNSCOM for three reasons.

"First, it's about disarmament. I've spent a lifetime *talking about* disarmament—passing resolutions, extending treaties, and so on. Now I'll be able to roll up my sleeves, get my hands on some weapons, and do some actual, physical disarmament. Everything I've argued for in the past compels me to do this real job.

"Second, I understand from Rolf that it's a fabulous job with real flexibility of operations. I gather I'll have my own budget, my own staff, even my own airplane—greater independence, in fact, than anyone else at a comparable level in the UN system." I wondered subsequently whether Kofi Annan wasn't listening closely at this point in our conversation. Had he been, he might have recognized the implications of what I was saying. As it turned out, he later regretted the degree of freedom I enjoyed as executive chairman of UNSCOM, possibly thinking that I had abused it.

"Third," I concluded, "I accept the job because *you* asked me." I meant this sincerely. I was very committed to Kofi Annan as secretary-general, and I wanted him to know this. I knew I would need his support in return.

Annan was pleased. "Fine," he said, "it's agreed," and in due course he proceeded to consult with the members of the Security Council about appointing me formally. Meanwhile, I informed my home government of this agreement, stating that I proposed to accept a two-year appointment to the post starting on June 1, 1997. I told Canberra that the appointment would be at the level of under secretary-general on the usual terms and conditions that applied to that level.

My only political concern about putting it to Canberra was that the Australian government might be worried about a possible effect on international trade—specifically, on Australian exports of agricultural products like sheep, lamb, and wheat. (Australia doesn't need much oil from the Middle East.) But there was a bigger problem. The UN personnel office belatedly told me that, of course, it was understood that the sending government would pay my salary. This was the precedent established with Rolf Ekeus. In fact, the same was true with virtually all UNSCOM staff: Their salaries were paid by their sending governments, not by the UN itself.

In discussing the position with me, Rolf had never made completely clear the financial arrangements that went with the job. When our conversation ended, I'd concluded that Sweden paid an allowance to help defray Rolf's rent in New York but that otherwise he was paid, in the normal way, by the UN. Now I learned that this wasn't the case.

So a day after my initial cable to Canberra, I had to send a follow-up cable saying, in effect, "Oops, sorry! I didn't realize. Australia will have to pay my salary." It amounted to some $200,000. The UN would pay my duty-related travel and expenses. In fact, this was the opposite of the impression I'd formed after talking it over with Rolf.

This caused quite a problem. Foreign Minister Downer waxed indignant, claiming he'd been misled, that I'd known all along about the financial arrangements but had tried to deceive Canberra. This was wrong. But Prime Minister Howard was gleeful about having an excuse for not supporting my appointment. Canberra sent a cable saying that I could accept the job, but only if the UN paid the salary. Not surprisingly, the UN refused, and a fairly nasty squabble ensued.

In the end, it was settled when Madeleine Albright called Downer and said, in effect, "I don't believe it. You are thinking of denying us the services of Richard Butler, who is so eminently suited to this important and necessary job—and why? Because Australia 'Can't afford it'?! It's ridiculous." I had no knowledge that Albright made the call until sometime afterward.

Downer was duly persuaded—or, at least, embarrassed into agreement—and Australia approved my appointment. Kim Jones, then deputy secretary of the Australian Foreign Ministry, wrote to Joseph Connor, the UN's under secretary-general for administration, saying Australia had decided to support me—but his letter was couched in regretful, niggardly tones. The letter specified that Australia would agree to pay the money only if the funds went into a special UN account from which the salary could then be drawn—as if it were a matter of high principle that the Australian government should not pay Richard Butler directly.

This detail having been settled, and with the members of the Security Council in accord, my appointment was announced at a press conference in New York, attended by both Rolf Ekeus and me. The journalists present, mostly experienced UN-watchers, were well aware of our differing reputations. He was seen as circumlocutory, I was seen as blunt. One asked, "How is it that a mild-mannered, conciliatory sort of diplomat like Rolf Ekeus is to be replaced by the blunt-speaking, uncompromising Richard Butler?

"People change," I answered.

Just ten minutes later, Rolf was asked to comment about his experiences in negotiating disarmament with Iraq. He responded bluntly that he'd found the Iraqi leaders to be a gang of despicable liars and cheats. Fred Eckhard, Kofi Annan's spokesman, turned to me with an ironic glance and a nod in Ekeus's direction. I said to Fred, with a grin, "*This* is the mild-mannered one?!"

A LTHOUGH, AS YOU'VE SEEN, UNSCOM's executive chairman was appointed by the secretary-general, I did not report to him but rather to the Security Council. Oddly, officially I was not a UN employee. Thus, a bit paradoxically, my U.S. diplomatic identification card described me as under secretary-general of the UN, but I could not contribute to the UN employees' pension fund—because I wasn't a UN staff member.

There was a rationale for these slightly complicated arrangements, which had been carefully and deliberately crafted at the time of the founding of UNSCOM to afford the executive chairman independence of action. When Kofi Annan later asked me to soften my stance toward Iraq, and I respectfully declined to do so, I wasn't disobeying my "boss"; Kofi Annan was in fact a colleague, one of unique importance whom I should recognize as such, but I was not formally bound to obey his directives.

This deliberate independence was essential to UNSCOM's success, but I found that it caused serious envy and resentment toward me and UNSCOM on the part of Annan's senior staff—though I do not believe that the same was true of him personally. Whatever our disagreements—and they became serious—Kofi Annan always treated me with courtesy, and in any case he is a far larger man than some of those around him. When I made decisions that were opposed by particular countries—especially Russia, China, and France—my special status caused grumbling among staff around Annan that ultimately escalated into demands for "more normal" political control of my office.

The spring of 1997 was a period of transition for me between my UN ambassadorship and the UNSCOM job. Rolf Ekeus had generously offered me any amount of his time to meet in the UNSCOM offices to examine records, to be briefed by UNSCOM staff, and so on.

These briefings were valuable, but perhaps most important was a dinner Rolf hosted one night at the Century Club in New York with a few of his staff who had high-level, intelligence-based knowledge of Iraq's arms program. The purpose of the dinner was to brief me on this knowledge and on the entire UNSCOM intelligence operation.

Rolf and his staff described for me the workings of the Concealment Unit, the special group within UNSCOM charged with tracking down information concerning Iraq's hidden caches of weapons, its undisclosed work on developing and manufacturing weapons, and its efforts at hiding and disguising both. Rolf told me that he'd accepted certain intelligence assistance—electronic and otherwise—from particular member states in an effort to crack the Iraqi wall of deceit.

High-altitude surveillance using a U-2 spy plane was an example of the intelligence work UNSCOM had undertaken. Based in Saudi Arabia, the U-2 was owned and flown by the U.S. Air Force, but it was painted with the UN logo. Its pilot always carried documents saying he was on UN duty, and he followed a flight plan approved by the executive chairman of UNSCOM. (Once I took over the job, signing off on these plans became one of my weekly tasks, and the Iraqi government was always informed of the flight dates and the plans.) The resulting "film product" (i.e., the aerial photos of Iraqi facilities, structures, vehicles, and so forth) was the property of UNSCOM.

Similar arrangements were devised for the use of other intelligence resources—personnel, equipment—provided by member states. In each case, the details were intended to draw clear lines of ownership, control, and responsibility so that no one could truthfully claim that the resources or authority of UNSCOM were being placed at the service of any individual nation or were being used to further any cause other than the disarmament mandate established by the Security Council.

Rolf urged that I continue using this intelligence assistance. I listened carefully and subsequently decided to continue this practice, as he'd recommended.

IN MAY, shortly before my installation as executive chairman of UNSCOM, Tariq Aziz, the deputy prime minister of Iraq, made a visit to New York. I was invited to have a talk with him at the Iraqi mission to the UN on East 79th Street between Park and Fifth Avenues.

I learned later that he'd asked Egyptian Foreign Minister Amr Mousa for an opinion about my appointment. Mousa had offered this: "I know

Richard Butler, and he's tough. But he's also a decent and fair person from whom you can expect fair treatment." When I first met Aziz, his attitude toward me—courteous, even friendly—was probably guided by that advice.

Aziz began our talk by offering me a cigar. I declined. He lit up his own smoke—not for the last time in my presence. Tariq Aziz chain-smokes Cohiba cigars from Cuba, a strong and expensive brand. I don't know what the Iraqi government pays for them, but in the West they cost $50–70 apiece.

I can't say exactly what I expected from Tariq Aziz, but I recall I was surprised to discover how cloying he is—an impression that grew deeper and more intense with subsequent conversations. Basically, Aziz is a vain, arrogant bully, about whom there appears to be nothing decent.

On a physical level, Aziz's company is repulsive. In my meetings with him, he would sit behind his desk, puffing away on his Cohibas, with a big ashtray and a box of tissues at his elbow. Approximately once every two or three minutes, he would pluck a tissue from the box and expectorate into it a large globule of green phlegm. He would then drop the wadded-up tissue into the ashtray, where such tissues would pile up for the duration of our talk—all with never a word of explanation or gesture of apology.

When in New York, Aziz wore Western-style business suits (in Baghdad, I always saw him in military garb). His attitude at all times was very haughty: "How dare you ask me that question?" was his continual tone. He occasionally made vague attempts at reasoned argument: "You see, Mr. Butler, the reason this happened is so-and-so." But these attempts were brief and couched in a whining, dismissive tone. And as soon as he was challenged, he became abusive and threatening: "There will be grave consequences for your refusal to accept this truth," and so on, and so on.

I also found Aziz (like the other Iraqi leaders whom I met) to be utterly without humor. At times during our many confrontations, I'd try to break the tension with irony or self-mockery, which had worked for me in other diplomatic situations. (For example, if we were arguing over an apparent attempt to cover up some illicit arms manufacturing, I might quip, "Of course, we all know that no country has ever attempted a cover-up before!") I'm no stand-up comedian, but I've sometimes been able to elicit a chuckle at the right moment with lines like these. I never got so much as a smile out of the Iraqis. I often considered whether, if I were to write a book about this experience, I should title it *Dictators Don't Laugh*. . . .

In one way, Aziz stands apart from the others in Saddam's elite. He's a Chaldean Christian, a member of an ancient sect that acknowledges the religious sovereignty of Rome. They number about 10,000 members in Baghdad. Abraham, the biblical patriarch and progenitor of the Jews, was born in "Ur of the Chaldeans" (Genesis 11:31), and to this day the Chaldeans use Aramaic, the language of Jesus of Nazareth, in their liturgy.

Several weeks later, when we interrupted our first meeting in Baghdad for a break of a few hours, Aziz asked me how I'd use my time between sessions. I suppose I planned a shower and a nap in my hotel room, but I facetiously responded, "In prayer and reflection." (Another lame attempt at humor.)

Aziz didn't catch my ironic tone at all. Instead, he fell on me: "What religion are you?" he demanded.

"I'm a Christian," I replied.

"What kind?" he pressed on, "A Protestant or a Catholic?"

"I'm a Catholic," I told him, "by choice."

"Well, I'm a Christian, too."

"Yes, I'd heard you are." It was as close to a personal exchange on a human level as the two of us ever got. I mused later on whether the meaning of this exchange had been to demonstrate the truth of Jesus's reflection, "My Father's house has many mansions."

Aziz is the only Christian with a high post in Saddam's government. He has been an able promoter of the interests of the regime, especially as its representative in the West. He is fluent in English; in fact, he was once an English teacher. And because he's a Christian, he could never garner enough personal support to stage a successful coup against Saddam. Thus, his religion, which excludes him from the innermost circle of the Iraqi leadership, also makes him in some ways an ideal servant of Saddam.

I soon discovered another trait of Aziz: Whenever I gave him a new word or concept, he would seize it and use it against me.

During our first meeting in New York, I told Aziz that I thought UNSCOM's job should be carried out in an "objective" and "scientific" manner. I went on to explain that the issue was the location and disposition of certain weapons systems; that these were matters of fact, not of ideology; and that I wanted simply to find and dispose of the weapons of mass destruction in accordance with the UN mandate, not to score political points. This was what I meant by an "objective and scientific" approach.

Aziz promptly agreed and urged me to visit Baghdad as soon as possible after entering my post (which I did). I quickly found that he'd adopted the words "objective" and "scientific" into his own lexicon. Aziz started claiming that "objectivity" and "science" was *his* preferred approach, and he frequently declared that his quarrel with UNSCOM was that we were not being sufficiently objective or scientific. Of course, Aziz's notions of objectivity and science were somewhat different from mine. He later expropriated other words or concepts from me in a similar fashion and always to our disadvantage.

At one point during our New York meeting, I told Aziz that I'd be the happiest man on earth if, one day soon, I could wake up and find myself unemployed—that is, if the mission of UNSCOM could be successfully concluded. I said this because it was true, and I wanted to make it clear from the start that I was not interested in dragging out the disarmament process simply to provide myself with a sinecure. This was a suspicion that some of the Iraqi leaders may have had, if not about me, then about other members of the UNSCOM operation. Nikita Smidovitch is an example. He'd been a very senior Soviet disarmament official who'd found a new life in the United States as an UNSCOM official. The Iraqis often attacked Smidovitch unfairly, including on the basis that he would want the disarmament work to drag on indefinitely to support his new life in the West.

I concluded our New York meeting with the following, rather carefully planned, verbal olive branch: "One of the concerns I have about this whole business of UNSCOM and sanctions is that it all but obscures the fact that the Iraqi people are a great people and an ancient culture. Some call Iraq the cradle of civilization, and rightly so. The patriarch Abraham himself was born there. I hope that when I visit Baghdad, I'll have a chance to learn more about this culture and to visit your nation's historic sites, because I feel very positively and strongly about this aspect of Iraq."

To my surprise and dismay, Aziz showed no interest whatsoever in what I'd said—not even a word of acknowledgement or thanks for my compliments. Offhandedly, he remarked, "Well, if you're interested in such things, we can arrange for you to visit Babylon or Nineveh." There was no sense of any personal connection or reaction. My olive branch was probably my first (and not last) mistake with Aziz.

Of course, I'd also been trying to make a subtle political point: that the totality of Iraq's history and importance is not wrapped up and expressed in Saddam Hussein. One day, Saddam will be gone, while Iraq will remain. Aziz ignored this point completely. I don't know if this implication simply passed him by, or if he deliberately chose to disregard it. After all, though Tariq Aziz may be an Iraqi nationalist, he is above all a creature of Saddam Hussein—someone whose ambitions and destiny have been tied to those of Saddam with links of steel. The larger importance of Iraq as a nation is of secondary interest to such a man.

H AVING ENDED my first encounter with Tariq Aziz, I returned to the Australian mission to the UN and began preparing to move into my new offices, across the street at UN headquarters.

One more step remained, however, before I could undertake my new role. I had the right, as a retiring head of mission, to return to Australia for debriefing. I went home for just a couple of days to formally sign off from my job as UN ambassador and, indeed, the Australian foreign service.

While I was in Canberra, I received a final unpleasant surprise from the Australian bureaucracy. Philip Flood, the secretary of the Department of Foreign Affairs—not a political appointee but the permanent civil-service officer in charge of the Australian foreign service—told me I must retire altogether from government service. By contrast, when Rolf Ekeus had taken the same UNSCOM post, he'd been retained as a member of the Swedish diplomatic corps, simply being put on the so-called unattached list. I was to be given no such option. It was the final payback for my having "lost" the Security Council vote.

Flood begged me to understand the difficulty of his situation—trying to run a foreign service during a time of budget cuts and austerity. If I were to go, it would release a senior executive position making it eligible for abolition. In speaking with me, Flood's obvious assumption was that to leave his department must be a tragic prospect for me. My true feelings were just the opposite. I believed in the high importance of the work of international diplomacy—as I still do. And I was proud of the positive role Australia had played over the past two decades in helping to make the world safer, more peaceful, more secure. But serving in Philip Flood's foreign service had become awful. Under his and the new government's policies, the department had become so despairingly bureaucratic and so cheap that this expulsion felt more like a liberation.

I signed the required documents and walked out into the Australian sunshine with a spring in my step; the bureaucratic burden of being a member of what the Australian Department of Foreign Affairs had become was lifted from my shoulders. Soon I would be headed back to New York and then to Baghdad, where the challenges of UNSCOM and the secrets of Saddam Hussein were waiting.

5

WHAT HONEYMOON?

MY FIRST HIGH-LEVEL meetings with Iraqi officials in Baghdad took place toward the end of July 1997, just three weeks after I had begun my new job at UNSCOM. The team I led to the meetings was composed of senior policy advisers and the leaders of our scientific staff, so the discussions could cover both political and technical/disarmament issues. It included staff who'd visited Baghdad countless times and others who had been there less frequently. I was the only novice. Our nationalities were also mixed—we were from North and South America, Eastern and Western Europe, Asia and the Pacific. The one common denominator was that every member of the UNSCOM team was an expert, possibly unique, on one or another phase of Iraq's program to build and deploy weapons of mass destruction.

We traveled to Baghdad following the same route many previous UNSCOM teams had taken: via commercial flight from New York to Europe and then on to Bahrain, where UNSCOM maintained a field office. Then, because UN sanctions prohibited flights by commercial airlines in or out of Iraq, we flew a UN aircraft from Bahrain to Baghdad—a slow, noisy Hercules L-100 we'd leased from a private company, painted white and inscribed with the words "United Nations." Comfort was not a feature of this craft; the only seats it contained were paratrooper-type mesh hammocks, in which passengers arranged themselves as best they could. However, it had a large cargo capacity, which was frequently used to bring UNSCOM's heavier equipment and supplies in and out of Iraq.

Northern and Southern Watch are the two military surveillance units maintained by the Western coalition in the Gulf region, charged with enforcing the "no-fly zones" over Iraq's borders. Both units were always informed in advance of our flight plan, which had us over unpatrolled Iraqi airspace for only the last fifteen minutes of our two-and-a-half-hour journey. Iraq insisted that our flights always land at the military air base at Habbaniyah, some eighty-five miles northwest of Baghdad. This requirement was a violation of Iraq's obligations under the UN resolutions, which stated that UNSCOM should be able to land anywhere. But Iraq insisted on this arrangement and got away with it—one of its innumerable violations of the Security Council's requirements.

In some respects, however, entering Iraq through Habbaniyah was curiously appropriate. It was a vast and desolate airfield dotted with military aircraft of many different kinds and some tanks, almost all of Soviet origin. These machines were dirty and apparently in disrepair, but during our repeated flights in and out of Habbaniyah we would often see the fighter aircraft fly, mainly in "touch-and-go" (takeoff and landing) exercises. The hangar at which our aircraft parked that day in July had been splashed with the slogan "Down with the USA"—a resonant welcome to Iraq.

The Iraqi government provided transportation and a security escort for our drive from Habbaniyah into Baghdad. On this visit, my first to Iraq, they were particularly courteous, providing a senior protocol officer to accompany me—a man I soon came to think of as "Date Man." For some reason, starting with that first long drive into Baghdad, he spoke to me endlessly about the cultivation of dates in Iraq, describing Iraq's remarkable groves, numbering some 30 million date trees, and its nearly infinite varieties of the fruit. On every subsequent visit to Iraq he told me more—indeed, far more than I needed or cared to know—about Iraq's date crop.

I had decided to follow the routine of my predecessor, Rolf Ekeus, with respect to accommodation—that is, to stay with a small number of my senior staff in an Iraqi government guest house. The remainder of our team stayed in a fairly rudimentary hotel downtown.

The guest house was on the Tigris River not far from the main presidential area in Baghdad. It was a relatively large, two-story building dominated by a huge reception room the size of a tennis court, around the outer edges of which were some twenty garish couches. The rest of the building could house about six visitors, and besides sleeping in it we took our meals and held our preparatory meetings there. Iraqi plainclothes security officers carrying automatic weapons patrolled outside the building day and night, and we assumed that the inside was wired for sound. Thus, our planning sessions had to be highly circumspect in order to avoid the Iraqi side knowing, in advance, the approach we would take in discussions with them.

Our periodic visits to Baghdad were devoted largely to meetings between our teams and the Iraqi leadership. Before these began, I spent two days at UNSCOM's local office, the Baghdad Monitoring and Verification Center (BMVC), to consult with our resident inspection and monitoring staff. Those consultations with our resident staff were of immense value. These men and women represented the frontline of UNSCOM's efforts to find and destroy Saddam's array of weapons of mass destruction. Our staff worked hard, lived in tough conditions, and often encountered danger.

As I've mentioned, UNSCOM personnel were not employed by the UN; virtually all were provided and paid for by member states. UNSCOM paid a daily field allowance only. Some forty-five member states contributed. The executive chairman (first Ekeus, then me) would write regularly to the permanent UN missions of various nations in New York, requesting experts in particular fields: "We need an image reader . . . a biologist . . . a linguist . . . a computer expert." Eventually, some 200 long-term UNSCOM workers were recruited in this fashion, along with another 800 or so who served temporary roles on one or more inspection teams.

In addition to technical experts and policy advisers, UNSCOM employed a variety of support staff to handle essential, practical functions. For example, we maintained an auto pool in our Baghdad office that included about twenty land cruisers and a couple of trucks, which required a team of mechanics to keep them in good working repair. We also maintained a fleet of six helicopters provided by member states—first Germany, then Chile.

All told, the BMVC housed about 120 UNSCOM workers. Another fifty were in New York, while twenty-five worked out of our field office in Bahrain. We sometimes called the BMVC the Canal Hotel, since it was located in the building that was formerly a hotel with that name, and it is located beside a canal, usually dry. The building was a rough structure made of concrete blocks. One side of its first floor housed our administrative offices, including my office when I was in Baghdad, while the other side housed our technical facilities—a chemical laboratory, a biology room, a missile room, and office space for our colleagues from the International Atomic Energy Agency.

We also had a significant storage area in which we kept provisions and equipment of many kinds, including field rations supplied by various countries, including the French, German, and American armies, and supplies of drinking water in giant plastic bottles that we flew in from Bahrain. We also kept on hand stocks of all kinds of equipment: nuts and bolts, tools, wire, rubber bands, whatever, and vehicle parts for use by the motor pool team.

Finally, we maintained a little military museum, a single room displaying samples of shells, rockets, and other weapons we'd found. Visiting UN officials and dignitaries from member states would examine the various specimens that illustrated, in tangible form, the subjects of our inspectors' work.

Of necessity, UNSCOM was equipped to operate as a largely self-sufficient organization, especially since we knew that Iraq might choose to withdraw its cooperation and assistance from us at any time. We had our own doctor, an excellent professional whose services might be necessary at any moment, because we never knew when one of our inspectors might be contaminated by toxic chemicals encountered on a mission. (In fact, one German officer who served as part of UNSCOM's helicopter crew is still seeking compensation from the UN, claiming that he was severely exposed to chemical weapons agents at several sites throughout Iraq.) One of our helicopters was set up as a medical rescue unit, ready to go at a moment's notice. It was a truly impressive facility; in fact, we could have performed heart surgery in it if needed. This helicopter was also used for medical emergencies by other UN agencies in the area. The five other helicopters in our little fleet were mainly used for aerial inspections. They'd all been brought to Iraq on a Boeing 707 cargo plane, and they were flown and maintained, during my tenure, by a team of forty Chilean air force personnel.

WHILE I WAS AT the BMVC on the day prior to the scheduled beginning of consultations with the Iraqi side, I received word that I was to be favored with a private conversation with Tariq Aziz before formal consultations started. Of course, I accepted. It was the first of many private conversations I'd have with Aziz in Baghdad over the next two years.

Saddam Hussein himself never agreed to meet with me. Rolf Ekeus had received the same treatment. In 1997, there was a hint that Saddam might meet me—perhaps a honeymoon blandishment—but that never transpired. No reason was ever given for this attitude toward the head of UNSCOM, but all the signs were that such a meeting was considered to be below Saddam's dignity, his sense of which is massive. Besides, any meeting with the head of the United Nations disarmament effort would have involved an implicit concession by him that there actually *were* disarmament issues to discuss. He would never have been prepared to concede this so clearly.

Although my meeting with Aziz was to be a one-on-one session, the Iraqis insisted that the whole of our team go to the Foreign Ministry at the same time—a demand that was not atypical in its arbitrariness. This meant that my colleagues were obliged to sit about and wait while Aziz and I chatted over coffee in his private office.

The encounter lasted some thirty minutes. It began with Aziz making a series of declarations to the effect that Iraq had already met its obligations under the UN disarmament resolutions. He said this must be recognized without further delay, so that the UN sanctions against the Iraqi people could be lifted.

I wasn't surprised by Aziz's position. I'd been warned that the Iraqis had refused to acknowledge that they owed anything to the UN or to the world at large, and I'd decided not to begin my first visit to Baghdad with a debate over that issue. Without agreeing or disagreeing, I repeated what I'd told Aziz several weeks before in New York—that, in my view, what was at issue were largely scientific and technical matters. For this reason, the hallmark of UNSCOM's future work should be scientific objectivity. Aziz made no comment.

Although Aziz sought to conduct this tête-à-tête in what he considered to be a pleasant fashion—he was on his best behavior—his manner had a saccharine quality, like that of the overly sweet, cardamom-spiced coffee that was always served in his office. Paradoxically, it also had an underlying atmosphere of threat. Aziz was clearly accustomed to conveying to others the idea that you *will* do what I say—or else. Nonetheless, the relative cordiality of this first meeting gave me reason to hope I might enjoy a honeymoon of sorts—at least a brief period of cooperation between Iraq and UNSCOM—on the basis of which a constructive working relationship might be built.

When we concluded our private conversation, Aziz invited me into the adjoining room to meet his senior colleagues: the generals who ran Iraq's missile, chemical, and biological weapons programs, as well as the lesser general who ran an office called the National Monitoring Directorate (NMD)—the bureaucracy charged with shadowing UNSCOM inspectors. Aziz's successor as foreign minister, the extraordinarily unctuous Mohammed Al-Sahaf, was also present, as was his deputy, Riyadh al-Qaysi, whose style was that of an Oxford law professor, sporting tweed jacket and pipe. Following introductions and a brief, studiously jolly exchange of small talk, we moved into the large conference room to begin our formal consultations.

I described the sinister atmosphere of the setting in the first chapter of this book. On the occasion of this first meeting, the room was much as I depicted it there, with one difference: Video cameras were not yet in place around the room—at least not visible ones.

I asked permission to begin with a formal opening statement, to which Aziz agreed. I wanted no misrepresentation of what I would say at the beginning of this journey—new for Iraq and for me. I was also aware that the media would want to know about this first exchange, and I wanted an accurate text to be available to them.

In my opening statement I used "time" as the major leitmotif, repeating the word in several contexts. I said there had been a great loss of time in the disarmament of Iraq, the heaviest impact of which had been upon the ordinary Iraqi people, through the sanctions process. The sanctions, too, had gone on for far too long a time. As far as the timing of UNSCOM's concluding its work was concerned, we wanted that to be as quick as possible. Time, I emphasized, was of the essence.

I then noted firmly that the key to all of this was cooperation by Iraq: compliance with international law and with the resolutions of the Security Council and, especially, a decision by them to declare accurately and then give up their illegal weapons of mass destruction.

I'm no Churchill, but my little speech did involve thought and some attempt at persuasion. It sank like a stone. The Iraqis "noted" my comments and responded not at all. As I was beginning to learn, the boys in Baghdad are not about ideas and certainly not about sentiments. They want what they want, they want it now, and they're interested in nothing else. International law? UN resolutions? Disarmament? They would have none of it. They wanted the freedom to sell oil, to travel, and to trade without restrictions. They wanted, above all, to hold on to their weapons of mass destruction. All other topics merely bored and annoyed them.

Nonetheless, the UNSCOM team was in Baghdad to do a job, and we were determined to do it right. Accordingly, we began a two-day process of examining what remained to be accounted for in each of the pro-scribed weapons areas: missiles and chemical and biological weapons. Nuclear weapons were dealt with separately by the IAEA, with which UNSCOM worked closely.

For the first day, the behavior of the Iraqi side of the table supported the honeymoon theory. Not that affection or even respect for UNSCOM, or me, were involved. Aziz and his colleagues were testing whether or not they might get out of me a more lenient approach to ver-ification of their declarations of prohibited weapons, many of which were demonstrably false. Whatever the motive, however, the tone of the first day's discussion was businesslike and cordial.

We returned to our guest house at the end of the first day and dis-cussed among ourselves what had happened. Some of our experienced UNSCOM staffers were a bit troubled by the apparent coziness that had been displayed. My deputy, Charles Duelfer, was especially concerned. The following morning, he handed me a note he'd written the previous night. He said he'd been unable to sleep and had written his note instead, but also to have spoken what he wanted to say to me would have been recorded by the Iraqis. It stressed the need for us to remain "robust"—that is, tough and unyielding—in our demands for accurate disclosure. At breakfast, I thanked Charles for his note and said that I could see his point, although I told him I didn't agree with all of the comments he had written.

On the second day of the talks, I suggested to the Iraqis that we should agree on a "program of work" that would accelerate the process of disarmament and bring to final account all outstanding weapons issues. Aziz agreed to this approach, and a specific program of work, to be executed within six to eight weeks, was drawn up.

In the missile area, we agreed to re-excavate remnants of missile warheads and launchers to determine whether they had, in fact, been destroyed as the Iraqis had claimed. Iraq would also provide more information on the disposition of its proscribed missile force. In the chemical area, we agreed on the destruction of certain chemical weapons equipment and the key precursors for the development of those weapons. In the biological area, Iraq would provide a new declaration containing its full, final, and complete disclosure.

After the formal talks concluded, Aziz and I explained to the media, who had been assembled at the Foreign Ministry, what we had done and agreed. We both expressed our commitment to completing the program of work.

My team and I were scheduled to depart for Bahrain and New York the next day, but before we left for the Habbaniyah air base I was invited for another private talk with Aziz. He used this half-hour to try to pressure me into reducing the standard of Iraqi compliance, focusing especially on the proposed destruction of some chemical equipment our inspection teams had located, which, under the law, had to be "destroyed, removed, or rendered harmless." I had indicated that destruction, for technical reasons, was the best course of action. Aziz asked me to reconsider, claiming that the equipment could be used for production of agricultural pesticides and fertilizers. I took this under advisement and indicated I'd get back to him. Later, I rejected his request on the technical advice of UNSCOM experts. The equipment was then destroyed.

All in all, I felt that our first round of meetings in Iraq had been satisfactory. But the test, of course, would be in how the plans we'd laid were actually carried out.

T HE SPECIAL PROGRAM of work was acted upon immediately. Back in our New York offices, I authorized the required inspections and consultations with the Iraqi side in Baghdad in all weapons areas. Six weeks later, at the beginning of September 1997, I returned to Baghdad with our senior team to discuss the progress that had been made in resolving outstanding disarmament issues. The results, we found, were mixed at best.

The UNSCOM team had made some progress in the missile area. Specifically, we'd been able to clarify our records concerning the 819 SCUD missiles Iraq had imported from the former Soviet Union. We now felt we were able to draw up an account of the use or destruction of 817 of the 819 missiles. This was probably about as good as could be hoped for, given the orders of magnitude involved and Iraq's history of unilaterally destroying weapons.

But there were other serious sources of uncertainty in the missile area to address.

Iraq had refused to provide credible declarations and evidence on its indigenous production of prohibited missiles—the vehicles that could deliver biological, chemical, and nuclear warheads. There were also gaps in our knowledge about missile warheads and their contents, whether chemical or biological.

Iraq had announced in March 1992 that it had unilaterally destroyed production equipment and major components for its proscribed long-range missiles. It claimed it had disposed of several tons of missile materials at Al Alam, near the Tikrit military barracks. However, an UNSCOM investigation later forced Iraqi authorities to admit that this original declaration had been false. The commission's excavations at the site in September 1997 uncovered far fewer major engine components than Iraq had supposedly destroyed—just 10–15 percent of the quantity Iraq had claimed. Confronted with these facts, Iraq admitted that it had secretly removed the engine parts and production equipment from Al Alam in April and May 1992 in an effort to conceal the full extent of its missile program.

Then there was also the question of missile fuel—specifically, the kind of propellant that would fuel only a SCUD missile. Iraq had refused to give us an account of the disposition of some 500 tons of this propellant, saying it was irrelevant, as they no longer had SCUDs. They sometimes claimed the propellant was a general-purpose fuel that they could use in legal vehicles, a contention that was utterly false. The chemistry of SCUD propellant and the geometry of its engine are such that, if used in a short-range missile, it will quickly become too hot and explode, destroying the missile rather than launching it. Obviously, the only reason Iraq would insist on retaining SCUD-specific propellant would be if it either had concealed SCUDs or expected to acquire SCUDs in the future. Either step would be illegal. Thus, we had to know the whereabouts of the SCUD fuel—but Iraq continued to stonewall.

UNSCOM had also made some progress in improving its accounting of the substantial quantity of chemical weapons and chemical-warfare agents held by Iraq. Nevertheless, the chemical ledgers were far from complete. Particularly disturbing was the thoroughgoing attempt by Iraq to deceive UNSCOM about its manufacture of VX.

As I mentioned in Chapter 1, at first Iraq had sought to deny outright any manufacture of VX. When UNSCOM had demonstrated that this was false, Iraqi officials then tried minimizing the quantities involved, claiming they'd manufactured only some 200 liters of VX. After further detective work, we forced them to concede that a figure reaching some 3,900 liters was closer to the truth. However, they still refused to report the actual quantity they'd produced or where it had gone, claiming only that they had never "weaponized" VX—that is, deployed it in warheads or other delivery systems.

Finally, there was the area of biological weapons—a "black hole," as I described it to Aziz. For five years, Iraq had sought to deny that it had had any program for offensive biological weapons at all. Only when it became clear that this denial was not viable did Iraq present a purportedly accurate declaration concerning the program. UNSCOM had a team of international experts review that declaration as part of the program of work. They unanimously concluded that the Iraqi declaration hadn't a shred of credibility because it was incomplete and full of inaccuracies. It failed to provide critical information on the biological weapons program, including planning, procurement, research and development, and concealment.

We reviewed all this in a technical-level meeting I attended with UNSCOM experts and the Iraqis in charge of the biological weapons program. I then discussed the issue in a private session with Aziz. In the technical meeting, the Iraqi in charge, General Amir Sadhi, had told me that the reason their biological weapons program had been so "tiny and ineffective" was that Iraq had lacked the expertise to make it better (clearly implying that they would have happily made it bigger and better if they could). He was lying about the scope of the program, of course, and his audacity in frankly admitting that he wished it had been greater was appalling.

I complained to Aziz about this, and in an unguarded moment he revealed the official Iraqi attitude: "What's your point, Mr. Butler?" he asked, apparently genuinely puzzled. In other words, what was wrong with having a biological weapons program if you could do it really well?!

I then raised the question of concealment, the known Iraqi policy of undermining UNSCOM's disarmament mission by dividing Iraq's illegal weapons into two portions—that which would be concealed, perhaps literally underground, and that which would be revealed and then, presumably, removed. At certain moments, Iraq had conceded that there had been such a policy of concealment, particularly after Saddam Hussein's son-in-law, General Hussein Kamel, defected in 1995 and revealed crucial details about the policy. However, officials subsequently insisted they had ended the concealment campaign in 1995.

This was the stance Aziz now adopted. Furthermore, he said Iraq would refuse to cooperate with any inquiry or inspection in pursuit of what had been concealed as distinct from what was simply being misrepresented.

I appealed to Aziz to stop the obfuscation and come clean on Iraq's biological weapons program. I felt outraged, and I expressed this feeling, hoping perhaps to elicit at least a trace of remorse. "For four years," I pointed out, "as the main spokesman for Iraq, around the world and at the Security Council, you claimed that Iraq had no biological weapons program. You now admit it was a bald-faced lie—a lie you concocted and threw in the face of the entire world."

"That was a mistake," Aziz muttered. His meaning was clear. The mistake had not been in lying; the mistake was failing to get away with it.

There wasn't much point in further discussion. Frustrated, I indicated to Aziz that I would report the current state of affairs faithfully to the Security Council, and I departed Iraq.

UNSCOM WAS REQUIRED to report on its progress twice a year to the Security Council, and the first biannual report I would submit as executive chairman was due in early October. Well aware of this deadline, Aziz had sought to threaten me about the contents of this report, both across the conference table and in a more sinister way in private.

Publicly, he warned me merely that a report that did not begin to give Iraq a clean bill of health as to disarmament would be taken very hard in Baghdad. The threats in private were more ambiguous. Aziz suggested that my professional standing and reputation would suffer if I failed to meet his demands, but there also seemed to be a deeper, although vaguer, threat when he referred to his inability to know what "the reaction of the senior leadership of Iraq would be" if I did not report appropriately to the Security Council. He sought to draw a distinction between himself and the "hard men" around the president, who, he said, could get very angry and personal. So Tariq Aziz was the nice guy!

As soon as we arrived back in New York on September 10, 1997, I began to draw up the October report. At the same time, UNSCOM's regular cycle of inspections continued, including some inspections of sites where we thought the Iraqi concealment mechanism was in operation. I always authorized inspection of particular sites on the basis of our own analysis and reasoning and, occasionally, on the basis of information—provided by UN member states or defectors—suggesting that prohibited weapons or related documentation might be secreted at those sites.

For the first two months of my tenure at UNSCOM, these inspections had proceeded more or less routinely. Three days after I returned to New York, however, the playing field changed. Iraq began systematically blocking UNSCOM inspections, physically impeding our inspectors, willfully violating the commission's rights under Security Council resolutions, and even endangering the lives of our personnel. These actions sparked a crisis that would continue for the next eighteen months.

If there had been a honeymoon for the new executive chairman, it was clearly over.

UNSCOM typically created and deployed some forty to fifty inspection teams each year. Under Rolf Ekeus, UNSCOM had developed a core list of skilled inspectors whom we'd gotten to know and rely on. So from the beginning of my tenure, certain experts were on tap from various countries, mostly government employees of various kinds who might work at research labs or military facilities when not involved on an UNSCOM project. Of the approximately 1,000 people UNSCOM used during my administration, perhaps 250 were American; another 150 were British. Iraq would, not surprisingly, soon seek to make an issue of the nationalities of inspectors.

Each inspection team would consist of a number of specialists under the direction of a chief inspector, who was usually a permanent employee of UNSCOM. The rest were generally on temporary assignment. For a chemical weapons inspection, for example, we might recruit four or five chemical experts, a couple of linguists, a couple of computer experts (to scan databases in search of relevant information, for instance), a paramedic, and technicians to run the field telephone and other equipment.

Once the team for an inspection was recruited, members would first gather at our field office in Bahrain. There they would be briefed on the inspection plan and discuss any issues or problems they anticipated; team members who were new to UNSCOM would receive some basic training. Then everyone would board the L-100 for the flight to Baghdad, where they'd settle in to one of the local hotels.

In each case, the inspection plan would have been approved by me personally. We'd contact the NMD in Baghdad, meet with them around 8:00 P.M., and hand over one copy of the Notification of Inspection, which would say, "Inspection beginning tomorrow with a team comprising X number of individuals, to depart from our office at eight o'clock." Iraq would then put together its team of minders, which would meet us and accompany us everywhere. If it was a no-notice inspection, the plan wouldn't include locations, only the date and time of departure, the size of the team, and the number of vehicles. Each inspection had a number—"UNSCOM 150," for example—and its mission might include one site or several sites to be inspected over the course of one to two weeks. This protocol had been developed by Ekeus and was continued under my watch.

On September 13, UNSCOM sent out a combined inspection team, UNSCOM 199/203, so designated because the inspections represented the commission's 199th chemical mission and its 203rd biological mission. The target was the military barracks at Tikrit, Saddam's hometown. It was a large military area connected to both the chemical and biological weapons programs. The team assembled at our Baghdad office at 11:09 A.M., and Chief Inspector Brian Baxter presented a Notification of Inspection to the senior Iraqi government representative on hand. Minutes later, the official declared that the site was "sensitive." Under an existing UNSCOM protocol, the declaration of a site as "sensitive" triggered the application of the so-called modalities for inspection of sensitive sites, a set of special procedures Rolf Ekeus had given to the Iraqis in June 1996 following blockages of inspections at that time.

If there was a declaration of a sensitive site, then the number of inspection personnel to be admitted was limited to four. In this particular case, that was a ludicrously small number. The Tikrit barracks were a huge facility, covering some five square kilometers and including dozens of separate buildings; the idea that four individuals could adequately examine its contents was absurd. Nonetheless, the Iraqis insisted on this procedure, and they also stalled the entrance of the inspectors on various pretexts—tactics they'd used to hamper UNSCOM in the past and would use again.

One of the rules for inspecting sensitive sites required that all vehicular movement within or from such a declared site should cease until the inspection could be completed. The intention, of course, was to prevent the Iraqis from hiding, moving, or destroying evidence before the inspectors could get to it. On this occasion, however, while the UNSCOM team was awaiting admission to the site, they saw trucks and jeeps moving inside the barracks compound and saw others fleeing the area through back gates. They called this to the attention of the Iraqi officials present, but the movement continued.

During this standoff, one of UNSCOM's helicopters was circling above the site in support of the ground inspection. Our helicopter was piloted by one of our Chilean air force personnel and, in conformity with established practice, had an Iraqi pilot on board. The chief inspector radioed the helicopter and ordered the inspector aboard the aircraft to photograph the moving vehicles within the compound. The Iraqi pilot protested, declaring that photography was not permitted. When the aerial photographer tried to photograph a vehicle exiting the inspection site, another Iraqi government representative on board released his own flight safety harness and moved to physically prevent the photographer from carrying out his task. Alarmed by the Iraqi interference and fearful of a crash, the chief aerial inspector decided to land the helicopter. As the helicopter dipped to about 100 feet above the ground, the Iraqi pilot released his flight safety harness and moved toward the UNSCOM pilots in an apparent effort to interfere with the flight controls. The chief aerial inspector grabbed the Iraqi pilot, forcing him back into his seat.

The inspection team was finally granted access to the Tikrit barracks at 2:05 P.M.—almost three hours after they'd arrived. Two inspectors and two interpreters entered the site, where they found that documents had clearly been hastily removed from the premises, presumably in the vehicles our team had seen leaving the site.

There was a similar obstruction at the Sarabadi Republican Guard base two days later, on September 15. The incidents prompted me to send a letter to Tariq Aziz on September 16, 1997, detailing the two incidents and strongly protesting the violations Iraqi government officials had committed. I wrote:

> Apart from raising serious concerns about the commitment of the Government of Iraq to ensure the safety of the Commission's personnel, these incidents raise fundamental questions about the way in which the modalities are being applied by Iraq.
>
> The Commission has been working scrupulously within the terms of the modalities at sites declared by Iraq to be sensitive. As on a number of previous occasions, the events of 13 and 15 September indicate that Iraq is not.

I concluded by informing Aziz that these incidents would form part of UNSCOM's forthcoming progress report to the Security Council.

Aziz responded on September 17. He belittled the two incidents as "small" and unintentional but expressed the hope that similar problems would not recur. He promised that the two Iraqi officers involved in the helicopter mishap would no longer take part in UNSCOM flight missions and that he had issued instructions requiring adherence to the "modalities."

But the obstruction and concealment persisted. There was a particular flash point on September 27. Earlier that week, one of UNSCOM's senior biological inspectors had seized a briefcase from two Iraqi officials running out the back door of a laboratory. She found it contained biological test materials—namely, reagents for testing biological warfare agents such as anthrax and botulinim toxin—along with some correspondence related to a biological warfare program, bearing the letterhead of the Special Security Organization (SSO)—the military unit charged with personally protecting Saddam Hussein.

It was clear that we had a potentially significant discovery related to the Iraqi concealment program on our hands, one that needed to be explored further. After discussing possible steps with Scott Ritter (the leader of the UNSCOM Concealment Unit) and senior UNSCOM headquarters staff, I decided upon a two-step procedure.

First, we would provide the Iraqis with an opportunity to explain the meaning of the briefcase's contents. Second, if they refused to explain or offered an incredible explanation, as they so often did, I would authorize an immediate inspection of SSO headquarters. That inspection would be at night because the consultation with the Iraqis, consistent with their work habits, would take place at night. With Scott Ritter in-country leading our team, I authorized him to be the chief inspector in the event that an inspection was necessary. He would be accompanied by senior biological inspection staff.

The consultation with the Iraqis took place at the NMD and, as expected, produced only flat denials. Ritter therefore presented my Notification of Inspection and set off immediately with an inspection team in a small convoy of a half-dozen UN vehicles toward SSO headquarters in central Baghdad, about a mile from one of Saddam's palaces.

When the convoy got to within half a mile of the SSO building, it was stopped at gunpoint. Our staff were directly threatened. Weapons were cocked. A leading Iraqi General, Amir Rashid, arrived at the site to negotiate with Ritter, who then used a satellite telephone to call me at the UNSCOM offices in New York.

I had prepared for such an eventuality by laying out in our operations room, an array of U-2 photographs of the target area, and I was able to follow Ritter's account closely as we conferred by phone. Clearly, the situation was dangerous. Ritter tried to negotiate with General Rashid, pointing out that UNSCOM had a legal right to inspect the SSO building, but to no avail.

The matter was then moved upward, that is, to a telephone conversation between Tariq Aziz and me. Aziz began by denying we had any reason to inspect SSO headquarters. This involved one of our most ludicrous exchanges. Aziz noted that the biological test materials we had found had come from a food-testing laboratory, then added, "Mr. Butler, you know as well as I do that every government in the world has a section of their State Security Organization devoted to the testing of the food of the leadership." I could scarcely believe my ears.

"Could you please say that again? Are you saying that this program is for the testing of the food of His Excellency the President of Iraq?" Aziz repeated what he had said and confirmed that indeed the biological materials had come from a laboratory dedicated to testing the food served to Saddam Hussein.

I have not subsequently asked the representative of any Western intelligence organization whether they have such a laboratory within their institution. Frankly, I doubt that the FBI and CIA have ever devoted their resources to analyzing Bill Clinton's French fries or George Bush's pork rinds. But I have heard reports that Saddam Hussein does have a food taster, namely, the son of his leading chef!

Getting beyond this farce, I put it to Aziz that the test materials in the briefcase were actually not for food poisoning–type substances such as salmonella but rather were reagents for testing biological warfare agents. Aziz said that he was not himself a scientist but that his scientific advice was as he had explained it to me. "I think our scientists will need to have a talk about that," I told him.

I then indicated to him that, setting this "scientific" issue aside, it was important for us to inspect SSO headquarters because of the documentation that had accompanied the test materials.

Aziz shifted his ground and claimed—even more remarkably—that the building no longer existed: "It is an empty shell, it has no roof, there is no point in going there!" he declared.

Turning to my U-2 photo material, I said that was not what my information suggested to me: "I have a photograph in front of me at this moment that seems to suggest that the building is in fine shape."

Aziz shifted ground a second time. "You're wrong," he insisted. "The building is dilapidated. Nevertheless, it is within a presidential site. For reasons of the national dignity and sovereignty of Iraq, UNSCOM can never be allowed to visit any presidential site."

I referred again to the U-2 photograph, explaining to Aziz exactly where I knew our vehicles to be. They were a half-mile from the SSO building, with the front entranceway to the presidential palace a mile farther down the road. "How can you tell me that this is a 'presidential site'?" I demanded. I even mentioned the date of our U-2 photograph, which had been taken only a month earlier.

Aziz replied, "Mr. Butler, there are presidential sites—that is, environs around presidential palaces—from which UNSCOM must be perpetually excluded. This must be understood." It was a transparently ludicrous situation, but Aziz refused to budge.

We'd clearly reached a stalemate. Furthermore, our people on the ground were being restrained by the threat of force and were in genuine danger. I called off the inspection in the interest of the safety of our staff.

THIS WAS THE FIRST time that Tariq Aziz had introduced the notion of "presidential sites" that should be free from any weapons inspection. This new concept, together with the mixed results that had been obtained under the program of work, made it obvious that there were very definite limits to Iraq's willingness to complete the disarmament task.

At this moment, it also became clear to me that the claim that Saddam Hussein's regime wanted above all to rid Iraq of economic sanctions was false. Iraq's priority, I now realized, had always been to retain weapons of mass destruction—and, perhaps in particular, a biological weapons capability. Because disarmament and relief of sanctions are tied together under international law, this means that Saddam's ability to hold on to such weapons is far more important to him than the welfare of 22 million ordinary Iraqis.

On October 1, 1997, I wrote another letter to Aziz to protest Iraq's continuing violations. I stressed that Iraq had no right to prevent UNSCOM from carrying out inspections at what the Iraqis now called "presidential/residential sites." Further, I pointed out that the modalities for inspection of sensitive sites had never been part of a bilateral agreement between UNSCOM and Iraq, as Aziz had suggested. In fact, Rolf Ekeus had unilaterally issued the modalities in 1996 "in an attempt to demonstrate respect for Iraq's legitimate security concerns." I wrote in part:

> Respect for Iraq's legitimate security concerns does not inevitably place certain sites out of bounds for inspection. To do so would represent a major restriction on the Commission's effectiveness in carrying out its mandate, would contradict the decisions of the [Security] Council and would harm the credibility of reports the Commission might make to the Security Council on Iraq's fulfillment of its disarmament obligations. I continue to assume that Iraq has an interest in the Commission's reports being credible.

I pointed out that Iraq was increasingly applying the sensitive-site modalities on a selective basis. There had been four cases during the previous three weeks in which, following the declaration of sites as "sensitive," Iraqi personnel had then further claimed that they were unable to act in accordance with the modalities.

The special rules for sensitive sites, in other words, were no longer working. Instead, they were merely being manipulated by Iraq to thwart legitimate inspection efforts. I threatened to abandon the sensitive-site modalities altogether and to return to the original—far more sweeping—inspection rights established for UNSCOM in 1991.

Aziz reacted badly. He wrote to the Security Council, complaining that I was proposing to dishonor agreements and understandings that had been previously made and kept. As the modalities had not been "agreements," or been respected by Iraq, this was pure propaganda.

M Y OCTOBER 1997 REPORT to the Security Council was submitted in the midst of these violations. Nevertheless, I tried hard to provide a balanced account of UNSCOM's work during the previous six months. I explained that there had been some progress in the missile and chemical areas but that biology remained the black hole. I also made very clear, however, that UNSCOM was in no position to give Iraq a clean bill of health even in the missile and chemical areas, since the further evidence and information we had requested from Iraq and had set forth in the program of work during July were still nowhere to be seen.

Furthermore, I explained, two disturbing issues of access had now arisen. First, the category of sensitive sites had been arbitrarily expanded, and the rules in relation to inspection of them had been routinely abused. Now, we were also confronted with the idea of presidential sanctuaries, a notion absolutely contrary to the resolutions of the Security Council. Second, my report mentioned that we had been the subject of further blockages of inspections and threats to our helicopters.

The Security Council's consideration of this report was tortuous, which was a real departure from past history. Previously, virtually all resolutions on Iraq had been adopted unanimously. And when there had been transgressions like those of September 1997, the Security Council had always declared Iraq in breach of its obligations, even when such a declaration brought the possibility of military action or, at least, intensified sanctions.

On this occasion, however, the Security Council drafted a resolution, No. 1134, that failed to condemn Iraq in unequivocal terms. In declaring its "grave concern" over Iraq's continued intransigence, the council specifically avoided using language like "material breach," those being the words that could be used to justify military action.

As for new sanctions, it merely sought to impose travel restrictions on senior Iraqi officials who were responsible for Iraq's noncompliance with

UN resolutions. It did postpone sanctions review—that is, consideration of whether or not the existing sanctions might be alleviated—for a
period of six months. These steps, as some sardonically observed at the
time, were about as powerful as threatening to lash Saddam with a wet
noodle.

When Resolution 1134 was put to a vote, an even more disturbing—
and unprecedented—event took place. Ten members of the Security
Council voted in favor while five abstained, including three permanent
members—Russia, France, and China. Because these were abstentions
and not negative votes, they did not prevent the adoption of the resolution. Nevertheless, this action sent the clearest possible signal to Iraq—
namely, that the Security Council was wavering in its resolve to enforce
its own law.

Russia's pronouncements during the Security Council deliberations
typified the tepid response of the three Iraqi sympathizers among the
permanent five. As Russian Ambassador Sergey V. Lavrov put it, Russia
remained committed to Iraq's compliance with its obligations, but the
incidents of the previous months did not justify an immediate adoption of
additional sanctions. It was a shocking change of heart. During the preceding months, Iraq had trampled on the Security Council's law in some
five or six different ways. Now it was official: Iraq had gotten away with it.

Perhaps recognizing that the only real beneficiary of a division among
lawmakers is the outlaw, Iraq moved quickly to capitalize on this failure
of the Security Council. It moved into high dudgeon, declaring the resolution and its "egregious" new sanctions—the wet noodle—an offense
against the dignity and sovereignty of Iraq. Therefore, Iraq announced,
a mere six days after the adoption of the resolution, that it had taken
some new policy decisions.

In a letter dated October 29, 1997, Tariq Aziz informed the President
of the Security Council that the government of Iraq was

> ready to continue the cooperation with the Special Commission
> and to arrive, with the Commission, at balanced arrangements
> enabling it to fully discharge its task in accordance with the legal
> framework and without excessiveness provided that no individuals
> of American nationality shall participate in any activity of the Spe-
> cial Commission inside Iraq, particularly the activities of inspec-
> tions, interviews, aerial and ground surveillance. We shall put this

decision, not to deal with the Americans working with the Special Commission in these activities, into effect at 1:00 A.M. on 30 October 1997. We also demand that all the aforementioned persons leave Iraq within seven days from that date.

In other words, Iraq now claimed the right to approve or disapprove of members of the UNSCOM team based upon their nationality.

Iraq focused on the United States for several reasons. Of course, Iraq still was angry with the United States for rallying the world to Kuwait's defense and then leading the assault that quickly ended Iraq's occupation. But Iraq had other concerns, too. Most of UNSCOM's concealment inspections had largely been led by one chief inspector, Scott Ritter, who happened to be an American. Moreover, the United States supplied the U-2 that UNSCOM used for aerial reconnaissance of key Iraqi sites. Aziz's response to the new sanctions also sought to put an end to U-2 surveillance flights.

The Iraqi demands reflected a growing anxiety about UNSCOM's continuing inspections. They also signaled Saddam's renewed campaign to conceal his weapons stockpiles. Aziz claimed that UNSCOM was

an institution influenced to a large extent by America's hostile policy aimed at fulfilling its illegal and illegitimate objectives. Therefore, the Special Commission, in terms of its composition, activities and rules, is no longer a neutral institution operating impartially and objectively to implement the provisions of Security Council resolutions.

Having already blocked inspections, threatened UNSCOM personnel, unilaterally altered the inspection rules, and introduced new and arbitrary restrictions on UNSCOM activities—and apparently gotten away with all these breaches of the law—the Iraqi regime was clearly determined to demand even more. In less than three months from my beginning the job of seeking to bring Iraq's weapons of mass destruction to final account, Iraq had decided to enter into new, full-combat levels of resistance to our work. And the voting on Resolution 1134 in the Security Council showed that Iraq had acquired powerful allies for the war against UNSCOM from within the heart of the council itself.

6

THE RUSSIANS MAKE THEIR MOVE

ALTHOUGH I TRAVELED to Iraq periodically to meet with UNSCOM inspectors on the ground and to review our progress—or lack thereof—with Tariq Aziz and the other representatives of the Iraqi regime, I did most of my work in New York, at UNSCOM offices in the UN headquarters building. Of course, despite the vast distances involved, nothing of significance related to disarmament activity in Iraq happened without my prior approval and daily review.

I began each day by scanning the overnight reports from the field. Then, at 9:15 A.M., key UNSCOM staff would meet in what we called the Bunker, an internal conference room with special locks for added security—a dull-gray space equipped with a whiteboard and a videotape player; the walls were plastered with blowups of U-2 photos.

Attendees at the daily meeting would include virtually all staff present in New York, but certainly my deputy, the policy advisers, our lawyer, the public affairs chief, and the heads of our technical departments. It was the task of these technical heads to propose inspections within their areas of expertise, and the resident teams in Baghdad reported to them about the results of those inspections, usually by computer or via secure, coded fax communications.

The daily meeting was begun by Danny Rouse, a colonel in the U.S. Air Force who was my chief of operations. Rouse arrived early each morning, spoke to our offices in Bahrain and Baghdad, and then came to the Bunker, where he would post on the whiteboard a description of that day's activities. These activities would already be almost completed; Iraq is eight hours ahead of New York. Rouse always posted the temperature in Baghdad (which could have a significant effect of our operations), the numbers identifying the day's active missions (usually five or six at any one time), and a brief description of the missions: where the inspection team had traveled, what they'd observed, and any notable incidents or problems.

Rouse would open the meeting by summarizing the day's activities. The department heads would add other details, sharing information they'd gleaned from their own staffs' reports. We'd then move on to other issues. I might turn to our policy people and ask for a political report: "What's happening in the Security Council? What are the representatives of the key countries saying?" And toward the end of the meeting, I'd allocate tasks. For example, if the due date for one of our biannual Security Council reports was approaching, I'd assign portions of the preparatory work to various members of the team. After ten to sixty minutes, the meeting would end.

Often, I'd meet in the Bunker later in the day with specific members of our leadership team to talk through technical issues or other developments. Political questions might also be discussed there, in part because the Bunker was a more secure speech area than was my office.

Nowadays, no conversation in an office with windows can be considered truly secure; new technology involving laser-guided microwaves can read conversations by picking up the vibrations caused by voices on window glass. There's no way to block these microwaves completely, although drawing the blinds helps. Sometimes the best way to have a truly private conversation is to take a walk outside and find a random place to chat—a park bench, the steps of the public library. I found that, in a pinch, the UN staff cafeteria, filled with noisy conversations and the clatter of plates and glasses, worked fairly well.

The close links between our New York team and our field operatives in Iraq were important, especially during the periodic crises that erupted throughout my time at UNSCOM. Saddam's capacity for violence, the fact that our mission had been forced to become increasingly investigative and confrontational, and the volatile nature of politics in and around the Middle East—all added to the atmosphere of tension surrounding UNSCOM's work. By the end of October 1997, with Iraq having decided to intensify its resistance to the UN disarmament effort, the world community was watching closely and with more than a little trepidation.

O N NOVEMBER 2, 1997, the first test of Baghdad's determination to rid UNSCOM of Americans arrived. An UNSCOM aircraft landed at the Habbaniyah airfield that morning, with two American inspectors among its passengers. The Iraqi officials present refused to allow them to leave the aircraft. I had issued instructions that, were such resistance to occur, those denied admittance to Iraq should return with the aircraft to Bahrain.

I'd also consulted on this possibility with the IAEA in Vienna, knowing that a United States national who worked for IAEA would also be aboard that flight. Iraqi officials did not seek to prevent the IAEA official from entering the country, but in accordance with our agreement that UNSCOM and IAEA should stick together, that official also returned to Bahrain.

I advised the Security Council of this event in writing, noting that Iraq, by this action, had extended the policy announced in its letter of October 29—that is, it was seeking not only to expel UNSCOM officials from the United States already at work in Iraq but also to prevent the entry of any such persons into Iraq.

On the same day, Nizar Hamdoon, the Iraqi ambassador to the UN, addressed a curious letter to me. He referred to Iraq's decisions of October 29 with respect to U.S. nationals and the U-2 aircraft; he wanted to draw my attention particularly to the U-2 decision "because of its importance." He again proposed that the U-2 be replaced by an Iraqi aircraft. According to Ambassador Hamdoon, the U-2 flights were connected to the "military aggression" the United States would soon conduct against Iraq. I was therefore urged to cancel the U-2 overflights scheduled for November 5 and 7 of which I had given Iraq notice. Ambassador Hamdoon then delivered his punch line:

> I hope it will be clear that you will bear the responsibility for the consequences that will ensue from any decision to send the spy plane to Iraq, especially in circumstances where our anti-aircraft defences are being activated everywhere and are being made ready to meet the possibility of aggression.

In other words, if Iraq felt obliged to shoot down a U-2 plane, I would have pulled the trigger.

UN Secretary-General Kofi Annan became understandably exercised about the tense situation developing. In a discussion in his office, he first asked me a question that frankly surprised me: Why couldn't UNSCOM work without United States inspectors?

I explained that there were two reasons why Iraq's demand should be resisted. First, inspectors of U.S. nationality often possessed a significant portion of the required expertise in specific technical fields. Such expertise was to be found in relatively few countries, and not all of them were willing to help UNSCOM. If the Americans were to be summarily removed, this would immediately diminish our technical competence.

Second, were Iraq to succeed in singling out any one nationality, it would contradict a well-established principle that the receiving state in a circumstance like this should not be able to dictate to the sending authority, that is, the arms-control agency, the composition of its inspection and monitoring teams. Such a precedent would be wrong and dangerous.

In any case, I argued, it would be contrary to the spirit of the UN as well, given its rules against discrimination on the basis of nationality. I thought this latter argument would reach Kofi Annan. After all, he was the chief officer of the United Nations and the person most directly responsible for its integrity. He didn't forcibly disagree with me, but he didn't agree, either. Instead, as the crisis wore on, he repeatedly asked me the same question: Why couldn't we do our inspections without Americans?

When the issue came up again with Annan, I waxed slightly more philosophical. Iraq's position, I said, seemed to assume that arms-control work was subjective rather than objective. I contended that any competent scientist, of whatever nationality, if he or she considered the same data objectively, would come to similar conclusions. Was Iraq claiming that American scientists were incompetent? That would be absurd. Was Iraq claiming that they lacked objectivity? Practical experience and the testimony of countless unimpeachable sources showed that this would be false. Or was it that Iraq actually wanted *subjectivity*—that is, inspections by scientists who would arrive at the conclusions Iraq desired, irrespective of the facts? I said I thought that this was the most plausible explanation.

The secretary-general's main concern was to find a solution to the political dilemma Iraq's demand had created. He was aware that Iraq's position fundamentally had nothing to do with serious scientific objectivity or even the proper way to accomplish the job at hand. Iraq simply wanted out from under its UN obligations and was seeking to weaken UNSCOM through any tactical means.

Events now moved quickly on both fronts, in Iraq and New York. As for Iraq, I continued to authorize U-2 surveillance flights, sending the standard Letter of Notification to the Iraqi authorities. Meanwhile, UNSCOM inspection teams went into the field to carry out their work in each of the main areas of concern—missiles and chemical and biological weapons. All of those teams contained U.S. nationals, not by plan or through any wish to provoke the Iraqi government, but because American personnel happened to have the technical skills required. I took no action to remove them, deciding to send the teams into the field as normal.

On November 3, a missile inspection team reached its site, the Al-Karama State Establishment, which was involved in producing Iraq's Al-Samoud missiles. Iraqi officials blocked the inspection on the ground that the team contained personnel of U.S. nationality. In accordance with my instructions, the team's British chief inspector, Brian Baxter, told Iraqi officials that his mission could not proceed without all its members and that the team would return to base. As I'd directed, he also contacted the other teams en route to their inspection sites, who then stopped and returned to base. This process of UNSCOM seeking to do its work in the normal way and then being blocked continued over subsequent days. It was frustrating, but I wasn't prepared to allow Iraq's policy to be implemented in any circumstances.

ALSO ON NOVEMBER 3, Kofi Annan decided to act. He wrote to Saddam Hussein, calling his attention to the Security Council's concerns about Iraq's decisions of October 29; he also noted that the foreign ministers of France and the Russian Federation had urged Iraq to rescind them unconditionally. He emphasized that he had "full confidence in UNSCOM, whose personnel are recruited on the basis of expertise and integrity, not nationality." And he advised Saddam that he had appointed three personal envoys to travel to Baghdad in hopes of defusing the growing crisis.

Kofi Annan's envoys were three diplomats: Lakhdar Brahimi, Jan Eliasson, and Emilio Cardenas. The team leader was Brahimi, a former foreign minister of Algeria and a trusted confidante of Kofi Annan. Jan Eliasson had previously been Swedish ambassador to the United Nations in New York and had then crossed the street to join the UN Secretariat, where he had served for two years as under secretary-general for humanitarian affairs. Later, he'd been appointed permanent head of the Swedish foreign ministry. Emilio Cardenas had been the Argentine ambassador to the UN and had served on the Security Council for two years. He'd recently returned to Argentina, where he entered the private financial sector.

The team was an interesting and potentially volatile mix. Brahimi was sympathetic to Iraq. Eliasson, a Social Democrat, was primarily interested in the humanitarian situation; in other words, while perhaps concerned about Saddam's weaponry, his deepest sympathies would be with those suffering as a result of sanctions. Cardenas was a modern, post-Falklands Argentinean who had developed a distinctly pro-Western outlook. He had formed a particularly close relationship with Madeleine Albright during his time on the Security Council. His voice, I thought, might be the strongest among the three in support of UNSCOM's mission.

Before the envoys were dispatched to Baghdad, Kofi Annan asked that they be briefed by UNSCOM. Recognizing the important role they could play, I made sure that our best staff were involved, and I took an active part in the discussions.

The briefing sessions were largely straightforward, but Brahimi signaled transparent hostility toward UNSCOM. He was impatient with our presentations on the weapons issues and seemed skeptical about the data we presented, even though he had no expertise in the field. The man was determined not to allow facts to modify his prejudices. It was apparent that Brahimi was going to Iraq with an agenda that excluded any serious attempt to address Iraq's obligations in the field of disarmament.

Another minor problem revealed in these briefings was Eliasson's preoccupation with the impact of sanctions upon the Iraqi people. I shared Eliasson's humanitarian concerns, but in the Security Council resolutions on Iraq, a clear connection had been drawn between Iraq's willingness to comply with its disarmament obligations and its release from sanctions. Eliasson knew this well, but, a deeply humanitarian man, he wanted to find a way to alleviate the suffering of the Iraqi people—no matter what happened on the arms front.

UNSCOM made arrangements for the three envoys to travel to Baghdad and provided them with local staff support and facilities. However, the three seemed reluctant to take much advantage of UNSCOM staff while in Baghdad, and Brahimi was positively hostile to accepting anything other than the most menial assistance from UNSCOM officials.

At Kofi Annan's request, I also agreed to postpone the November 5 and 7 U-2 overflights, which would have taken place while the three envoys were in Baghdad delivering his message to Iraqi authorities. Notwithstanding this concession, Iraq continued each day to block our attempts to conduct inspections.

Iraq also took steps to interfere with our ongoing monitoring inspections, whose purpose was not to verify disarmament declarations but to check that dual-use facilities were not being used for illegal purposes. For example, cameras would be installed to observe activities within a chemical plant, and air-sampling devices were used to check for the presence of illicit compounds. We'd have to visit the facilities from time to time to change videotapes and to make sure that machines and equipment hadn't been moved. Now, on November 5, UNSCOM staff in Baghdad observed, through our remote monitoring system, that Iraq had begun moving proscribed equipment out of sight of our monitoring cameras. In certain establishments, monitoring cameras had been tampered with; lenses had been covered and lights had been turned off to prevent photography.

I apprised the Security Council, pointing out that movement of equipment without prior notification was prohibited under its monitoring plan. Such interference could indicate an immediate problem with Iraqi compliance. In the biological context, for example, it would take mere hours to adapt fermenters, once moved out of camera range, to the production of seed stocks of biological warfare agents.

In response, Iraqi Foreign Minister Al-Sahaf denied that Iraq had in any way interfered with UNSCOM's equipment. But then, in obvious self-contradiction, he acknowledged that authorities had "taken certain measures" in preparation for "military aggression by the United States of America against Iraq," claiming that the equipment had been moved to undisclosed sites to prevent their damage during an American attack.

The Security Council urgently considered these reports on November 6 and decided to call upon Iraq to stop these actions and to obey the law. The best it could agree upon was a statement by the president of the Security Council—not a resolution—expressing support for the work of the three-man diplomatic team and saying that the council "does not wish to see any situation that is detrimental to the solution of the question."

Meanwhile, the Iraqis maintained pressure on me. Saeed H. Hasan, the chargé d'affaires of the Iraqi mission to the UN, sent another letter on November 6 to warn me that the U-2 might be shot down by Iraqi antiaircraft defenses. According to him, I would bear "the responsibility for the consequences that will ensue from any decision by you to send the spy plane to Iraq."

Annan's three envoys finished their work in Baghdad on November 7. Iraq had taken up the overwhelming portion of their time with extensive briefings, including "documentary" films about the way in which UNSCOM conducted its work. The Iraqi government's contention was that UNSCOM's work was essentially ridiculous, its employees dishonest and incompetent. The content of these briefings amounted to elaborately contrived propaganda.

The envoys held a press conference at the end of their visit to Baghdad. Much of it was dominated by Brahimi speaking in Arabic, a language that his two colleagues did not understand. Very little was said during that conference, except that Brahimi mentioned that the Iraqis had requested the personal intervention of the UN secretary-general to improve the situation. Tariq Aziz then reiterated the Iraqi position: The government would not back down from or alter its policy decision of October 29. Iraq considered UNSCOM a mere instrument of U.S. policy against it, and UNSCOM's makeup must change.

If Kofi Annan's personal envoys had indeed tried to engage Saddam's regime in serious discussion over disarmament obligations, they'd obviously failed.

The secretary-general's decision to send the envoys to Baghdad was a perfectly conventional approach to try to solve a problem. Such action is one of the many options open to the secretary-general. Crucial determinants of the success of such a mission are: Is there a basis or willingness for constructive discussion? Were those selected for the job appropriate? Was the contact properly organized?

I've already commented on aspects of each of these determinants, as they played out in this case, particularly on the first of them where, demonstrably, Iraq had no interest in the discussion other than the opportunity it provided to attack UNSCOM.

To simply point out that this diplomatic effort failed is to miss its real and far graver effect. The secretary-general's decision to send the envoys was seen by Iraq as further confirmation that Annan was committed to a diplomatic solution to Iraq's recalcitrance, without obliging it to be disarmed. Iraq's new policy of enhanced resistance to and then destruction of UNSCOM was given a boost. The next step was, thus, obvious.

Before departing, the envoys were handed a letter addressed to the secretary-general and signed by Tariq Aziz. It purported to be a message from President Saddam Hussein and focused on what Iraq considered to be UNSCOM's misconduct, which was juxtaposed to "the suffering, hardship and injustice we have endured for more than six and a half years." UNSCOM personnel, Aziz declared, had been "directly responsible for jeopardizing Iraq's security and for prolonging the embargo, in service of the objectives of their State," this last phrase being a reference to the United States.

A set of demands was attached to the letter. These included an immediate determination by the Security Council that Iraq had been disarmed and that, therefore, the sanctions should be lifted. To carry this out, Iraq proposed establishing a team of representatives from the Security Council's five permanent members to discuss the "accomplishments" of the past six and a half years. It also proposed that UNSCOM teams, both at headquarters in New York and at the BMVC, should henceforth be constructed on the basis of strict balance among various nationalities and that there should be a deputy executive chairman appointed for each of the five permanent members of the Security Council to "undertake specially with the Executive Chairman the responsibility of decision-making and the direction of the activities of the Commission." In other words, this panel would ride herd on the executive chairman. There was a proposal for the resumption of sanctions reviews and suspension of visits to any "sovereign or sensitive sites" until the Security Council had studied Iraq's achievements to date.

Finally, another proposal asked that the U.S.-supplied U-2 be replaced by an airplane from a neutral country.

These demands provided a snapshot of the mind-set prevailing in Baghdad. It was also a preview of things to come.

W ITH SURPRISING UNANIMITY, the Security Council adopted a firm response on November 12, 1997. Resolution 1137 condemned Iraq's attempt to exclude staff from UNSCOM based on the ground of their nationality, its implicit threat to the safety of the commission's reconnaissance platform, and its removal of dual-use equipment from sites under monitoring. The Security Council not only demanded that the Iraqi government rescind its decisions of October 29 but also backed it up by implementing its threat to prevent senior Iraqi officials from traveling internationally. This new sanction, the council declared, would terminate one day after the UNSCOM executive chairman reported that Iraq was allowing UNSCOM immediate, unconditional, and unrestricted access to all areas, facilities, equipment, records, and means of transportation that it wished to inspect, in accordance with its mandate.

Baghdad responded with another defiant gesture. General Nils Carlstrom, the director of the BMVC, provided to UNSCOM by Sweden, was summoned to the Iraqi Foreign Ministry on the afternoon of November 13, 1997. Adnan Malik, the head of Iraq's Department of International Organizations and Conferences at the Foreign Ministry, handed General Carlstrom a letter instructing American personnel of the BMVC to "leave Iraq immediately today . . . via Baghdad-Amman highway." It meant that all of our staff of American nationality had to be across the border—some 500 miles away—by midnight.

This was an outrage, and I resolved to oppose this Iraqi attempt to divide our American and non-American staffs. I immediately instructed General Carlstrom to inform the Iraqis I had decided to remove virtually all UNSCOM personnel, leaving only a small skeleton staff led by him. All inspection and monitoring staff, irrespective of nationality, would depart on an UNSCOM aircraft due to land at Habbaniyah at 7:15 A.M. the next day (November 14) to depart for Bahrain at 8:00 A.M. Under these circumstances, I asked the Iraqi government not to insist that our American personnel leave by road to Amman but to accept instead my assurances that they would leave as soon as the UNSCOM aircraft arrived the next morning.

The response came quickly: flat-out refusal. Iraq was going to make it as hard as possible on UNSCOM, especially the Americans. Our American staff would be obliged to drive northwest to the border. Six Americans, a Briton, and an Australian packed a few belongings, and we hastily assembled a motorcade of cars. After I sought assurances on their safe transit—the Iraqis provided four police Mercedes to accompany the motorcade—they left for the border and crossed safely into Jordan through the Karameh Desert after a ten-hour drive. Virtually all other UNSCOM personnel, some seventy-nine people, left by air the next day for Bahrain.

This evacuation of staff turned out to be the first of three during my watch. In each case, my paramount concern was ensuring the staff's safety and dissuading Iraq from resorting to brutal or hostile measures (such as hostage-taking). The logistics of these evacuations were managed from my office at UN headquarters in New York. A small team, including my deputy, one or two policy advisers, and the chief of operations, would be in constant contact with our office in Bahrain and with the military authorities monitoring the southern no-fly zone. Given the time difference between Baghdad and New York, these operations typically involved a sleepless watch, through the night, until our people safely crossed the border.

Some eyebrows were raised, to say the least, at the immediacy and scope of my decision to pull out all inspectors. I had no hesitation over this decision. Had I allowed Iraq to cut out any group from our team, on the basis of their nationality, a dangerous precedent would have been set—the receiving state determining the composition of an international arms control and monitoring team. This leaves aside the question of when, if ever, we would get persons of that nationality back into Iraq. What happened subsequently proved it to be the right decision. Iraq had played a risky card. I called it and they folded.

My decision to evacuate UNSCOM personnel attracted immediate criticism from Russia, France, and China, although China was slightly muted on this occasion because it occupied the presidency of the Security Council during November 1997. In that role, the Chinese ambassador wrote to me the next day, accepting an offer I'd made to brief the council on UNSCOM's ability to perform its duties under the circumstances and asked for my views on the need for an emergency meeting of the Special Commission, that is, UNSCOM's board of advisers.

Action took place quickly. On November 19, I assembled a group of UNSCOM's most senior biological, chemical, and missile experts for this unusual opportunity to brief members of the Security Council. Using U-2 photos and overhead slides of tables and graphs, UNSCOM's experts set forth in clear, precise terms the major unresolved issues in each weapons area, demonstrating the extent of Iraq's recalcitrance. So as not to lose the issue in the slew of technical data being presented, I asked experts to separately highlight Iraq's vigorous concealment policies. We emphasized Iraq's failure to provide credible information regarding the disposition of SCUD missile propellant, the production of VX agent, and the full extent of its biological weapons program.

The discussion that followed made it clear that the Security Council members now had at least a slightly improved understanding of the practical aspects of arms control and, specifically, the problems Iraq's concealment policy had created. I was attacked strongly by the representatives of Russia, France, China, and one or two other nonaligned states for my decision to withdraw UNSCOM from Iraq. This seemed far more important to them than what they were being told about Iraq's resistance to the council's own disarmament requirements. They argued that I'd acted without Security Council approval.

I maintained that as executive chairman it was my responsibility to take the evacuation decision and that I'd acted appropriately given the council's recent resolution condemning Iraq's attempt to discriminate against a given nationality. Moreover, UNSCOM still had a skeleton staff and a monitoring system in place that would continue to operate. I hoped that these measures would only be temporary—but this would depend on the resolve of the Security Council.

M EANWHILE, 8,000 miles away, Russia was preparing to take a more active role. Perhaps this was not a surprising development. Post-Soviet Russia has many reasons for valuing a close relationship with Iraq. In the tradition of the "Great Game"—the historic competition among European nations for control of Central Asia—Russia has long viewed Iraq as one key to the oil-rich Middle East and access to Persian Gulf ports. Iraq had been an important Russian trading partner, especially in such strategic goods as weapons and oil. Maintaining a positive connection with an outspoken Muslim regime could help reduce the chances of an explosion by Russia's own restive Muslim minorities. And—perhaps most compelling—Russia shares with China and even France a deep resentment of American power in the so-called unipolar post–Cold War world. In this context, the absence of any relationship between Iraq and the United States provided Russia an opportunity to act as a Great Power in settling problems, whereas the United States could not.

For all these reasons, and on the basis of its assessment that Iraq posed no threat to Russia, Moscow was happy to maintain Saddam as a client and to defend his interests on the world stage. Furthermore, as I'd recently learned, the Russian leadership had other, more personal reasons for wanting to placate Iraq.

A few months earlier, in late September 1997, I'd accepted an invitation from the Russian ambassador to the UN, Sergey Lavrov, to visit Moscow, where I would meet with Foreign Minister Yevgeny Primakov. I went with a small team to Moscow.

Our first engagement was a working luncheon hosted by Deputy Foreign Minister Viktor Posuvalyuk at the foreign minister's mansion. Like his chief, Posuvalyuk was an Arabist; he'd spent much of his career in Baghdad. (He was also an active musician; at the time of his recent death, his music was popular among Muscovites.) The luncheon talks with Posuvalyuk centered on the question of finding new and, by implication, more lenient criteria for judging Iraq's compliance with disarmament obligations.

Later that afternoon, we went to the Foreign Ministry, where we were received in the executive conference room by Foreign Minister Primakov and his key advisers. Having made several visits to the Soviet Union in the past to discuss disarmament issues, I found the Russians' approach to the conversation entirely familiar: dogmatic, very self-interested, and unrelieved by even a superficial acknowledgment of higher principles.

Primakov began, declaring that "Russia wants the Iraq problem solved." He saw UNSCOM as having a key role to play in achieving this objective—by finishing its disarmament work as soon as possible. For this purpose, it should consider new criteria for judging Iraq's compliance with the law. "You mustn't be rigid," he urged. "You must be more flexible, more understanding." The onus of proof, he made clear, was as great upon UNSCOM as upon Iraq—if not greater. This constituted a dramatic reversal from what the Security Council's resolutions provided.

To exemplify his argument, he made an extraordinary assertion: If an UNSCOM inspection revealed no weapons at a suspected site, then it should conclude that none had existed there in the first place. Under these circumstances, only when UNSCOM can *prove* that weapons exist should the Security Council hold Iraq accountable for them.

Rather surprisingly, Primakov made the Russian motivation for this stance very clear. Without being asked, he stated that Iraq owed some U.S.$8 billion to Russia for military equipment. For this reason, Russia wanted the disarmament phase ended and the oil embargo lifted. Russia needed that money badly, and it would not be paid unless Iraq was able to sell oil freely.

I told Primakov that I shared his view that the disarmament phase of this work needed to be brought to conclusion without further delay, but I argued that there was a need for Iraq to be brought into compliance with international law. I was not certain that new, more flexible criteria could be introduced, but I did offer the assurance that UNSCOM, while I was in charge, would not behave in an unnecessarily fastidious way. We were not hostile to Iraq; we simply wanted to fulfil our duties as objectively and as quickly as possible.

This exchange seemed to be more or less satisfactory at the time, but two aspects of it were of particular concern to me. First, Primakov's attitude was overbearing and somewhat bullying, redolent of the hard-line Soviet techniques I had experienced in prior undertakings. Second, the notion of making it easier for Iraq to comply with the law seemed to be the thin edge of a wedge—or maybe something worse: a willingness to cook the books.

I returned to New York both educated and troubled by my experience in Moscow. The real shocker arrived, however, a few days later. I received reliable intelligence reports concerning Primakov's relationship with the Iraqi regime. The reports indicated that Primakov had been receiving personal payoffs from Iraq. Naturally, I was disturbed by this information, and I questioned my sources intensively. They insisted their facts were rock-solid. They could confirm the details of the payments, the times, the amounts, and the accounts to which they were sent.

Over the next eighteen months, I occasionally asked intelligence authorities if they were satisfied with the accuracy of these reports about Primakov. Could there have been a mistake? I was informed repeatedly that the reports were verifiable and, a year later, was told that fresh evidence further confirmed the accusation.

I'd been exposed to political corruption—for example, during my time as Australian ambassador to Thailand—and I was well aware of the somewhat chaotic political and economic circumstances in Moscow. Of course, no misbehavior by the Saddam Hussein regime could be considered surprising. So the idea that a high-ranking Russian official might be on the take from Saddam wasn't implausible. But it worried me because of the effect it might have on what we were trying to achieve.

Russia probably knows more than any other nation about the status of Iraq's weapons systems, having been Iraq's major weapons supplier. Now, their foreign minister was seeking to bury known facts that were essential to the disarming of Saddam, and not only for reasons of Russian political interest but also, apparently, for personal gain.

THE RUSSIAN DESIRE to shield and support Iraq came to center stage just as the evacuation crisis reached its height. Tariq Aziz visited Moscow on November 18 and 19, 1997, and Presidents Boris Yeltsin and Saddam Hussein communicated directly during the same period. In Moscow, Aziz held what were characterized as extensive talks with Foreign Minister Primakov. On November 20, Aziz and Primakov announced that an agreement had been reached whereby Iraq would accept the return of UNSCOM to Iraq, with its full complement of members, to resume its work.

Of course, there was a quid pro quo. Primakov voiced the right words about the need for Iraq to implement the Security Council resolutions, but he also promised that Russia, in fulfillment of these ends, would take active measures to "enhance the effectiveness" of UNSCOM's work while respecting the sovereignty and security of Iraq. This was code-language for weakening UNSCOM. The joint Russian-Iraqi declaration stressed that Russia would work actively for a speedy lifting of the sanctions against Iraq, especially those related to disarmament.

On the same day, it was reported that Saddam Hussein had chaired a meeting of the Revolutionary Command Council in Baghdad, the titular ruling body of Iraq. It had issued a decision to invite UNSCOM to return to Iraq.

The foreign ministers of four of the Security Council's permanent five hastily gathered in Geneva (China was represented by an ambassador). Meeting at 4:00 A.M. on November 20, they agreed to support the joint Russian-Iraqi declaration. Under these circumstances, I instructed all UNSCOM personnel to return to Baghdad from Bahrain and resume work. The first major crisis on my watch was over.

The emergency session of the whole Special Commission, which had been agreed to as part of the resolution of the crisis, was convened on November 21 in New York. In addition to its permanent staff, UNSCOM was a formal commission—the Special Commission—comprising the executive chairman and twenty commissioners drawn from UN member states and appointed in their individual capacity by the secretary-general. I chaired its meetings, their purpose being to advise the executive chairman.

The emergency session began with a technical briefing similar to that provided to the Security Council a few days earlier. The Special Commission then deliberated the contents of a draft report prepared by my office for the Security Council. During the discussion a major dispute erupted. The Russian commissioner, Gennady Gatilov, argued that Iraq was substantially disarmed and that many of the concerns raised in the briefing by the UNSCOM experts were illusory. He went on to present an interpretation of the data that involved ignoring some facts, distorting others, and dismissing still others as unimportant, all of it adding up to an argument in favor of giving Iraq a clean bill of health and winding up UNSCOM's disarmament work.

Several of the other commissioners were angered by this blatantly political maneuvering, and a heated argument ensued, with facts and accusations thrown in all directions. The dispute ended only when I intervened, saying to the Russian commissioner, "Your point of view has been fully stated, I think. Now, if you insist on having the official report of this emergency session record that point of view, the report will also have to record in extenso the alternative points of view. That would have to include a full discussion of Iraq's concealment activities. Shall we proceed?"

He backed off. The result was a report as close to the facts as diplomacy would allow and it confirmed that the disarmament task had not been completed.

The report of the emergency session also contained a series of recommendations ostensibly to make UNSCOM more "effective." These weren't ideas I endorsed but rather were ideas advocated by one or more of the commissioners, sometimes with obvious political motivations. They ranged from relatively innocent proposals, such as providing better training and equipment for UNSCOM personnel, to favorite Iraqi objectives—promoted by the Russians and the Chinese—such as expanding the number of nationalities taking part in UNSCOM's work. They also pushed for the possibility of "enhancing" UNSCOM aerial operations by introducing "other assets," all of which was code for replacing the U-2 spy plane with an aircraft of another national origin. This report was subsequently presented to the Security Council and endorsed unanimously.

D URING THESE FIRST few months of my tenure at UNSCOM, Iraq had taken a number of diplomatic and political risks. Nearly all had paid off handsomely. Iraq benefited greatly from the split vote in the Security Council in late October, which no doubt encouraged Iraq to eject the United States nationals from UNSCOM. The Security Council's adoption of a resolution condemning this action reflected a brief return to at least superficial unity, but it did not seriously harm Iraq or exert much pressure on Iraq to return, even approximately, to compliance with the resolutions. Ironically, it seemed that the more recalcitrant Iraq's behavior, the greater the support it attracted, especially on the part of Russia (but also from France and, to some extent, China).

The emergency session of the Special Commission did not, however, go in Iraq's or Russia's favor. That was a short-term setback for sure, but it was far from a total loss, as the resulting report opened UNSCOM operations to a new degree of scrutiny. Thus, political attention would increasingly focus on UNSCOM's behavior rather than on Iraqi noncompliance. This was a major achievement for Iraq and its supporters.

Baghdad's relentless propaganda machine, especially through newspapers, cultivated the new situation assiduously. Concocted or distorted stories of offensive behavior by UNSCOM inspectors began to multiply. For example, the Iraqis trumpeted with horror the fact that we'd conducted inspections at a convent and a nursery school. Although these were completely legitimate visits—Iraq had stored weapons in such places—and were brief and inconsequential, they were represented by Iraq as examples of how UNSCOM had simply gone mad.

Iraqi propaganda began to have its effect at the UN Secretariat. Kofi Annan's senior staff increasingly argued that the source of the problem in regard to the disarmament process was not Iraq, or Saddam Hussein, or his weapons—but UNSCOM. It was argued that UNSCOM was run by a bunch of out-of-control cowboys, a posse bent on frontier justice. Annan's trio of envoys helped confirm this view. They returned with videotapes, provided by Baghdad, of UNSCOM staffers interviewing Iraqi officials, tapes edited to make our inspectors appear like latter-day inquisitors.

Gradually, the terms of discussion began to shift in Iraq's favor. Reference to Iraq's weapons, its capabilities, and its past use of those weapons—including on its own people—diminished daily. Now the debate focused on the humanitarian crisis, the political stalemate between the Security Council and Iraq, and the deplorable conduct of UNSCOM.

In this charged atmosphere, Secretary-General Annan began to signal, very clearly, his personal interest in the Iraq issue and the possibility that he would intervene to fix it.

7

THE RESISTANCE STIFFENS

URING THE FINAL months of 1997, with the first major crisis of my UNSCOM watch averted, we were back on the ground in Iraq, conducting inspections and continuing our efforts to piece together the truth about Saddam's weapons programs and bring them to final account. But the new Iraqi policy of designating certain locations as "presidential sites," off-limits to UNSCOM, was deeply disturbing. Clearly, these sites were ideal for the storage and manufacture of weapons. Some members of the Security Council now shared my concern, in particular the United States and the United Kingdom, and after some debate I was urged by the council to visit Iraq to address this issue.

I wrote to Aziz on December 1, 1997, proposing arrangements for meetings in Baghdad, at both the technical and policy levels, to take place immediately. I referred to concerns I had already expressed regarding key weapons issues in October 1997, but I stressed that now it was more important, in light of Iraq's presidential sites policy and the repeated violation of inspection modalities for sensitive sites, to discuss access issues.

The next day, Aziz replied evasively. He claimed that the proposed time for my visit was inappropriate because a number of concerned Iraqi officials would be away, attending an Islamic conference in Tehran. He proposed that the visit take place later in December. Completely ignoring the access issues, he demanded that the meeting focus on closing the missile and chemical disarmament files, including VX. He also wanted us to agree on a schedule for completing the verification of Iraq's biological declaration, while offering no new information or materials to make such action meaningful.

Aziz further stipulated that my professional staff should be accompanied by UNSCOM commissioners and technical experts from countries represented in the Security Council, who should take part in our discussions. He maintained that the presence of these actors would "have the advantage of expanding participation and of increasing the transparency of the operation, lending it credibility and strengthening its international character. This is an important feature of the work of the United Nations." Of course, Aziz's goal was to reduce UNSCOM's independence by ensuring that diplomats of a variety of political persuasions would be on hand to at least second-guess and possibly seek to modify our actions.

Aziz concluded by suggesting that the sole political topic that needed to be discussed was the removal of the U-2 surveillance flights and their replacement with "an aircraft of a neutral country."

I responded to Aziz on December 3, 1997, with one of the stronger letters I addressed to him. I accepted the postponement of the meeting but pointed out that his letter did not address the main purpose for our discussions—to arrive at a negotiated agreement on full access to all sites in Iraq. The members of the Security Council specifically intended our discussions to focus on improving the implementation of the so-called modalities for inspection of sensitive sites. I made clear that there could be no progress in other areas unless these issues were discussed first.

I kept the Security Council fully informed of this exchange and forwarded the correspondence. I also proposed that there be a council meeting immediately upon my return, that is, on December 18, to consider the results of the visit.

The United Nations security office, which always provided a small contingent of guards for our visits to Baghdad, had become deeply concerned about the safety of our mission, especially with respect to our accommodations. After much discussion, we decided to have the core team visiting Baghdad—my deputy, Charles Duelfer, a few other senior officers, and I—stay in our offices instead of the Rasheed Hotel or an Iraqi government guest house. The message was sent ahead to the BMVC, which made arrangements for sleeping spaces and portable cots. It meant that we were less in the hands of the Iraqis, that our transport problems and comings and goings were simplified, and that we were now in a compound where we could control the perimeter. But such an increase in our safety was marginal at best.

One of Aziz's first actions when we met in Baghdad was to ridicule our decision. With broad sarcasm, he protested that it was unthinkable that any person in Baghdad would dream of doing us harm.

The UNSCOM team left for Baghdad in the second week of December. For the first time, I included three commissioners in UNSCOM's contingent of senior professional staff members. These were Michel Saint-Mleux of France, Gennady Gatilov of Russia, and Paul Schulte of the United Kingdom.

It transpired that Iraq had something new for us. At our December 14 and 15 meetings, five video cameras were aimed at our delegation to record every word and gesture. I asked Aziz, "What is the purpose of this?" He replied that Iraq had decided merely to keep a video record of our conference-room discussions and that we would be provided with a copy.

Concerned about the potential for selective video editing making its way into the media, I asked for and received assurances that the tapes would not be released to the news media. Of course, within a few weeks, heavily edited footage from our discussions aired on Iraqi television and was later carried on international outlets, particularly CNN, which was well established as Iraq's preferred Western media conduit.

In spite of Iraqi resistance, we began the talks by discussing the issues of access. I made two main points. The first was the inspection modalities for sensitive sites. UNSCOM had been repeatedly prevented from fulfilling its mandate because Iraqi officials did not abide by the established rules. Iraq's sole discretion to designate a particular site as "sensitive" had been abused; and limiting the number of persons allowed into any given site to four was absurdly restrictive. UNSCOM inspectors had often been held up for too long at the front gate of a disputed site, and we'd often seen cars and trucks driving within and out of sites, some of them obviously removing documents or prohibited materials. All of this had to stop, or the modalities must change.

"That is not possible," Aziz responded. "The modalities were agreed in negotiations between the two sides. You cannot change them at will, Mr. Butler!"

"You're wrong," I told him. "The modalities were never part of any agreement. They were declared unilaterally by UNSCOM's previous chairman, and their text states that UNSCOM has the right to review them in the event they were not working effectively. They are *not* working effectively, and as far as I'm concerned, they are over."

Second, I pointed out that Aziz, following the blockage of the SSO headquarters inspection in September, had indicated that there was now a new, previously unidentified category of sites that Iraq considered as sanctuaries, never to be inspected. I said that UNSCOM "is entirely prepared to behave in a way that respects the legitimate national security, sovereignty, and dignity concerns of Iraq, but this did not mean that there can be sites perpetually free from any entry or inspection."

Aziz exploded. He launched into a long diatribe, recounting the many crimes UNSCOM had committed against Iraq. "We will not tolerate any more of this, Mr. Butler," he declared. "Iraq is not a defeated country, UNSCOM is not an army of occupation, and you are not General MacArthur!"

Biting my tongue, I replied quietly that I found this historical analogy somewhat fatuous, given that Iraq consisted of some 22 million people, while at any given moment UNSCOM had only some 200 employees—hardly enough to make up an army of occupation.

Aziz was not finished. I was wrong, he said, in stating that Iraq had simply defined certain locations as perpetual sanctuaries. In reality, there were five categories of sites within Iraq: normal; national security; presidential and sovereign; civilian; and foreign.

This elaborate array of categories was a brand-new wrinkle. I asked Aziz to explain the nature of each category as well as the kind of access he had in mind for UNSCOM. Unsurprisingly, as Aziz unfolded his new system, it turned out that it would drastically limit our ability to find and monitor Iraq's weapons systems.

UNSCOM would have full access, as required in the Security Council resolutions, only to "normal sites." As Aziz defined them, these were mainly manufacturing establishments—factories, food-processing plants, warehouses, and the like—but Aziz acknowledged that they might include places at which, at least in the past, prohibited activities had taken place.

"Civilian sites" and "foreign sites" included private residences, embassies, the homes of foreign nationals, and offices or workplaces owned by non-Iraqi companies. These were beyond the jurisdiction of Iraq, according to Aziz, and therefore off-limits to UNSCOM inspectors. In a democratic country with reasonable rules of private property and limits on government intrusion, this might have been believable, but it was an utterly incredible statement in Saddam's dictatorship.

"National security sites," according to Aziz, were locations where the old sensitive-site modalities must be applied. He included in this category sites related to the Republican Guard, the Special Republican Guard, the military and civilian intelligence agencies, and the national security apparatus. These were the very organizations responsible for managing Saddam's clandestine weapons programs. Thus, the idea that inspections of these sites ought to be limited was tailor-made to assist Saddam's concealment efforts.

At this point, I had to fight back. I insisted that the way in which the sensitive-site modalities were being applied to national security sites needed to be altered. After a long argument, Aziz agreed that UNSCOM could increase the size of entry teams to such sites beyond the prevailing limit of four persons, if the size of the site warranted it, as decided on a case-by-case basis. Iraq would also attempt to reduce the delay of entry to such sites and ensure that vehicular movement was frozen.

Having made these minor "concessions," Aziz went on to warn me, "Understand—even if access is granted to national security sites under the sensitive-site modalities, there may well be special or secret rooms within those sites to which access can *never* be given!"

Finally, we came to Iraq's crown jewel—the "presidential," or "sovereign," sites. "These sites aren't clearly defined," he conceded, "but they are sites associated with the presidency, and they are well known, very well known to all Iraqis. They include sites, offices, and resorts at which the head of state lives or works. These areas can never be inspected or overflown by UNSCOM under any circumstances."

The other restrictions Aziz outlined had been arbitrary and tendentious, but this absolute prohibition was unworkable. I told Aziz so. He responded, "I am not surprised to hear you say this, Mr. Butler, but Iraq's position is absolute."

I made several attempts to resolve the issue through creative redirection. I proposed that we develop special arrangements for inspecting the presidential sites, designed in consultation with Iraqi officials and planned to take into account Iraq's legitimate security, sovereignty, and dignity concerns. But Aziz was impassive. *No* conceivable arrangements, he insisted, could ever cover Iraq's concerns.

I tried another angle. I asked Aziz if Iraq would provide UNSCOM with a list or map of the presidential sites so that we could better understand the magnitude of this proposed exclusion. He refused, claiming that such a map would assist the United States in bombing those sites. When I pressed him, Aziz said that if I obtained a written guarantee from the president of the Security Council that such bombing would never take place, then a list or map could be made available. He knew that such a ludicrous request would never be fulfilled.

Our talks then turned to aviation. I made no concessions concerning our use of the U-2 aircraft for aerial reconnaissance, and I asked, as I had before, whether Iraq would be prepared to honor the law and allow our aircraft to land at the Rasheed air base in Baghdad and at Basra in the south, rather than being restricted to the Habbaniyah air base. Aziz rejected these requests on the spot, saying that he saw no need to make any concession to UNSCOM until the sanctions were lifted. What was being asked for, of course, was not a "concession." Then Aziz, with a straight face, cited one of the most serious examples of the harm done by sanctions: that he, personally, was no longer able to fly out of Iraq in his private jet. When he was able to resume such flying, he said, he might reconsider UNSCOM's landing rights.

When the meeting turned to technical and disarmament issues, Aziz proposed settling outstanding differences in the weapons fields through a series of "seminars" in which international experts would participate along with Iraqi experts. He said that UNSCOM could continue its normal work but that these seminars would hold the key to bringing, in particular, the chemical and biological areas into final account.

One of the more fascinating statements Aziz made in this discussion referred to biological weapons. "The government of Iraq," he declared, "possesses not one gram of biological agents, not one gram of biological weapons, in Iraqi government hands in the territory of Iraq."

A literal examination of the sentence raised two possibilities. If there was a biological weapons capability in Iraq, it might not be, formally, in government hands. Or it might be that a government-owned biological weapons capability had been moved outside the territory of Iraq. I favored the latter interpretation because of intelligence materials I had seen indicating that Iraq may have transferred some of its biological weapons equipment in shipping containers for safe storage in another country. Then again, the entire sentence might simply have been another Tariq Aziz lie.

Answering Aziz's proposal for "seminars," I made clear that I would not accept any arrangement that called into question either the responsibility of UNSCOM to the Security Council or its professionalism and objectivity. I then made a counterproposal: to convene technical evaluation meetings (TEMs) with the Iraqi side. I'd invite qualified and objective international experts chosen from countries having the necessary expertise. UNSCOM would prepare all relevant basic materials for the TEM, including materials provided by the Iraqi government. Its discussions would be conducted in an open manner, but its conclusions would be forwarded to me. I would then have the right to incorporate them into reports to the Security Council, which I would share with Iraq. I saw no other way of maintaining our link to the Security Council and of setting aside Aziz's notion that objectivity in a scientist meant that he or she was from France, Russia, or China.

Aziz agreed to these proposals, and we arranged to proceed immediately with TEMs, beginning in January 1998. I indicated that the first TEMs would cover the area of missiles and VX nerve gas, with a TEM on biological weapons to follow as soon as practicable.

I was not sure that this new methodology, the TEM, would lead anywhere. As usual, it would depend on how much truth Iraq would tell. I was sure, however, that the formulation Aziz had proposed was disingenuous.

Before leaving Baghdad, I agreed to another tête-à-tête over coffee with Aziz. It would turn out to be our last. As you can imagine, these sessions were becoming more and more strained and unpleasant, dominated by Aziz's hectoring about UNSCOM's crimes and insensitivities and the evils being committed against the Iraqi people.

As I arrived at his ministerial suite, I felt that I'd had enough of the hectoring which had taken place in the conference room. I decided to try to divert Aziz by asking for his wider, more philosophical, views on the Middle East.

Aziz took this up with alacrity. He began with Saudi Arabia. "The country is unstable," he announced. "It is only a matter of time before the people will be able to shake off the corrupt rule of the House of Saud."

With respect to Kuwait, he explained to me that the Kuwaitis were "deceitful and aggressive people." Iraq, he said, needed to be strong because it was "surrounded" by such neighbors. I was stunned by the apparent conviction with which Aziz, a leader in the regime that had invaded and terrorized Kuwait, described the victims as "aggressive."

He then turned to the Iranians. He referred to them as "the Persians," presumably to underline that they are not Arabs or to make some other ethnocentric point. Iran, he said, had theocratic ambitions. The Iranians wished to dominate the region not only for political or economic reasons but also for religious reasons. Specifically, they coveted the five places in Iraq that were holy to the Shiites, and they ultimately wanted either to seize Iraq or to dismember it in order to gain control over those sites.

In one of the few more or less honest remarks he ever made to me, Aziz went on to say that this was why it had been so important for Iraq to have missile and chemical weapons. Those weapons had saved Iraq from the Persians. He pointed to Iraq's use of missiles during the Iran-Iraq War, the so-called War of the Cities. The same was true of its use of chemical weapons in the south. He stopped a trifle short of saying that Iraq would be ready to use such weapons at any time in the future, but he was quite frank about the fact that they had used them on Iran in the past.

He then mentioned the other great external threat to Iraq: the "Zionist entity," which he described as an illegitimate state and an enemy that wished to do Iraq harm. The existence of this well-armed Zionist entity had forced Iraq to develop biological weapons.

So what had begun as a slightly facile distraction by me resulted in some real coin. Aziz had stated quite plainly that Iraq had used chemical weapons on Iran, that it maintained biological weapons, and that these were intended specifically for use against Israel. The world picture he painted was one already familiar from Saddam Hussein's speeches. There is an Arab world, an Arab ethnos, led perhaps by shaky governments in some quarters, but that needs to be united and vigilant against the Persians in the northeast and the Israelis in the southwest. Iraq was fitted for the task of leading and defending the overall Arab ethnos. For that purpose, it had sought, obtained, used, and would use again in the future weapons of mass destruction.

O N MY RETURN to New York, I reported my findings to the Security Council, which discussed my report briefly and then authorized the council president to make a statement in response. That statement reiterated the council's demand that Iraq cooperate fully with

UNSCOM and its obligation to provide immediate, unconditional access to any site or category of sites. The council's authorization of a presidential statement on its behalf was far weaker than a resolution that might induce or encourage Iraq to comply.

I proceeded to plan a series of inspections in Iraq that would both pursue key disarmament objectives and test Iraq's renewed and expanded application of the sensitive-sites modalities. In planning these inspections, designated as UNSCOM 227, I took care to ensure that each site to be inspected had a clear and justifiable relationship to UNSCOM's disarmament mandate, and I made certain that the composition of our teams was mixed in terms of nationality as far as possible without either bending to Iraq's illegitimate demand that there be no Americans, or compromising the technical effectiveness of the teams. For example, the inspection team for UNSCOM 227, deployed for January 12–16, 1998, consisted of forty-four persons drawn from seventeen nations.

Two features of these inspections proved to be of particular concern to the Iraqis. First, their leader was an American—Scott Ritter. Second, one of the sites we planned to visit was the Abu Ghraib prison, where we'd heard, from Iraqi defectors, that biological weapons had been tested on inmates during 1994. (In planning, I'd also authorized the inspection of sites near our office in Baghdad, because we believed that we were under electronic or other surveillance from those buildings. Iraq did not prevent us from doing this. I'd also authorized the inspection of an intelligence headquarters, the Directorate of General Security.)

But UNSCOM 227 was short-lived, being blocked on the first day. While Iraq never provided any clear or convincing reason for their interference, Nizar Hamdoon, the Iraqi ambassador to the UN, offered an explanation on the following day, January 13. He claimed that the inspection team falsely tried to "demonstrate the existence of alleged connections between the Iraqi security services and dubious activities." In an amazing piece of reasoning, he wrote:

> That the team was made up of Americans and British confirms this fact, since it is the United States and British authorities that are giving currency to false allegations with regard to certain activities with a view to misleading the Security Council and world public opinion concerning the true state of affairs in Iraq.

The main reason for Iraq's decision to halt the work of this team until such time as it is restructured in a balanced manner is not the nature of the sites that it inspected, since we allowed it to complete the work of inspection for 12 January. The reason is that its composition lacks balance and that this lack of balance has an essentially political significance. As long as the composition of the Special Commission and the composition of the inspection teams reporting to the Security Council remains thus, the embargo will remain in place and will continue to murder Iraqis in the service of the declared United States policy against Iraq.

Apparently, citizens of the United Kingdom were now added to the purgatory once reserved for Americans.

The UNSCOM 227 team had been divided into several parts, and the group that was to visit the Abu Ghraib prison was to be led by the senior UNSCOM biologist, Dr. Gabrielle Kraatz-Wadsack. I had given her strict instructions to go only to the administrative building of the prison to search the records. She should avoid speaking with prisoners or behaving in other ways that would allow Iraq to complain, for example, either that we were assuming the role of the International Committee of the Red Cross or that we were seeking to suborn or intimidate prisoners.

On arrival, Dr. Kraatz-Wadsack indicated to the prison director that her sole purpose was to examine the administrative building. She was permitted to do so. The director inquired whether she would care to extend her visit to include a personal inspection of the amputation room, of which he seemed proud. Dr. Kraatz-Wadsack is a strong person and could have stomached the spectacle, but she politely declined this offer.

Her examination of the file-storage room in the administrative building proved intensely revealing. There were continuous records for prisoners at Abu Ghraib with the exception of only a single year—1994—the year in which we were most interested. The arrangement of the other files indicated that the missing files had been removed very recently.

Our Iraqi minders were not fools. As the purpose of Dr. Kraatz-Wadsack's visit became clear, Iraq quickly moved to shut down her inspection, to block Scott Ritter's inspection at another site, and then to demand that UNSCOM 227 as a whole be terminated. Once again, they sought to justify their decision by arguing that the inspection teams were improperly constituted, containing "too many" Americans and British.

Not surprisingly, tensions between UNSCOM and Iraq were escalating. Immediately following these incidents, the Security Council met and, in a brief statement, authorized the council president to express continued support for UNSCOM and its executive chairman. It also endorsed a proposal I had made to visit Baghdad again to explain to the Iraqis the views of the Security Council concerning Iraq's attempt to exclude presidential sanctuaries.

For this visit to Baghdad (January 19–21, 1998), I continued the innovation of taking UNSCOM commissioners along with the professional team, this time Ron Cleminson of Canada, Zhou Fei of China, and GianPiero Perrone of Italy.

As the date for our visit neared, the virulence of Baghdad's anti-American, anti-UNSCOM rhetoric became even greater than usual, especially in the state-controlled media. In newspapers like *Babel*, which is owned by Saddam Hussein's son, Uday, the personal invective against me reached new heights. At one point, *Babel* wrote that the "time has come to chop the tongue of this dog." Simultaneously, the United States and the United Kingdom began strengthening their armed forces in the Persian Gulf, persuaded that another crisis was in the offing.

Shortly before our arrival in Baghdad, the BMVC was attacked with a rocket-propelled grenade. The single projectile did little damage, but it did hit an outside wall immediately adjacent to the cafeteria where staff normally took meals. The Iraqi authorities said they had no idea who had done this. Fortunately, no one was hurt, but this event heightened the tension, which by now was a constant backdrop to our work.

The set of talks at the Iraqi Foreign Ministry that now began were very tense. I started by expressing our grave concern about Iraq's blockage of UNSCOM 227. I recalled that the president of the Security Council had once again reiterated that Iraq must fulfill its obligations and that the council itself had rejected the strictures on inspections that Aziz had laid out in December 1997. Finally, I referred to a January 17 speech by Saddam Hussein setting a six-month deadline for the lifting of sanctions regardless of Iraq's disarmament status. I and members of my staff had heard that speech being delivered (with an English translation) while in Bahrain three days earlier. What were we to make of this speech?

By this time, I had become well accustomed to Tariq Aziz's circuitous answers to straightforward questions. He didn't disappoint on this occasion. He refused to comment on Saddam's public statements. When I pressed the issue of access to presidential sites, Aziz suggested a post-ponement of further disarmament work—fieldwork—until my next biannual report to the Security Council, due in April. In the meantime, he said, we should work solely through the TEM process to bring closure, once and for all, to all three disarmament files. If this was achieved and reported to the Security Council in April, the council might then proceed toward a decision to lift the oil embargo. Under these conditions, Aziz would be prepared to meet me in April to discuss access to presidential sites, which would then be the last remaining issue blocking a lifting of all the sanctions.

The motive of Aziz's proposal was transparent. He was stalling to buy time. All he was promising with respect to access was that we would meet in April and have another conversation. He gave no indication of what the likely outcome of that conversation might be.

Patiently, carefully, I walked Aziz through his own argument, discussing the status of each weapons area individually. I asked him to clarify what he was saying about conducting a TEM in the missile warhead area. If the TEM reported a satisfactory account of the disposition of Iraq's past SCUD warheads, would that mean the entire missile file was closed? Yes, Aziz said. I asked the same sort of question with respect to the chemical and biological areas and was given the same response.

I shook my head. Iraq was asking me to abandon an important part of the commission's work—the inspection of all possible sites for production and maintenance of weapons of mass destruction. Only the Security Council could direct that, I said. And if the council asked me, I would describe this latest proposal as a way for Iraq to avoid its obligation to provide unconditional access to any site UNSCOM wished to visit. I found his request deeply disappointing and disturbing.

Aziz fought back. He was fully aware of the Security Council's decisions and the language it had used on the issues of access in the various resolutions adopted since 1991. But in his view, the disarmament work could be completed through scientific and technical means—that is, expert-level discussions—without the need for any further inspections. In any case, inspecting the presidential and sovereign sites was certainly unnecessary.

Aziz went on to repeat his claim that the government of Iraq no longer possessed weapons of mass destruction and was not seeking to produce them. And, he added, "You understand, Mr. Butler, that the government of Iraq is working with the Special Commission in order to get sanctions lifted. If there is no prospect of this happening, why should we continue to cooperate? We are ready to face the consequences, including war. Tell the Security Council I said so." I reported this stance and its bellicose posture to the Security Council.

I'VE DESCRIBED the contents of these talks, but I haven't conveyed the sheer hostility Tariq Aziz managed to express. He made many long, tendentious statements filled with untruths, half-truths, and distortions to which no reply was invited or allowed. At other moments, he spewed abuse and denigration of UNSCOM and its professional officers, blaming UNSCOM solely for the fact that the disarmament tasks had not been completed and the sanctions on Iraq remained in force. The entire performance was redolent of the style of those two role models of Iraqi propaganda, Goebbels and Stalin: Tell the Big Lie, tell it often, and threaten unspecified hostility.

The lie in this case was breathtakingly audacious. Aziz spoke at length about how Iraq had divested itself long ago of all of its weapons of mass destruction, of their components, and of the means to produce them. This, despite Iraq's own written declarations and innumerable confessions made to UNSCOM about unaccounted weapons and weapons capability and their practice of lying often.

In fact, Aziz claimed that UNSCOM had been about to declare Iraq disarmed in mid-1995, until an "idiot" had upset the applecart. He was referring to the late Lieutenant-General Hussein Kamel, Saddam Hussein's son-in-law, who had defected from Iraq. Kamel had left behind, at his chicken farm, an extensive cache of documents on Iraq's prohibited weapons program. This came into UNSCOM's possession in August 1995.

Of course, Aziz' claim about UNSCOM's intentions in mid-1995 was untrue. At the time, Rolf Ekeus had been in the process of reaching some understanding with Iraq on the missile and chemical files—not the biological files. However, the bases of this potential agreement were destroyed by the discovery of Kamel's cache of documents. The contents of these documents, which spelled out in detail Iraq's weapons concealment program, had prompted the creation of UNSCOM's Concealment Unit. Iraq never seriously disputed the authenticity of the chicken-farm documents or the findings resulting from UNSCOM's subsequent investigations based on them. Those investigations resulted in a much clearer and changed picture of Iraq's prohibited weapons program, showing that it was larger and more advanced than had been thought previously. Aziz's histrionics about the disappointment of 1995 amounted to regret over having been caught in a lie, yet again.

At the conclusion of our January 1998 talks, I asked Aziz to put on the record his answer to key questions. Was he stating that Iraq had *no* weapons of mass destruction or the means to produce them? Had Iraq given UNSCOM *all* relevant materials? Was there nothing more to give, and would there be nothing more? And finally, was Aziz alleging that these facts, assuming all his answers were in the affirmative, remained unrecognized only because UNSCOM had refused to accept these facts?

Aziz's response to each question was Yes! Yes! Yes! Yes!

It was now clear that Aziz, under the direction of Saddam Hussein, was beginning to implement a policy of maximum resistance—of cut and run. He was making patently false declarations about Iraq's weapons capability, apparently calculating that Iraq could stand on this ground. It could attack UNSCOM as the enemy of the truth and get away with it.

Why did Iraq choose this path at this time? What made Saddam think that he could adopt this stance and defend it with impunity?

There are two key reasons. First, beginning with the split vote in the Security Council in October 1997, Saddam had every reason to believe that Russia, and possibly France and China, would support him vigorously within the Security Council. Second, Iraq was receiving signals from the UN secretary-general and the UN Secretariat that they would be amenable to some kind of diplomatic solution. Their motivation was to see sanctions come to an end and the political problem of Iraq dissolved; true disarmament was apparently of secondary concern.

When Aziz stood firm in refusing UNSCOM's access to presidential sites, he knew this would further exacerbate the atmosphere of crisis. There was no wiggle room on this issue. The sites in question were not only the places where President Saddam Hussein and his security operatives lived and worked; according to our information, they were also the sites from which his program for weapons of mass destruction was designed and operated and where the physical components of the program were probably stored as well.

Early in 1998, Iraq mounted an elaborate propaganda campaign to obscure these facts. Presidential sites were routinely described in public as Saddam Hussein's "palaces." Journalists and friendly diplomats were invited to tour two palaces to witness their tasteful and benign character. And as the days lengthened, the ongoing crisis continued, and the prospect of bombing by the United States and the United Kingdom got ever closer, ordinary Iraqi citizens were shown on television flocking to the palaces to express their support and to proclaim that they were prepared to camp there as human shields against their destruction.

M Y TALKS WITH Aziz had been harrowing, lasting some eight and a half hours. I began to breathe more easily when our plane lifted off from the Habbaniyah airfield and felt fully relieved only when, two and a half hours later, it touched down in Bahrain. We went immediately to our hotel, where we planned to work on our reports for the Security Council for the rest of the afternoon and evening before taking the midnight flight to New York. As usual, I had also agreed to a detailed program of briefings for interested ambassadors in Bahrain and the Bahraini foreign minister before the journey home commenced. These were carried out, lasting several hours.

On arrival at our hotel, Dennis Grimm, the UN security guard closest to me personally on this journey, swung into action, quickly checking my room to ensure that it was secure and did not contain any uninvited guests. As Dennis checked the bathroom, I turned on the television set, relieved to be out of the censored news space of Baghdad and hoping to see some news from the real world. Indeed I did.

Within seconds, I stood transfixed, watching the first reports from Washington about an alleged sexual affair between the president of the United States and a young White House intern named Monica Lewinsky.

Shortly before this visit to Baghdad, my wife and I had attended an advance screening in New York of the film *Wag the Dog*. The storyline of the movie was this: In response to an observed incident where the president sexually approached a young female visitor to the White House, he is persuaded by his advisers to launch a fabricated war, on film only, against an odious Third World regime as a way of distracting the public from his own shortcomings and restoring his stature as an heroic leader. This satire on the relationship between politics, public relations, and show business was one that many reviewers and commentators had found chillingly close to reality. The conjunction of the release of *Wag the Dog* and the revelation of the Lewinsky affair immediately raised in countless minds the idea that President Clinton might be tempted to stage an external diversion from his domestic travails.

Having finished his checking, Dennis Grimm, a salt-of-the-earth character, arrived at my side. He focused on the news from Washington and, moments later, exclaimed, "Jesus, boss, it's *Wag the Dog*." I had no idea that he'd seen the movie or was aware of its plot. We'd never discussed it.

As I watched the news, my heart began sinking: We didn't need this distraction; we needed resolve to back us up. Where would this end, where would it leave us? I feared that the consequence of this affair might be a weakening of U.S. resolve, a backing away from the threat to enforce the law against Saddam, precisely in order to avoid an accusation that the tail was wagging the dog. "I don't know, mate," I shot back at Dennis, "maybe it's just the opposite." In truth, I had no idea where this would lead.

8

KOFI ANNAN GOES TO BAGHDAD

THE LEVEL OF CONCERN about Iraq's defiance was rising sharply at the beginning of 1998. Informal discussions among Security Council representatives were dominated by the issue, and the United States and the United Kingdom were undertaking a considerable military buildup in the Persian Gulf. As senior Iraqi and American officials exchanged public accusations, U.S. Secretary of Defense William Cohen spoke of large-scale attacks being planned against Iraq.

Now UN Secretary-General Kofi Annan began actively exploring a role for himself in diffusing this crisis, including proposing a visit to Baghdad for direct negotiations with Saddam Hussein. At the same time, he was increasingly making his own policy preferences known. On February 1, 1998, Annan presented a supplementary report to the Security Council on the implementation of the UN humanitarian program for Iraq, in which he recommended more than doubling the Oil for Food program. While this decision addressed humanitarian problems, Annan went farther. In pronouncing that he opposed any linkage between the UN humanitarian program and Iraq's violations of Security Council resolutions, he was departing from the letter of the Security Council's resolutions. This was the start of an attempt to accommodate Iraqi recalcitrance, to come to terms with, or appease, a state that was refusing to fulfill its legal obligations.

Saddam's government is intensely realist and calculating in its view of international affairs. It rightly assumes that significant statements and actions reflect the ebb and flow of relative power among states and key actors. So, the new flexibility in offering aid was interpreted by it as a weakening in the political resolve to enforce either disarmament or sanctions. It was therefore unsurprising that Tariq Aziz fulsomely encouraged Kofi Annan to travel to Baghdad. In his talks with Annan in early February, Aziz had been utterly dismissive of UNSCOM and of me. According to Aziz, the real goals of certain "elements" within UNSCOM were not to obtain the truth about Iraq's weapons status (conceding that up to this point there had been lies!) but to promote American and British interests by isolating Iraq and to prolong sanctions.

Aziz sought to paint a picture of a benign Iraq, willing to cooperate with virtually any international institution other than UNSCOM. He told Annan that I had caused a lot of damage by playing a negative role in the disarmament process, "not a UN role," as he put it, citing the controversy caused by my comments in an interview with the *New York Times* editorial board. I'd been quoted as saying that a single appropriately armed Iraqi missile could "blow away Tel Aviv." Annan agreed with the Iraqis that my remarks had been inappropriate, ignoring the facts. What I was reported as saying was both true and had been stated previously in a written report by Ekeus to the Security Council; furthermore, the newspaper had published only a portion of what I had said, which distorted the meaning of my comments. (The newspaper subsequently published an apology for having done this.)

Aziz insistently repeated his claims that Iraq was disarmed, had nothing to hide, and had no intention of rearming. He suggested that Iraq was prepared to show the presidential sites to "any group of people" to prove to the international community that they were not hiding any prohibited weapons, as UNSCOM was alleging. This is why the Iraqis wanted the secretary-general to visit Baghdad to help resolve the conflict: "It would be in your hands. Leave UNSCOM aside." Iraq's assessment was that it could recruit Annan to its side.

The Russians and the French were also active in promoting the Iraqi cause at this time. Russian Foreign Minister Yevgeny Primakov supported the Iraqi proposal for having UNSCOM inspectors accompanied, at presidential sites, by a special team of diplomatic representatives from the permanent members of the Security Council and other countries (this subsequently occurred). Primakov also proposed that this special team should be led by a "prominent international political figure." It was then suggested that I could become that person's deputy.

At the same time, the French were working on a similar proposal, one that would see the sites inspected by a core technical team accompanied by diplomats to ensure that nothing would offend or impugn Iraq's sense of national dignity. In one instance, the French actually discussed the sort of clothing that might be worn on these occasions. (Perhaps only the French would make inspector couture a priority.) This led to the French idea of diplomatic accompaniment being described in the UN corridors as the "white-glove brigade."

Faced with similar, competing proposals, Secretary-General Annan asked me for a comparative analysis of them, which I provided on February 9. I emphasized that the main difficulty of diplomatic accompaniment was that arranging it in advance would give prior notice to Iraq of any future inspection, effectively depriving UNSCOM of one of its key tools: no-notice inspections. I said that any proposal, if it was to be viable, must include the following: A very restricted number of presidential sites would be designated; all other areas of Iraq would be open to all UNSCOM activities; the presidential sites should be open for the purposes of ongoing monitoring and verification; and all work of technical substance should remain UNSCOM's responsibility.

I never received a formal reply to this advice. And it was ignored. As the debate continued, the basic goal of Secretary-General Annan and his senior staff was to solve the crisis and avert military action. Two principles guided them.

First, Annan's advisers detached the goal of conflict resolution, as such, from the fundamental requirement of disarming Iraq. Furthermore, the conflict to be resolved was one-dimensional: everything would be alright, the advisers seemed to say, if only Iraq didn't feel so put upon. Thus, they focused on establishing the least challenging basis for a possible agreement. The only terms in which proposals were addressed was whether or not they might lead to agreement with the Iraqi government. The disarmament standards set by the Security Council resolutions were virtually disregarded. I feared that this act of disconnecting diplomacy from substance held great dangers.

Second, whenever my office would try to introduce facts about the disarmament process into the discussion, Kofi Annan and his senior staff would try to marginalize them. These "details" were considered unnecessarily complex for what was perceived as a pure diplomatic project. Eyes would literally glaze over when we would attempt to make clear that there were specific technical requirements for any given site inspection, document examination, or one-on-one interview concerned with Iraq's illegal weapons programs—and that these details mattered.

Of course, this second point was connected to and derived from the first. In detaching diplomacy from the substance of disarmament, the secretary-general's advisers effectively treated the technical details as irrelevant. When they did ask about technical matters, their questions betrayed a shocking degree of ignorance. Ignorance is no crime; one purpose of dialogue is to inform and educate. But Annan's staff also displayed impatience with such dialogue and the answers they were given on weapons-related issues. It was all too hard.

One of the more disturbing aspects of the secretary-general's preparation for his intervention in Baghdad concerned the so-called presidential sites. Obviously, it was crucial to identify and describe these sites. Where were they? How large were they? What did they comprise? We desperately needed precise answers to these questions. In the second week of February 1998, Kofi Annan told me that Tariq Aziz had asked him to provide UN surveyors to draw up maps of Iraq's presidential sites. Secretary-General Annan asked me for advice on how this might be done quickly. I told him that we already had a notion of what those sites were, and at his request I provided a written list. This was based partly on discussions held in Baghdad during the preceding two months, partly on our prior work, in which we sometimes sought to visit buildings located on these sites. We listed eight sites with a description of the buildings and the approximate area involved: the Kharkh Presidential Area, the Republican Palace Presidential Area, the Radwaniyah Presidential Area, the Tharthar Presidential Palace Area, the Tikrit Presidential Palace Area, the Auja Presidential Palace Area, the Jabal Makhul Presidential Palace Area, and the Mosul Presidential Palace Area. In our estimation, the presidential areas encompassed a total of seventy square kilometers and 1,500 permanent structures.

I certainly didn't object to providing this list, but the idea that the UN should take formal responsibility for mapping and describing the presidential sites Iraq claimed as sanctuaries, immune from inspection, struck me as strange. This was another diversionary tactic by Iraq, and I said so.

Nonetheless, after several more phone conversations with Tariq Aziz, the secretary-general told me that he was disposed to accede to Aziz's request and put together a team of UN surveyors.

On February 11, I addressed a brief note to Annan, expressing my serious concerns. Aziz was claiming that Iraq did not possess adequate maps, which was absurd. Iraq had an extensive cartographic capability supported by aerial reconnaissance. We knew that Iraq had a cartographic office in the Special Republican Guard that regularly prepared maps of sites in Iraq for the president. I pointed out that an UNSCOM officer had been in that office on one occasion and had personally seen and held in his hands relevant maps of very high quality. In fact, we had in our possession photographs of parts of Iraq taken by Iraqi aerial survey planes and given to us by Iraq. General Nils Carlstrom, the director of our office in Baghdad, could pick up whatever maps Iraq was prepared to provide and send them back to New York by secure means at an hour's notice. I wrote:

> Under these circumstances, it would appear that Tariq Aziz has sought to mislead you. For this serious reason but also because it would be appropriate both in terms of saving essential time and because it is Iraq that is demanding that certain sites in Iraq be identified as sites for which a special form of inspection should be designed, I suggest Tariq Aziz be told that Iraq must provide, as a matter of urgency, identification of the sites it has in mind and maps thereof so that you could know the exact nature and extent of those sites.

There are, of course, times in diplomacy when it makes sense to agree to trivial requests because, psychologically, it can grease the wheels for the bigger deal. But this was not one of those cases. The UN secretary-general was being lied to, played for a fool. If he accepted such lies, it would augur badly for any future negotiations in Baghdad.

Annan rejected my advice and proceeded to assemble a team of UN surveyors, provided by Austria, but including a French photo interpreter selected by the secretary-general's staff. He also decided that the team should be led by a senior UN official, Staffan de Mistura, who had recently ended a posting at the UN humanitarian office in Baghdad and then been appointed as the secretary-general's representative in Rome.

The survey team went to Baghdad immediately and worked with great speed to cover all the sites involved, by land and air, within the space of some four days. The team conducted its last inspection on February 20 and forwarded its report to Annan the next day. He, in turn, forwarded the report to the president of the Security Council and Tariq Aziz.

The survey team then traveled immediately to New York, bringing along the maps it had drawn up and some 500 new photographs. These materials were afforded the sort of protection one might expect for the Dead Sea Scrolls. UNSCOM was not allowed to hold them. Instead, they were guarded on the thirty-eighth floor of the UN Secretariat in the name of the secretary-general. Vladimir Gratcheff, a Secretariat official from Russia, was appointed as the gatekeeper during the brief period Security Council members could view the maps. Earlier I wrote that the Iraqis we dealt with were humorless, but surely not on this occasion. Saddam Hussein must have fallen down with laughter at how the UN protected these contrived maps. Indeed, it was as difficult for UNSCOM to see them as it was for us to inspect a site in Iraq. The leadership of the UN had become a facilitator of Iraqi concealment.

THE INCREASING involvement of the secretary-general and his immediate staff raised the political quotient of every decision and action regarding the disarmament of Iraq. The involvement of Gratcheff, who worked close to Annan but clearly reflected Russian interests, underscored this danger.

In contrast with many UN agencies, UNSCOM had always sought to insulate itself, to the extent possible, from national political interests. This wasn't easy to do. Naturally, every UN agency must draw its staff from specific national sources, which unavoidably produces political coloration. Yet we tried to minimize this through the character of the people we recruited.

My immediate policy staff were first-rate, objective professionals. However, after being in place for a year, I had to accede to political pressure to accept a Russian and a Frenchman within that staff. This was designed to inhibit me, and to some extent it worked. I had to recognize that my actions were the subject of regular insider reports to the Russian and French governments, which were increasingly hostile to UNSCOM's mandate. Of course, this reality was never openly discussed—every staff member was always treated with courtesy and professional respect—but it introduced the need to be guarded about what was said and written in my executive office.

It wasn't only policy experts who could be assumed to pass along information to their national governments; clearly, the staff in technical areas did the same. The UN Charter specifies that staff members shall not take advice from any government, but this is an empty rule. UN staff have always walked both sides of the street, pursuing the interests of their home countries while ostensibly serving their official international mission. It's a well-known fact, but one that is publicly ignored, and perhaps that's how it has to be.

Occasionally, however, the conflicts become too flagrant to ignore, and Vladimir Gratcheff was a case in point. During UNSCOM's repeated crises, it became clear to me that Gratcheff was feeding the secretary-general distorted reports about Security Council debates— reports that tended to be consistently negative in respect to UNSCOM. I had positive evidence of this misbehavior, and I took it up both with Kofi Annan and with Sir Kieran Prendergast, the under secretary-general for political affairs and the most senior Briton in the UN. I knew that Prendergast was concerned about aspects of the secretary-general's handling of the Iraq issue, and so I considered him a colleague I could turn to.

Prendergast investigated by examining some of Gratcheff's handwritten notes for Annan and, convinced I was right, pointed out the misleading statements to the secretary-general. Annan was struck by Prendergast's warning and said he'd "take it into account" in evaluating what Gratcheff told him in the future.

Prendergast later told me, "It's well known that Gratcheff is close to the Russian mission." But despite Prendergast's warning, Gratcheff remained a member of Kofi Annan's senior staff until the day I left UNSCOM.

W ITH THE MAPS and photos in Gratcheff's care, arrangements were also made for Staffan de Mistura, the diplomatic leader of the surveying project, to personally report his team's findings to the Security Council. I was present. De Mistura entered the chamber bearing a glossy Morocco leather folder and dressed in elaborately formal garb, including a perfectly folded pocket handkerchief and pince-nez. His appearance set the tone for the discussion that followed.

De Mistura described at length the warmth and hospitality he and his team had received from their Iraqi hosts. He described vividly the grandeur of the presidential palaces they visited, although he discreetly hinted that perhaps the Carrera marble and other adornments were a touch overstated. He said that it was very clear to him that these palaces were deeply popular in Iraq; the people *wanted* their great leader to be accommodated in luxury.

De Mistura indicated that the sites identified by UNSCOM that I'd listed for the secretary-general were indeed the presidential sites at issue. However, the UN surveyors' measurements had resulted in a smaller area and number of buildings. According to de Mistura's team, the overall area consisted of some thirty-five square kilometers and slightly more than 1,000 buildings. This adjustment to UNSCOM's earlier estimate was presented in a way that suggested our team had committed some egregious error. This was, of course, amplified by Iraq, which subsequently accused us of greatly exaggerating the size and scope of the problem posed by the presidential sites.

Although de Mistura had been sent to Iraq for a strictly technical purpose—surveying the presidential palaces—he dwelled on the political, social, and cultural revelations of his trip. One detail particularly seemed to fascinate him: that some of the presidential palaces distant from Baghdad contained substantial kitchens with fully stocked larders. At one site, he said, the pantry could be readily supplied with fresh venison (of which Saddam, he'd been told, was especially fond) from a specially maintained game park adjacent to the palace. In each case, de Mistura assured us, there was a complete kitchen and household staff waiting at all times in case the leader might decide to drop in.

De Mistura went on to observe that these were perfectly normal conditions, as he'd learned through his long diplomatic experience in various parts of the world. A great leader was expected to live well, lest crucial "cultural values" be offended.

When de Mistura's presentation had ended, U.S. Ambassador Bill Richardson asked de Mistura whether he had any views on the evident disparity between the amount of money Saddam Hussein was prepared to spend on his own palaces and the parlous economic state of the Iraqi people. Did he think this was right?

De Mistura responded in sardonic tones. He said there were, of course, many in the room with wider diplomatic experience than his own—it was implied that he did not include Richardson in that category—but he felt there would be widespread agreement in the room that it was characteristic of countries like Iraq to have such leadership compounds and palaces. The people were proud of these monumental buildings. And while he could not go into the economics of the issue, he did not personally find what he had seen in any way strange or incongruous.

Richardson remained silent. I thought of Oscar Wilde's response to a fatuous claim: "Sir, your argument does not deserve the compliment of rational discussion."

When the Security Council meeting ended, Annan invited me to an informal luncheon at his residence, where de Mistura would be the featured guest. As soon as we had taken our places at the luncheon table, de Mistura regaled the secretary-general with what he considered to have been the extraordinarily naïve exchange that had just taken place in the Security Council. He ridiculed Richardson as a person whose question only betrayed his ignorance of the world of diplomacy. I am sorry to record that Kofi Annan and his chief of staff, Iqbal Riza, seemed amused by, and took no issue with, de Mistura's posturing.

FROM EARLY TO MID-FEBRUARY, the secretary-general consulted extensively, especially with the permanent members of the Security Council, on the question of whether or not he should go to Baghdad. Only later were states other than the permanent five included, a fact that angered many.

On the afternoon of February 16, the secretary-general was consulting with the permanent members in his private conference room on the thirty-eighth floor of the UN Secretariat. I received a telephone call in my office, eight floors below, and was summoned to attend the meeting immediately. Upon taking my place at the table, I was straightaway put a question by the Russian ambassador, Sergey Lavrov. Lavrov began by giving the briefest description of what had been discussed among the permanent five and the secretary-general for the last hour or so and then asked me if I believed that UNSCOM would be able to carry out its work effectively if presidential sites were inspected with diplomatic accompaniment.

Suspecting that I was being ambushed, I began my answer by asking for further clarification of the proposed conditions. Lavrov merely repeated the same information he'd already given.

Under these circumstances, I decided to give a careful answer, beginning by saying that I could reply only on the basis of a narrow band of technical arms-control and monitoring criteria. If the elemental technical capability and responsibility of UNSCOM were preserved, then I believed we could do our job under the circumstances that Lavrov had sketched. Lavrov seemed satisfied with this answer, and the meeting soon broke up. Oddly, the U.S. and British ambassadors remained silent.

Downstairs in my office, I reflected on what had happened. I had indeed been ambushed. I'd been told nothing of the more substantial discussion of the various proposals for inspection of presidential sites, in particular how these might have differed. Lavrov had decided to run for the money. He'd asked me, point-blank, a question designed to get a response he could claim as an unqualified affirmative answer.

I decided that I needed to dig myself out of this hole. I wrote a letter to the secretary-general and the permanent five overnight, clarifying the answer I'd given the previous evening. In political terms, this was difficult because it might seem that I was trying to backslide. So I stressed that I believed it was important for me to address the issues involved in the previous evening's question more completely than I'd been able to do on that occasion.

I made four main points. First, the Security Council's own resolutions gave UNSCOM immediate and unrestricted access to any site, document, or person in Iraq. Second, the determination of where, when, and for how long such access should be sought was assigned to me, as executive chairman of UNSCOM, under the direction of the Security Council. Third, the overall conduct of UNSCOM's business in all aspects, including the composition of inspection teams, was also my responsibility. And finally, it was my responsibility as executive chairman to report on all aspects of our work directly to the Security Council.

I then expanded these comments by stating that, had I been present during the earlier portion of the consultations, I felt sure I would have stressed the following additional points. Iraq had used the June 1996 modalities for the inspection of sensitive sites to reduce UNSCOM's rights of immediate, unconditional, and unrestricted access. A clear distinction should be drawn between a small number of palaces, which would be given special treatment in consideration of Iraq's sovereignty and dignity, and the wider areas around them. All areas other than the designated palace buildings should be treated as normal sites in the future for the purpose of UNSCOM inspections. The clarification of what constituted designated palaces or presidential sites would make it possible to abandon the previous notion of sensitive sites. If this did not occur, the council would have formally agreed to at least one, and possibly two, major exceptions from its own principles of access. Finally, the delineation of palaces or presidential sites should be carefully considered, because they represented significant places of work, not just places of entertainment or grandeur. They held documentary records of Iraq's weapons of mass destruction program and were also places where Iraq could and did retain prohibited materials, about which they had repeatedly made false declarations. If UNSCOM inspectors had to be accompanied by diplomats, then so be it, but if this meant any dilution of expertise or seriousness of purpose, then UNSCOM's task would have been trashed.

The Russians, French, and Chinese reacted with anger. Lavrov, who'd thought his ambush had succeeded, wrote to me complaining that I'd sought to alter the views I'd given the night before. Ambassador Lavrov's letter essentially provided a defense of Iraqi interests:

> We cannot accept your thesis that if a clear distinction is able to be drawn between a small number of Palaces and the wider areas around them then all areas other than the designated Palace buildings should, in [the] future, be treated as "normal" sites for the purpose of UNSCOM inspections. This approach could represent a very radical and absolutely unnecessary change of procedures, taking into account the nature of these sites. We cannot accept the idea of abandoning the modalities for sensitive sites which have been worked out as a practical solution aimed at providing UNSCOM with access while taking into account Iraq's legitimate security concerns as stipulated in relevant Security Council resolutions. . . . We consider any attempt to renege on the existing modalities as entirely unwarranted and totally counterproductive.

The French and Chinese ambassadors, in other, less formal ways, made clear that they, too, had been extremely discomforted by what I had written. They feared that my comments implied that the plans they were cooking up to deal with the current crisis might come apart.

M EANWHILE, the technical evaluation meetings—the so-called TEMs that I had earlier arranged with Tariq Aziz—were being held in Baghdad during February 1–6. The purpose of these meetings was to review the available information on proscribed missile warhead remnants and their possible chemical and biological agent content, especially the chemical-warfare agent VX. Teams of international specialists from countries with expertise in these areas attended, including representatives from the permanent members of the Security Council and experts from both UNSCOM and Iraq.

On February 18, I informed Iqbal Riza, Annan's chief of staff, that the final reports of these meetings had been received. They showed that Iraq had not provided full disclosure on proscribed missile warheads, on chemical and biological agents, or on its production of VX. The level of verification that UNSCOM had been able to achieve was unsatisfactory in all areas. Further verification would be required.

It is important to underline the state of affairs prevailing at this time. Iraq had introduced the notion of sanctuaries that would be free from any arms control. It had blurred the important material and legal issues this raised by characterizing it as a matter of national dignity—Saddam's palaces! It had succeeded in giving a key supporting role in this play to the UN itself by obtaining the secretary-general's agreement that the UN would map Iraq's sacred sites. The actual player, Staffan de Mistura, performed admirably—central casting would have been proud! As you will see later, the maps proved to be wrong. Perhaps, in the circumstances of such a farce any other result would have been implausible. Far more important, however, was that clear signs of what Iraq was about were available, including by lying to the secretary-general. But those signs were set aside in the name of diplomacy, as were fundamental arms control requirements. To cap it all, simultaneously with this political play, Iraq was blocking UNSCOM's arms control work. This fact should have been taken very seriously both because of its intrinsic importance and as a sign of Iraq's real motives in seeking direct engagement by the secretary-general. It was ignored.

On February 16, the secretary-general consulted with the permanent five and, later that day, with the other members of the Security Council; an understanding emerged permitting Annan to journey to Baghdad without objection from the Security Council. He was given no specific instructions but merely a generalized blessing to see if he could make some headway with the crisis.

The composition of the team accompanying Kofi Annan was predictable. It included his senior political and legal advisers, such as Hans Corell, under secretary-general for legal affairs, and Fred Eckhard,

Annan's spokesman. Mike Wallace, of the TV news magazine *60 Minutes*, was also included, styled in the delegation list as "journalist accompanying the official delegation." Most notably, the group also included Lakhdar Brahimi, who had led the diplomatic trio to Baghdad three months earlier. Brahimi came to be one of Annan's closest advisers during the visit to Baghdad (that is, if constant physical proximity to the secretary-general is any measure; Brahimi was always at Annan's side, riding in his car from meeting to meeting).

When I offered the secretary-general the presence of senior UNSCOM officers in his delegation, I was at first rebuffed. In further discussion it was agreed, however, that it might be appropriate for one UNSCOM commissioner to accompany the secretary-general, and I arranged for Ambassador Johan Molander, the commissioner from Sweden, to fill that role. I'd long known Molander to be of outstanding intellect as well as a highly skilled diplomat with deep knowledge of weapons of mass destruction. Molander had been a member of the original staff of UNSCOM.

I also proposed that one of my senior advisers, Gustavo Zlauvinen of Argentina, accompany the team. The secretary-general's chief of staff refused the offer, fobbing me off with a patently bogus excuse—the delegation list had already been printed! This was not the first or last occasion on which Iqbal Riza tried to deceive me, often claiming—falsely— that his actions had been directly authorized by the secretary-general.

After leaving New York, the delegation made an overnight stop in Paris for consultations with the French government, which then provided the delegation with a private jet for the leg to Baghdad. Unlike UNSCOM flights, this plane was permitted to land in the downtown Baghdad airport, where Kofi Annan alighted and announced to the assembled press that he had come on a "sacred mission."

The details of what happened in Baghdad—how negotiations were conducted and with whom—have never been made very clear. Much of the discussion took place between Kofi Annan and Tariq Aziz, who used much of that time to complain about UNSCOM. Some of their discussions took place during out-of-town tours to presidential areas, where the two men would take tea, sometimes at a presidential palace, while they continued their talks.

Meanwhile, Hans Corell was hard at work with his Iraqi legal counterparts crafting an agreement between Kofi Annan and Iraq. As those negotiations neared their conclusion—perhaps when Tariq Aziz felt that he could take the text upstairs to his boss—the participants in Baghdad and the world media focused on the somewhat breathlessly awaited meeting between Kofi Annan and Saddam Hussein.

That meeting took place on February 22. Only a few photographs were taken. They show Kofi Annan introducing to Saddam Hussein a small entourage, a member of which found it appropriate to bow deeply to the great man.

Annan and Saddam then apparently withdrew and spoke in private for several hours. They shared several Cuban cigars. Soon thereafter, Fred Eckhard, the secretary-general's spokesman, announced from the balcony of Kofi Annan's Baghdad quarters that he was confident that a breakthrough had been achieved and an agreement reached.

The text of the Memorandum of Understanding (MOU) was ceremoniously signed by the secretary-general and Tariq Aziz on February 23. Annan signed "on behalf of the United Nations," a curious and somewhat dubious formulation, given that neither the Security Council nor the General Assembly had officially authorized him to act on their behalf. The secretary-general and his party departed immediately for New York to present the agreement to the Security Council.

Upon his return to UN headquarters, Annan received a hero's welcome from several hundred of the Secretariat staff who had gathered in the foyer of the building at the urging of posted notices, e-mails, and public-address announcements. Annan later sent an e-mail to UN staff members thanking them for their support, proclaiming the triumph of the agreement to which all had contributed and dismissing criticism in advance:

> It was not unexpected that there would be some criticism of us and misrepresentations of what we have done in Iraq, but you must not be disheartened. The alternative to the agreement would have ended UNSCOM's work. The Memorandum of Understanding has strengthened it. I want you, therefore, to treat our critics with sympathetic understanding.

While enjoying this euphoric welcome, the secretary-general did not know that Tariq Aziz, at that moment, was sending a letter seeking to change the terms of the Memorandum of Understanding. Like the MOU itself, Aziz's letter was also dated February 23. So even as the ink was drying on the page, Iraq had thought better of it.

Annan went straight to the Security Council to report on his mission to Baghdad and to commend the agreement he had signed. Arrangements were then put in motion for the Security Council to, in some way, adopt or endorse the agreement (and thereby solve the problem created by the secretary-general, who purportedly signed on behalf of the whole United Nations when there had been no clear or political agreement for him to do so).

Immediately after his Security Council meeting, Annan held a press conference in which he said that Saddam Hussein was a man "I can do business with." Elsewhere, he repeated Iraq's charges that UNSCOM's inspectors had become a bunch of "cowboys," meaning roughnecks who were out of control and trampling on Iraqi sensitivities. Of course, the term also clearly suggested "American," a resonance with which Saddam would have had no difficulty.

The MOU itself was a short document comprising seven paragraphs. It had three main parts: an unconditional commitment by Iraq to cooperate with UNSCOM and IAEA; a broad-brush description of arrangements for the inspection of presidential sites, specifically to include diplomatic observers; and an acknowledgment that in all other respects UNSCOM's work in Iraq would be conducted in accordance with procedures hitherto established. Because of its historic importance, and curious character, I reproduce its text in full:

1. The Government of Iraq reconfirms its acceptance of all relevant resolutions of the Security Council, including resolutions 687 (1991) and 715 (1991). The Government of Iraq further reiterates its undertaking to cooperate fully with the United Nations Special Commission (UNSCOM) and the International Atomic Energy Agency (IAEA).

2. The United Nations reiterates the commitment of all Member States to respect the sovereignty and territorial integrity of Iraq.

3. The Government of Iraq undertakes to accord to UNSCOM and IAEA immediate, unconditional and unrestricted access in conformity with the resolutions referred to in paragraph 1. In the performance of its mandate under the Security Council resolutions, UNSCOM undertakes to respect the legitimate concerns of Iraq relating to national security, sovereignty and dignity.

4. The United Nations and the Government of Iraq agree that the following special procedures shall apply to the initial and

subsequent entries for the performance of the tasks mandated at the eight Presidential Sites in Iraq as defined in the annex to the present Memorandum:

(a) A Special Group shall be established for this purpose by the Secretary-General in consultation with the Executive Chairman of UNSCOM and the Director General of IAEA. This Group shall comprise senior diplomats appointed by the Secretary-General and experts drawn from UNSCOM and IAEA. The Group shall be headed by a Commissioner appointed by the Secretary-General.

(b) In carrying out its work, the Special Group shall operate under the established procedures of UNSCOM and IAEA, and specific detailed procedures which will be developed given the special nature of the Presidential Sites, in accordance with the relevant resolutions of the Security Council.

(c) The report of the Special Group on its activities and findings shall be submitted by the Executive Chairman of UNSCOM to the Security Council through the Secretary-General.

5. The United Nations and the Government of Iraq further agree that all other areas, facilities, equipment, records and means of transportation shall be subject to UNSCOM procedures hitherto established.

6. Noting the progress achieved by UNSCOM in various disarmament areas, and the need to intensify efforts in order to complete its mandate, the United Nations and the Government of Iraq agree to improve cooperation, and efficiency, effectiveness and transparency of work, so as to enable UNSCOM to report to the Council expeditiously under paragraph 22 of resolution 687 (1991). To achieve this goal, the Government of Iraq and UNSCOM will implement the recommendations directed at them as contained in the report of the emergency session of UNSCOM held on 21 November 1997.

7. The lifting of sanctions is obviously of paramount importance to the people and Government of Iraq and the Secretary-General undertook to bring this matter to the full attention of the members of the Security Council.

An annex, or side agreement, to the MOU specified the eight presidential sites that the regime agreed would be subject to the inspections.

These sites consisted mostly, but not entirely, of the same sites that my office had identified earlier. The differences were not significant. I immediately analyzed the text of the MOU, taking brief notes. The trepidation I'd felt about Annan's mission had been borne out, and I was dismayed by the language I read. What seemed particularly important was paragraph 5, which included the statement that all the work of UNSCOM would be conducted under the terms of agreements hitherto reached. This meant that our strenuous efforts to eliminate the invidious and now frequently violated sensitive-site modalities had been to no avail.

Paragraphs 6 and 7 gave particular attention to Iraq's concerns. First, the MOU referred, somewhat amazingly, to the recommendations of the Special Commission's emergency session of November 21, 1997, characterized as being designed to improve "the efficiency, effectiveness, and transparency" of UNSCOM's work. This was a distortion of the facts, as the main substance of that report had detailed Iraq's failure to meet its disarmament obligations.

In paragraph 7, the sanctions issue was treated in a language and tone quite different from that found elsewhere in the MOU. Specifically, the statement that "the lifting of sanctions is obviously of paramount importance to the people and government of Iraq and the Secretary-General undertook to bring this matter to the full attention of the members of the Security Council" was new. I later asked Kofi Annan about paragraph 7, observing that it was in a different tone and language from the other provisions of the MOU. I drew particular attention to the use of the word "obviously," saying that it seemed to import a subjective or judgmental element into an otherwise flat text.

Annan seemed pleased with this question and immediately claimed authorship of paragraph 7, saying that the person whose voice was heard in the word "obviously" was his own. He wanted to indicate to Iraq that he understood that the relief of sanctions was of principal importance, and that is why the paragraph went on to state that he, personally as secretary-general, was committed to bringing this matter to the attention of the Security Council.

U.S. Secretary of State Madeleine Albright telephoned me at home early that morning, seeking my reaction to the MOU. I went through my notes, calling attention to what I thought was the misleading aspect of the seventh paragraph. Iraq's behavior had made perfectly clear that Saddam's fundamental concern was not relief from sanctions but to maintain weapons of mass destruction. If relief from sanctions had been his main concern, he could have achieved that quickly, years before, by cooperating with the disarmament requirements. I feared that paragraph 7 contained the seeds of what would be the popular interpretation of the MOU, leading to a further breakdown of the disarmament effort. Albright thanked me for these views.

And then there was Aziz's letter of February 23. In that letter, Aziz proposed changing the meaning of paragraph 4(b), which stated that detailed procedures would be developed in line with the special nature of the presidential sites. Attempting to expand Iraq's control of the inspections, Aziz claimed that there had been an *understanding* in three areas:

1. For the purpose of coordination and rendering support for the work to be carried out by the Special Group, Iraqi personnel will accompany the Group according to practice hitherto followed.

2. The work to be carried out by the Special Group at the Presidential Sites shall comprise the determination of the presence or absence of proscribed weapons, equipment and/or production relating thereto. To that end, the Special Group can use any necessary equipment, including underground probing equipment, and, if necessary, immediately carry out excavations. The experts can take soil, water, plant and leaf samples, which shall be shared by Iraq and the parties members of the Group (senior diplomats). An analysis of these samples shall be performed at the Baghdad Centre of Monitoring and Verification of UNSCOM with the participation of representatives of Iraq and parties represented in the Special Group. Such analysis, on the basis of the same modality, can be carried out abroad by reputable experts when necessary. State documents shall not be subjected to the verification in question. Photographing activities shall be restricted solely to the technical work of verification.

3. Iraq shall provide all the necessary accommodation, transport and other requirements to the Special Group.

On February 26, the secretary-general replied that Aziz's reference to a certain "understanding" was wrong. The agreements Aziz had described were not and could not become a part of the Memorandum of Understanding. In a welcome show of robustness, Annan wrote:

You will recall that, during the discussions which led to the Memorandum of Understanding, the Iraqi representatives proposed the inclusion in the Memorandum of language along the lines that appear in paragraphs 1, 2 and 3 of your letter under reference. On the United Nations side, we explicitly stated that we were not prepared to include this language in the Memorandum. We pointed out that the provisions related to technical aspects into which we were not prepared to enter.

Before my departure, I informed you that upon my return to New York, I would immediately address the question of specific detailed procedures referred to in paragraph 4(b) of the Memorandum. I specifically reiterated to you that I was not prepared to discuss the subject matter in substance, and that I would revert to you with the required procedures, which are presently being prepared in the Secretariat.

In the light of the above, I should like to make clear that the language contained in paragraphs 1, 2 and 3 of your letter does not constitute an "understanding" between United Nations and the Government of Iraq.

Kofi Annan's response to Aziz may have been influenced by the U.K. ambassador, Sir John Weston, who had become aware of the letter from Aziz. He quickly approached Annan to express his deep concern about the idea that there had been side-understandings in Baghdad. The secretary-general rejected that contention and subsequently replied in strong terms to the Iraqis.

Subsequently, the office of the secretary-general ordered an internal investigation into how Weston had obtained a copy of Aziz's letter. This included an interview of me by UN investigators. I was never shown their report.

O N MARCH 2, 1998, the Security Council adopted Resolution 1154 in response to the secretary-general's actions. It endorsed the Memorandum of Understanding and looked forward to its early and full implementation. In that context, it asked Annan to finalize the procedures for presidential-site inspections in consultation with UNSCOM and IAEA, stressing that Iraq needed to comply with all of its obligations under Security Council resolutions and warning that any violation would carry the "severest consequences for Iraq."

The drawing-up of regulations and procedures for the MOU's implementation—particularly with respect to presidential-site inspections—began under the auspices of a small group comprising Kofi Annan's senior advisers, UNSCOM's legal adviser (John Scott), and me.

What should have been a routine job turned out to be peculiarly revealing. First, we were instructed by the secretary-general not to describe the inspections as such but to call them "entries." We then discovered that Annan's advisers were not sure that the word "entries" should be plural, that is, they thought the inspections might not need to be repeated, even though the MOU referred to "subsequent entries." An extended battle erupted in which I insisted that the reason for inspections was both disarmament, which could be relatively quick if Iraq cooperated, and monitoring, which could not be a brief procedure but had to be of indefinite duration. I said it was outrageous that the words "inspection," "disarmament," and "monitoring" were not permitted to be used. In the end, Annan's men reluctantly agreed to a footnote stating that UNSCOM's mandate included both disarmament and monitoring.

You could be forgiven for laughing or crying or both about this kind of word witchcraft so typical of diplomatic negotiation. In fact, what I've just briefly related was deadly earnest. Simply, the undertakings given about the word "inspection" and the fudging of the singular versus plural of the word "entry" had an ominous meaning. I achieved the footnote only by dint of angry argument, and it stated the right things. But I had no illusions about what had happened—UNSCOM's mandate had, at least in part, been bargained away in Baghdad.

Meanwhile, letters were being sent by the UN secretariat to members of the Security Council and other UN members that maintained embassies in Baghdad. They were invited to consider placing their diplomats on the roster of those that might be drawn upon to accompany UNSCOM inspectors, if and when they went to visit presidential sites.

Early in March, the stage was being set for the first inspection (or "entry") of presidential sites. The procedures for visiting these sites had been discussed with Iraq, which immediately attempted to amend them to further reduce UNSCOM's role. These efforts were rebuffed. The procedures were approved by the Security Council on March 9 they provided for the composition of the Special Group, functions of senior diplomats, functions of UNSCOM experts, the rights of the Special Group, and reporting procedures.

Kofi Annan had decided to appoint Jayantha Dhanapala as the under secretary-general for disarmament affairs, who would lead, at least in title, the Special Group constituted under the MOU. The regulations also included, at my insistence, the position of "head of the technical team," to be held by a senior UNSCOM official, who would be responsible for all substantive aspects of the conduct of inspections. I appointed my deputy, Charles Duelfer, to this role. We also assembled a separate technical team under his supervision with key people in each weapons area; most had experience in the field, some for a number of years. But before I could focus on preparing my team for these new inspections, I had to contend with a series of events that posed a serious threat to UNSCOM's technical objectivity and organizational independence.

Annan announced on March 5 that he was appointing Prakash Shah, former Indian ambassador to the UN, as his special envoy in Baghdad; this was the same man I'd battled with over the Comprehensive Nuclear Test Ban Treaty two years earlier. Within his own government's administration Shah had for some years been the senior official responsible for Indian oil policy. The letter Annan addressed to the president of the Security Council announcing Shah's appointment opened with a paragraph that illustrates both the stilted silliness of much diplomatic language and something of deeper significance in the political context of the moment:

I have the honor to refer to the difficulties arising from time to time in the relations between Iraq and the United Nations; and to the need for improved lines of communication between the Government of Iraq and my office in order to help avert the development of such difficulties into full-fledged crises threatening to undermine international peace and security in the area.

The use of the euphemism "difficulties" and the evident commitment to avoiding conflict at all costs accurately reflected the attitude of sympathy toward Iraq that prevailed in the secretary-general's office.

Annan went on to say that Prakash Shah would basically follow closely everything of interest to the United Nations in Iraq and "lend his support" to the work of arms control. Shah's appointment was widely described as a step toward crushing the independence of UNSCOM and its executive chairman. Perhaps this is what the letter meant in another passage: that Shah would give "special attention" to "any crisis or problem" that "might benefit from intervention" by UN headquarters.

Five days later, another troubling development took place. The secretary-general conveyed to the president of the Security Council, Ambassador Abdoulie Momodu Sallah of Gambia, a request he had received from Ambassador Lavrov of Russia. Lavrov recommended that UNSCOM establish an additional post of deputy executive chairman; of course, he nominated a Russian for it. The secretary-general kicked this ball to Ambassador Sallah, asking him to take it up with members of the Security Council as president and advise him (Annan) of any decision taken. No decision was taken and the Russian proposal was shelved.

O N MARCH 1, CNN, in its TV series *Impact*, broadcast in the United States a documentary report about Iraq's attempts to defeat and deceive UNSCOM. Entitled "High Noon in Baghdad: The Inspector's Story," the program was televised worldwide the following day. It was based largely on archival footage, but it also included, with my approval, interviews with UNSCOM staff members Charles Duelfer, Nikita Smidovitch, and Scott Ritter.

Iraq was not pleased. On March 7, Foreign Minister Mohammed Al-Sahaf wrote to Kofi Annan, complaining about this use of the media and claiming that UNSCOM staff had violated UN rules:

It was clear that those who participated in the programme were attempting to prove allegations of "concealment" made against my Government, with a view to claiming that Iraq still has stores of weapons of mass destruction and the materials and means to produce them. The participants did not hesitate to discuss the details of the work currently being undertaken in this regard by Iraq and the Special Commission, which is highly sensitive. Groundless allegations were made about Iraq which are shown to be unsubstantiated by the work of the Iraqi side. Official Special Commission archive materials, such as video film, documents and aerial photographs taken by U2 aircraft, are being used to substantiate these allegations. This material is the property of the United

Nations and is confidential, since it relates to a Member State. It should not be used without authorization for purposes of propaganda.

Iraq's attack was as unsurprising as it was ludicrous, considering the extensive use of the media by Saddam's regime throughout the decade. But I didn't expect the reaction I received from Iqbal Riza. He called to rebuke me and demanded to know what disciplinary action I would take against the UNSCOM officers who had given interviews.

I told Riza that I would take no disciplinary action whatsoever. What the officers had done had been authorized by me. Moreover, the CNN report had been basically accurate. Why should I or anyone else apologize for it? After we exchanged a couple more irritated messages, the matter was dropped.

I N THE LIGHT of the spirit that had been developed around the MOU, I wrote to Tariq Aziz on March 6 and 9, asking Iraq to make a serious effort to bring to account outstanding issues: "I am convinced that we [UNSCOM and the government of Iraq] need to seize this moment in order to advance our work together. We have already started this process, by conducting efforts such as sample collection in the chemical area and the excavation of warhead remnants in the missile area."

I also proposed to both the Security Council and Iraq that I should visit Baghdad at the end of March, immediately before the first planned inspections of presidential sites. I thought it was important to address some substantive disarmament issues before those inspections began and, equally, that I should leave the country before they did, leaving the team to get on with their work.

At only four days, this turned out to be my shortest visit ever to Baghdad. Only two plenary meetings and two separate technical meetings took place. I also traveled to Nibai, some thirty kilometers south of Baghdad, to visit a missile and warhead destruction site, accompanied by General Amer Rashid, the person in charge of chemical weapons and missiles. Perhaps fittingly, his very large Mercedes, which he drove himself, included its own modest arsenal—a .45-caliber pistol and an AK-47 assault rifle.

During our discussions, I made clear to the Iraqis that there were important discrepancies in the account of the unilateral destruction of missile warheads Iraq had undertaken. The Iraqi side acknowledged these difficulties and promised to provide the information required soon. I further noted that there remained important ambiguities in the field of indigenous production of missile engines and a full accounting of missile propellants. Again, the Iraqi side, in a relatively moderate way, said that it would seek to provide the information needed.

In the chemical weapons area, our discussions focused exclusively on the chemical agent VX. We agreed to a further technical evaluation meeting on the entire issue of VX to be held later in the year, possibly in May. However, when I mentioned that there remained other outstanding issues in the chemical area, Aziz was uncomfortable, saying that he preferred to concentrate first on VX and consider other issues only later. We agreed to leave discussion of biological weapons aside until the TEM, then under way in Vienna, had completed its work.

These meetings were overshadowed by the imminent first "entry" into the presidential sites, which was to begin on March 27, the day after our talks ended. I flew from Baghdad to Bahrain on that morning. When I arrived, I was handed telephone messages saying that the presidential-site inspections had already run into difficulties with respect to our use of helicopters and photography. The MOU had clearly provided for UNSCOM to have all of its established rights, including aerial photography. Within hours, Iraq was seeking to challenge precisely those rights and thus to back away from its earlier promises to the secretary-general.

Soon I was on the telephone to Jayantha Dhanapala, head of the Special Group in Baghdad, and Kofi Annan, who was traveling in Europe. Dhanapala attempted to dissuade me from insisting on our photography rights, but I refused, and Kofi Annan backed me up fully on this point. We then continued to fly and photograph, as needed.

Our inspections of the presidential sites were eventually conducted over a period of ten days, and on April 15 a report on these "entries" (in the UN vernacular) was presented to the Security Council by Jayantha Dhanapala. It praised Iraq for its hospitable attitude and cooperation. However, such praise ignored the salient facts about the sites' preparation and the intense, inhibiting Iraqi scrutiny under which the inspections had been conducted.

The report showed that all buildings had been sanitized down to the point of removing even ordinary furniture. The visiting team, some seventy inspectors and twenty-five diplomats, was shown around what was probably the world's largest Potemkin village. They were shepherded at all times by Iraqi minders, who often outnumbered the inspectors themselves.

Charles Duelfer, the UNSCOM leader of the technical team, filed a separate report that raised another, deeply serious issue. During a conversation Duelfer held with General Amer Rashid toward the end of the inspection, the issue of whether or not the perimeters of the presidential sites might be altered in the future arose. Apparently, despite the extraordinary fuss over sending UN surveyors to map the presidential sites (not to mention the grotesque pantomime by de Mistura staged in presenting the surveyors' report to the Security Council), the maps had been wrong in some instances. Yet when Duelfer mentioned the need for the designated sites to remain as they were, or at least for UNSCOM to be given fair notice if they were to change, General Rashid said this could not be noted in any agreement between the two sides because it would imply that Iraq had conceded there could be further visits, or "entries," to these sites. It seems that Iraq had never intended that these sites would be placed under long-term monitoring. All that was intended was a one-time visit pursuant to the agreement with the secretary-general.

This was more than a simple misunderstanding. Iraq's stance, as announced that day by General Rashid and then reported to the Security Council, demonstrated that the agreement signed on February 23 had not been what the Secretary-General had thought or at least had represented it to be and was already dead.

Duelfer's report caused anger on the thirty-eighth floor, and Kofi Annan complained to me strenuously about its implications. When I argued that Duelfer was merely reporting the facts, Annan made clear to me that such facts were unwelcome.

It was at this time that I had perhaps my iciest meeting with the secretary-general. I had asked to see him to inform him of inspections I had authorized to what, I felt certain, Iraq would declare to be sensitive sites. Annan edged toward seeking to dissuade me from proceeding. I said the work involved was important, as such, but also it was a means of testing the other, non-presidential parts of the MOU. How would we know that

Iraq had been earnest in its commitment to full cooperation on all other aspects of UNSCOM's work if we didn't test it? He had himself said publicly that the MOU needed to be tested. Annan asked me to wait a while, but then said, "I can see you've already decided." I confirmed this. He was less than happy.

The inspections went ahead; they were declared sensitive but were not blocked. Annan was subsequently relieved, claiming that this showed Iraq was sincere about his MOU. This episode derived from my formal independence from him, but I believe it strengthened the feeling, at least in his office, that UNSCOM's independence was dangerous.

On April 16, 1998, I submitted my second biannual report to the Security Council, covering the period from October 1997 to April 1998. This was a detailed report of some thirty-five pages that carefully stepped through what had been achieved in each disarmament area and what remained unaccounted for. It also discussed political developments, including the implementation of the MOU and the inspection of presidential sites. To help the council focus on the fundamentals, I made four main points.

> First, while Iraq has claimed for some time that it no longer holds prohibited weapons or systems, this claim has perhaps never been voiced so categorically as in the period under review. That this claim has been made is perhaps not, in itself, remarkable, but the associated insistence by Iraq that it has already made available to the Commission all the materials and information by it is significant.
>
> Second, in particular during the period of crisis, Iraq repeatedly failed to comply with the Council's requirements, especially those relating to immediate, unconditional and unrestricted access to relevant sites, documents and persons. It was therefore of major potential significance that the Secretary-General was able to obtain Iraq's promise, in the Memorandum of Understanding of 23 February, to comply henceforth with the Council's requirements.
>
> Third, there was a significant trend toward substituting consideration of issues of process for consideration of issues related to the destruction, removal or rendering harmless of Iraq's prohibited weapons and systems.

Fourth, as is evident in the disarmament section of this report, a major consequence of the four-month crisis authored by Iraq has been that, in contrast with the prior reporting period, virtually no progress in verifying disarmament has been able to be reported. If this is what Iraq intended by the crisis, in large measure, it could be said to have been successful.

Iraq's response was an extended reply from Tariq Aziz on April 22. He insisted that Iraq had fulfilled all its obligations and that it was simply the incompetence or dishonesty of UNSCOM that prevented that fact from being reported. Aziz repeated Iraq's arguments in the usual strident language:

This report blatantly fails to demonstrate objectivity and fairness, denies and misrepresents facts, and flouts the basic precepts of dealing with the issue of disarmament. The report tendentiously ignores everything that Iraq has done over the past seven years to comply with the provisions of section C of resolution 687 (1991). It is full of blatant falsehoods and lies and has been designed from the outset as a political document aimed at justifying the behaviour of the Special Commission in deliberately prolonging its mandate under resolution 687 (1991), tendentiously blaming Iraq and justifying continuation of the unjust embargo. . . .

Iraq requests the Security Council to put a final halt to the false claims which are used to justify intrusive inspections and the Commission's position. The former are irrelevant to the disarmament process and are in fact for the purpose of collecting intelligence information for the United States of America, which is determined to launch a new military aggression against Iraq, justifying the failure to close files, and delaying the implementation of Security Council resolution 687 (1991) paragraph 22.

During the Security Council's discussion of my report, France and some other delegations had raised a question: whether I had a view on the travel sanctions that had been imposed upon Iraqi officials as a result of Resolution 1137 (October 1997). According to that resolution, the travel sanctions would be removed one day after I certified that Iraq had resumed cooperation with UNSCOM. The comical aspect of this was that the Security Council had never actually enforced the travel sanctions, even though it had adopted them by law.

I considered the matter and decided to report to the Security Council that in the period immediately under review Iraq had essentially given us unrestricted and unconditional access to the sites we sought to visit. Under these circumstances, my view was that the requirements of Resolution 1137 were at that time sufficiently implemented to allow the termination of the travel sanctions. The Security Council accepted this view, and those nonexistent sanctions were duly lifted. This passage of events was truly silly. I was thanked for it fulsomely, especially by the French.

Notwithstanding Iraq's practical termination of the Memorandum of Understanding only weeks after it had been signed, the secretary-general and his senior staff continued to insist that there was a new atmosphere in the relationship between the United Nations and Iraq. In some respects this was true, and I sometimes tried to talk up the situation publicly by saying that I perceived something of a new spirit of cooperation—always emphasizing however that this would need to be tested in practice.

However, I did seek privately to bring to the secretary-general's attention the fact that we were not making progress in disarmament. We needed to draw a distinction between superficial cooperation by Iraq—indeed, occasional bursts of relative pleasantness—and practical compliance with the law. The latter had little to do with demeanor and everything to do with allowing UNSCOM to get its disarmament job done. This, of course, wasn't happening.

I had difficulty in persuading Kofi Annan to take this distinction seriously. He would listen to me and seem to acknowledge the points I was making, then ask me to affirm that Iraq, notwithstanding the difficulties, was in fact cooperating and keeping the promises made to him in Baghdad back in February. An unwelcome reality, it appeared, might be overcome by pretending it did not exist.

9

ROAD MAP TO NOWHERE

B Y MAY 1998, we had been in a nearly continual crisis for
some six months. The first crisis began when Iraq decided
to expel U.S. nationals working with UNSCOM; it developed further when Iraq sought to establish presidential sites as perma-
nently free of any inspection or monitoring. Discussions at the United
Nations to address these crises had two main characteristics: inten-
sifying efforts to distinguish between diplomacy and substance, and increasing attempts by the friends of Iraq, including the Office of the
Secretary-General, to question the substance itself.

Baghdad presented voluminous papers and arguments to the Security
Council to "prove" that it had disarmed, but these were laced with
political attacks against the objectivity and motivation of UNSCOM
officials. Iraqi officials increasingly deflected attention from their lack
of cooperation in the disarmament process by using language that
the diplomatic community would value: "sovereignty," "security,"
"dignity."

As a result of Iraq's propaganda campaign, I was repeatedly
approached by members of the Security Council, in particular the Russian
ambassador, Sergey Lavrov, questioning UNSCOM's assessment of
Iraq's weapons status. Because critical issues of substance were at stake
here, I felt UNSCOM ought to make available to the Security Council a
current, definitive statement on Iraq's weapons status. The presentation
we'd made to the Security Council in November 1997 had provoked
interest among certain members, and Brazil's ambassador, Celso Luiz
Nunes Amorim, had asked several times whether UNSCOM could prepare
a more detailed technical briefing. For these reasons, I decided to brief

the Security Council for a second time on UNSCOM's material, technical, and scientific concerns.

I had a second objective in mind for this briefing. At UNSCOM, we
had developed the idea of presenting, informally, a "road map" that
would outline the outstanding issues that needed to be resolved if we
were to be in a position to declare Iraq disarmed. Designing the form
and contents of such a road map would not be easy. I recalled a breakfast
meeting I'd had with the U.S. deputy ambassador to the United
Nations, Skip Gnehm, on the day I took up the job as executive chairman. Gnehm had been at pains to warn me against giving Iraq a finite list
of disarmament requirements—something he'd feared Rolf Ekeus had
been about to do. His problem with a finite list was obvious: It would not
only reverse the onus of proof from Iraq to UNSCOM; it could also
contain the possibility of ratifying serious factual errors. Suppose we
were to tell Iraq that we were looking for a final account of, say, ten missiles. The next day, Iraqi soldiers would probably show up at the front
door of our Baghdad office with trucks loaded with ten missiles. Because
of the Iraqi history of concealment, we would never know whether the
real number had been, for example, fifteen missiles instead.

I understood and agreed with Gnehm's point. But now, only one year
later, the political landscape had shifted significantly. Several members
of the Security Council, and certainly the secretary-general, were calling
for precisely such a finite list. The escalating rhetoric about finding a
solution to the Iraqi problem, one leading to the lifting of sanctions and
allowing Iraq to "see light at the end of the tunnel," pointed toward providing an indication of what remained to be done. We essentially needed
to tell the Security Council and Iraq how many laps remained in this
race.

With Gnehm's warning in mind, we developed a road map that was
not intended as a finite list of disarmament and monitoring issues but
rather as an enumeration of the most important and controversial ones.
To emphasize this, I stated that the elements of the road map were *necessary* conditions for the completion of the disarmament tasks, as distinct
from *sufficient* conditions. These necessary conditions could prove to be
sufficient only if Iraq met all its obligations to provide materials, documents, and information relating to the priority disarmament issues and
could demonstrate it had ceased its concealment efforts. My colleagues
at UNSCOM, as well as key Security Council members with whom I

conferred informally, including the representatives of the United States and the United Kingdom, supported this approach.

On June 3, 1998, the Security Council met in an informal session in a larger conference room than the one normally used for its consultations. The UNSCOM team brought projection screens and other visual materials to give a thorough, two-day briefing. During the briefing, we took the Security Council through each of the weapons files—missile, chemical, and biological—as well as important issues blending policy and technical substance: the Iraqi program of concealment, the importance of documentation in verifying Iraq's claims, and the intelligence reports, especially U-2 imagery, that substantiated our concerns about concealment.

Although most of the discussion among council members was technical and objective, a different tone emerged when the issue of concealment was raised. Three permanent members—Russia, China, and France—and one or two nonpermanent members seemed deeply skeptical about the notion that the Iraqis were pursuing a concealment policy. Some of their arguments were far-fetched. For example, when we showed a series of high altitude photos of some 130 heavy trucks gathered at an isolated spot in the desert, where Iraq claimed only 10 were present, French Ambassador Alain Dejammet speculated that perhaps a truckers' picnic was taking place. We explained that these vehicles, painted in Special Republican Guard colors, had rushed away from a site that UNSCOM was approaching, but he remained unconvinced.

At the conclusion of the briefing and discussion, I carefully put forward our road map, in the form of a brief note entitled "Necessary Conditions for Resolution of Priority Disarmament Issues." The road map identified three areas of work under the missile file: warheads, propellants, and indigenous production. UNSCOM's understanding of Iraq's warhead status required the completion of the warhead material balance, the implementation of recommendations made by a technical evaluation meeting, and the provision of documentation requested in 1996 and 1997. The closure of UNSCOM investigations into Iraqi holdings of propellants required complete records documenting their program of unilateral destruction. Our examination of indigenous production called for an accurate accounting of major components with supporting documentary evidence, especially monthly production-status reports.

Four categories of work were targeted within the chemical weapons file. Iraq would have to account for its special missile warheads by providing UNSCOM with documents and data on the production, filling, and deployment of warheads. It would have to provide verifiable evidence of the disposition of unaccounted special munitions, including 155-millimeter mustard shells and R-400 chemical/biological aerial bombs. Iraq would have to confirm the full extent of its efforts to produce the chemical warfare agent VX by implementing the recommendations from the technical evaluation meeting on VX and providing supporting documents and evidence. Iraq would have to reveal the material balance of chemical weapons production equipment by documenting the use and status of equipment evacuated from chemical weapons facilities prior to the adoption of Security Council Resolution 687.

Finally, the road map for the biological weapons file required Iraq to help UNSCOM ascertain a material balance by providing evidence on the acquisition, production, and destruction of all materials, equipment, agents, and munitions.

I stressed two points as I discussed the road map's proposals. It was essential to distinguish "necessary" conditions from "sufficient" conditions, indicating that the end objective of the road map was to get to the point where an honest, unfudged paragraph 22 report on the disarmament of Iraq could be lodged.

I then emphasized that each of the items identified in the road map rested on substantial assumptions with respect to other related items. Some of those assumptions were more reliable than others, but they would stand only if the answers given in fulfillment of the road map were themselves credible.

In the chemical weapons area, for example, we wanted verifiable evidence of the disposition of unaccounted munitions, including mustard shells and R-400 chemical/biological bombs. An accurate account would provide confidence in our understanding of what had happened to all other related munitions. Conversely, a phony account of these munitions would call into question all of our other figures.

I recommended to the Security Council that I go to Baghdad as soon as possible with this road map, seeking Iraq's agreement to what would be the second special program of work I had offered Iraq as a means of coming to final account on the priority issues identified by UNSCOM. I was careful, however, not to ask for a specific endorsement of the road map. Had I wanted such formal political support, I would have had to supply the Security Council with even more elaborate documentation, and the resulting discussions might have lasted months—with no guarantee as to the outcome. And, of course, we did not have months, for the Iraqi weapons program was not frozen in time. The sites we had sought to inspect were not ancient ruins, lifeless and only of historical value. They were still active. While the UN fiddled, Iraq was not only hiding their past experiments with weapons of mass destruction but also busily rebuilding a future of chemical and biological arms.

Most of the Security Council approved my proposal, although the Russian and the French ambassadors emphasized there was no specific endorsement of the contents of my road map. China's representative, Ambassador Qin Huasun, was more negative. We debated the issue until, finally, I leaned across the table and remarked, "Mr. Ambassador, if I had wanted political endorsement for this road map, I would have proceeded in a much slower fashion, with the presentation of full documentation. That was never my intention." This comment seemed to do the trick. It certainly provided the assurance that China was signing up to nothing. Qin Huasun indicated that he would withdraw his objection.

I assembled an UNSCOM team of policy and technical officers and added to it four commissioners: Dr. Emile Vanden Bemden of Belgium, professor Benson Agu of Nigeria, Gennady Gatilov of the Russian Federation, and Dr. Roberto Sanchez of Venezuela. We arrived in Baghdad on June 11, 1998, road map in hand.

O UR LANDING at Habbaniyah air base seemed normal, but the situation changed dramatically within a few minutes. The leaders of our chemical team in Baghdad, who'd met our plane, asked me to step aside on the tarmac to examine a report they'd received from our resident technical expert, which they felt I should see immediately. It was a laboratory analysis we'd recently conducted on metal fragments from destroyed Iraqi SCUD missile warheads, showing indelible traces of the nerve agent VX. It was the first evidence that Iraq had weaponized VX, the most toxic of the chemical weapons of mass destruction.

As I mentioned in Chapter 1, Iraq denied for years that it had ever produced VX. In 1995, after we proved this was untrue, Iraq shifted its ground, claiming that it had made only 200 liters of the substance and then destroyed it unilaterally. However, our evidence demonstrated that Iraq made almost twenty times that amount. And although we knew that the Iraqis had acquired the necessary precursors for the production of VX—chlorine, phosphorus pentasulfide, and di-isopropylamine—they had never given UNSCOM a satisfactory explanation of their manufacturing program. Finally, Iraq had always insisted that it had never loaded VX into a weapon. Here was evidence exposing Iraq's final VX lie.

Our technical staff and I agreed that we should proceed very carefully with this evidence. We would discuss it with the Iraqis quietly at first, giving them an opportunity to explain. The chemists pointed out that Iraq, obviously, would challenge our findings on the ground that they came from a laboratory located in the United States; we would need to be prepared to have further tests done in other laboratories. We planned to seek alternative labs as soon as we arrived in our office in Baghdad.

We held four overall plenary meetings and two expert-level meetings over some fourteen hours between June 13 and 14, 1998. Deputy Prime Minister Tariq Aziz led a large, high-profile Iraqi delegation, including Mohammed Al-Sahaf, the minister of foreign affairs, General Amer Rashid, the minister of oil, General Amir Sadhi, an adviser to the presidency, Abdel Diaf Taiwiesh, director of the Military Industrialization Corporation (MIC), and General Hossam Amin, director of NMD, Iraq's National Monitoring Directorate.

I opened the plenary level talks at the Foreign Ministry in Baghdad by summarizing the briefing we had given to the Security Council. I then turned to the issue of the road map, asking Aziz that we concentrate our discussions on the list set out in the informal paper I'd presented to the Security Council on June 4. I made clear that UNSCOM's list was based only on the major outstanding issues.

Aziz responded by launching into the predictable statements about Iraq's having fulfilled all its obligations, the ongoing suffering of the Iraqi people under sanctions, and the dishonest work conducted by UNSCOM officials. Under these circumstances, he said, there would be no Iraqi agreement to any kind of road map.

I chose to ignore his comments, merely arguing that it was important for UNSCOM to list the priority issues upon which we might draw up a new accelerated schedule for work. Aziz agreed to proceed on that basis. In other words, we could talk about the road map so long as we did not call it that. This reminded me of the old literary joke: "The *Iliad* was not written by Homer but by a person of the same name." I decided not to try this joke on Aziz.

As we worked through the items on the road map, we did reach a measure of agreement. The key exceptions were with respect to missile propellants and VX.

Aziz and I disputed the relevance of accounting for the outstanding quantity of SCUD-specific missile propellant—some 500 tons. Aziz argued that, as Iraq no longer held any SCUDs, the missile propellant was irrelevant. I contended that the opposite was true. The presence of SCUD-specific propellant probably implied either the existence of SCUDs, possibly concealed, or their planned acquisition.

Now the bombshell—our lab findings concerning VX. Assuring Aziz that I would not make a public fuss about it, I proposed that these findings first be considered privately at a technical level.

As we expected, Iraq angrily rejected the laboratory findings, insisting that they must be wrong because Iraq had never weaponized VX. We agreed to take further samples from destroyed warhead remnants and send them to other laboratories. I indicated that I'd already authorized UNSCOM to inquire whether laboratories in France and Switzerland would be available to do the work. I made clear, however, that while I had no objection to seeking further opinions and analysis, the outcome from other laboratory analyses, whatever they were, would not negate the need for the first laboratory finding to be explained. VX had been in contact with at least some Iraqi warheads—that much was certain.

Finally, I told Aziz that even if there was satisfactory progress on all of the topics in the schedule for work, we would still need to discuss the Iraqi policy of concealment. Aziz became very angry and abusive. When his verbal pyrotechnics ended, however, he said he might be prepared to have a conversation with me about concealment if satisfactory progress were achieved on all of the substantive issues on the schedule for work. He proposed that I return to Baghdad in about six weeks, and I agreed.

The final day of these talks had been particularly difficult for me personally. Shortly after waking up early in the morning, I realized I was ill. We'd eaten dinner in the Rasheed Hotel the night before. It was the same meal we'd always taken—chicken. My food had been brought to me by the head waiter somewhat separately from that of other members of our team. The sickness I felt was quite unlike any other I'd experienced. It was a sense of ebbing vitality. I also had stomach pains and, as the day went on, a dangerously high temperature.

I was determined to complete the talks, so at the BMVC I asked our doctor to prop me up. He did so with various injections to prevent my ejecting whatever at each end of my body.

I got through the morning talks but, literally, collapsed in the afternoon, fortunately at our office, where I stripped and lay in a cot. The doctor monitored me for three to four hours and my temperature slowly came down. With more injections, I made it through the evening session of talks, but always on the edge and with a strange sense that my grip on physical life was slipping away.

After the talks ended the doctor came to the hotel and gave me another shot. I slept reasonably well and, somewhat shakily, did a press conference in the morning. Our doctor, from the Australian defense forces, wondered whether I'd been poisoned. He sent my blood for testing. The result was inconclusive.

I was ready to leave Baghdad when one last issue surfaced. UNSCOM staff called my attention to Iraqi activities aimed at either converting their Volga missiles from surface-to-air to surface-to-surface capability, or enhancing both Volga and Al-Samoud engines (the Iraqi version of the SCUD) to extend their range beyond the legal limit.

It was a new twist on the theme of Iraqi recalcitrance. Rather than merely impeding the disarmament process, Iraq was now seeking to break out of current and future restrictions, even though it was made clear to them that this was illegal and could possibly sink a paragraph 22 report. I raised this issue directly with General Amer Rashid, and we had a long, heated argument about it. In the end, Rashid refused to stop Iraq's illegal work. I returned to New York and reported all this to the Security Council.

ON JUNE 24, 1998, the secretary-general's special envoy to Iraq, Prakash Shah, made his first statement before the Security Council, further revealing the type of thinking that was taking place in Kofi Annan's office.

What Shah said about the relationship between his office in Baghdad and the crises in the Iraqi disarmament process deserves full attention:

The establishment of my office coincided with the first ever visit of UNSCOM to the presidential sites, under the Memorandum of Understanding signed between the Secretary General and Iraq's Deputy Prime Minister Tariq Aziz. The Memorandum of Understanding, by itself, constitutes a new chapter in UN-Iraq relations. The Secretary General conveyed through the Memorandum of Understanding and his visit that despite the past historical baggage of suspicion and mistrust, it is necessary to look to the future in the interest of peace and development and to avoid, at all costs, the potential for any conflict situation that might involve the use of military force in the region.

He went on to parrot the Iraqi point of view about UNSCOM's work: "Iraqi authorities have conveyed to me that UNSCOM has carried out large numbers of inspections on a regular basis in the last three months and Iraq provided unconditional and unrestricted access for the inspections, in conformity with the Memorandum of Understanding." No mention was made of the fact that Iraqi authorities had shown mostly empty buildings to UNSCOM inspectors and diplomatic observers.

Shah's characterization of the Iraqi resistance to compliance as a quaint bit of "historical baggage," and the moral equivalency involved in the notion of mutual "suspicion and mistrust," was an accurate reflection of the thinking that was motivating the secretary-general and his senior staff, as was his insistence that the use of military force should be avoided "at all costs." As one member of the Security Council observed to me, neither Shah nor the secretary-general were in a position to put a blue pencil through Chapter VII of the UN Charter, which provides for military enforcement of Security Council resolutions, when necessary. Yet, this appeared to be what they were doing.

Meanwhile, in Iraq, yet another inspection crisis was brewing.

UNSCOM 244, led by Gabrielle Kraatz-Wadsack, was scheduled on July 18, 1998, to inspect Iraqi air force headquarters. Her team's mission was to seek information, especially documentation, to assist in verifying the disposition of Iraq's chemical and biological weapons programs. After a somewhat difficult negotiation on arrival at the site (one designated as "sensitive" by the Iraqis), Kraatz-Wadsack had led her team of sixteen people into this very large area.

During the course of the inspection, the operations room of the command of the Iraqi air force was declared as "especially sensitive." This meant that only the chief inspector, one other inspector, and an interpreter were admitted into the room. While they were there, they examined a safe containing a number of files, one of which listed munitions expended by the Iraqi air force.

It quickly became evident that four types of "special" munitions, together with conventional munitions, were included in this list—the term "special" being Iraq's term for weapons for chemical and biological warfare. Acquiring such information was one of UNSCOM's high priorities, because we knew that more than 100,000 special munitions allegedly consumed from 1981 to 1988 remained unaccounted for.

Rather than taking the document, which was UNSCOM's right, Kraatz-Wadsack decided that she would have a copy made. The senior Iraqi representative present initially agreed but changed his mind after a flurry of telephone calls, saying that the inspectors could only take notes or copy the document with certain sections blacked out. When Kraatz-Wadsack protested, the Iraqi official reacted by physically seizing the document and telling her that the team could examine no more documents.

Kraatz-Wadsack telephoned me in New York, and I instructed her not to leave the building without an authentic copy of the document. Iraq refused. I then spoke with General Rashid, the minister of oil (and missiles). We agreed that the document would be jointly sealed by UNSCOM and Iraq and stored in the custody of the NMD pending my visit to Baghdad, scheduled for two weeks later. I instructed Kraatz-Wadsack to finish the inspection and leave the site.

Meanwhile, however, Kraatz-Wadsack had been able to note the content of the document with the assistance of an UNSCOM interpreter. It numerically listed the Iraqi air force's use of chemical munitions to an extent never previously reported. This was significant in itself, and it directly contradicted other Iraqi declarations concerning its overall chemical weapons disposition. This document was a valuable find, underscoring the critical importance of unimpeded access to authentic documents.

A MEETING on Iraq's biological warfare program took place in Baghdad during July 17–23, 1998. When it was done, Aziz wrote to me saying that the meeting "did not succeed in closing the gaps between the two sides." Looking to the next high-level meetings scheduled to be held in two weeks' time, Aziz asked me to extend the time involved and bring with me as many experts as required so that we could "discuss intensively this matter politically and technically." Once again we were stuck.

Although Aziz accused me of dragging out the inspections process, and thereby prolonging sanctions, I had actually tried to streamline our inspections of Iraqi biological weapons. During the June road map meeting in Baghdad, I had proposed a new approach toward the problem of the biological file. The law essentially required a bottom-up approach. Verification of Iraq's biological disarmament status would begin with an examination of the raw materials for the program, such as the growth media, move on to manufacturing equipment, then to biological agents produced, and finally to weaponization in whatever numbers were involved. I put it to Aziz that this overall approach, while it was thorough and in accordance with the law, had possibly been a part of the problems the two sides had experienced. I therefore recommended a top-down approach. I asked him to tell us precisely what biological weapons Iraq had made and continued to hold. If we could verify those declarations, we might take a different attitude from a disarmament point of view with respect to the extant growth media and manufacturing capability, perhaps seeking to take care of those under a future long-term monitoring program. He agreed to this approach. But in the meeting that had just taken place in Baghdad, there was not the slightest evidence of this process being carried out. Iraq instead merely repeated past explanations for its biological program—fundamentally, a series of lies.

As I considered my travel plans for the August 3 meeting in Baghdad, my attention was called to the fact that I'd visited all of the permanent members of the Security Council except China. China's representative at the United Nations, Ambassador Qin Huasun, had mentioned this to me on one or two occasions. So I proposed to visit China en route to Baghdad, accompanied by a political adviser, Gustavo Zlauvinen, and UNSCOM's legal counsel, John Scott. We held talks in Beijing for a day and a half before proceeding to the Gulf.

In our talks at the Foreign Ministry, China reaffirmed its view that Iraq had basically fulfilled its obligations and that it was time for sanctions to be lifted. China's position reflected an abhorrence of multilateral intervention in the affairs of any state. Of course, China's concerns about Taiwan and Tibet—bluntly, its desire to claim and absorb both states free of international restraints—underlay its allergy to multilateral intervention.

Back in New York, I'd mentioned to Qin Huasun that I had a past relationship with Qian Qichen, who for the past ten years or so had been foreign minister and had recently been promoted to deputy premier of China with special responsibility for foreign affairs. I asked if it would be possible for me to call on him while I was in Beijing. Late in the afternoon of my visit, I received word that this would be possible.

My colleagues and I were then taken to one of the leadership buildings not far from the Temple of Heavenly Peace where we were shown into a classically decorated reception room. Qian Qichen sat on one lounge chair and I on another, separated by a small table on which cups of Chinese tea were placed. Our entourages sat several paces back on each side.

Through an interpreter, I recalled to the deputy premier the contacts we'd made in dealing with disarmament and Cambodia. He said that he remembered that I'd always spoken frankly with him about issues of common concern, and he hoped I'd do the same today. I laid out my concerns about Iraq's arms status and the need for it to obey the laws passed by the Security Council, and I asked him for China's support in the Security Council, acknowledging that China was a Great Power with a unique kind of influence.

Qian Qichen asserted that China considered a peaceful settlement of any disputes with Iraq to be very important. Iraq obviously had to meet the Security Council's requirements, but the time had come for the Iraqis to be released from the post–Gulf War state in which they remained.

I then tried on him a specific detail. "Mr. Deputy Premier," I said, "we need your country's assistance in our task of verifying Iraq's weapons declarations, because China has been a supplier of relevant weapons-related materials to Iraq. I've raised this issue with China's representatives in the past, but received no reply. Now I take the opportunity of asking you to see to it that Chinese officials provide us with the information we need. For instance, we need China's cooperation to verify claims about Iraq in the missile field. Of course, you have our assurances that we will retain the information you provide in strictest confidence."

Qian seemed disturbed by this request and spoke to some of his advisers in Chinese (our conversation had been in English). They, too, seemed agitated. The deputy premier then said to me that he had given instructions on the matter and that the Chinese mission in New York would be in touch with us. That never occurred. After the August 3 meeting in Baghdad, with all its consequences, China's stance in New York became even more resolutely in favor of Iraq.

B EFORE OUR ARRIVAL in Baghdad, the permanent representative of Iraq to the United Nations sent a statement to the Security Council on July 30, 1998. It was issued by a joint session of the Revolutionary Command Council and the Iraqi Regional Command of the Arab Baath Socialist Party, which serve as a combination cabinet-politburo presided over by Saddam Hussein. This statement recalled a similar one made by the same group in May 1998, threatening some serious action—unspecified—if sanctions were not lifted within six months. It also recalled two somewhat threatening recent speeches by Saddam.

In this statement, the Revolutionary Command Council escalated its attacks on UNSCOM. It denounced UNSCOM for perpetuating the "unjust embargo" in spite of Iraq's compliance with all Security Council resolutions. The statement went on to complain about sanctions and the way in which UNSCOM conducted its work. According to the Revolutionary Command Council, UNSCOM intended to "destroy and squander the property of the nation and to divert the State from its task of serving the people." It characterized the arrangements made under Kofi Annan's Memorandum of Understanding for presidential-site inspections as a shameful example of this unjust situation. Those inspections, nevertheless, helped to expose "the lies of Washington and London."

Most important and, as it transpired, ominous, the statement referred to the meetings that would take place in Baghdad within the next few days:

> The forthcoming meeting between the representatives of Iraq and [UNSCOM] will be an essential indication as to the outcome of the situation. Will [UNSCOM] recognize that the requirements of section C of resolution 687 (1991) have been met and will it submit its report requesting the Security Council to play its part and implement paragraph 22 in the near future? Or will it continue its

well-known methods of maneuvering, misleading people, raising marginal issues and dragging out its work interminably in the service of the criminal scheme of the United States the objective of which is the destruction of Iraq and its people?

The statement concluded with the words, "God is great. Let the despicable be spurned."

The choice UNSCOM would have to make was clear: Declare Iraq disarmed—or else.

Iraq had been in possession of the road map for almost two months. Never before had there been such a clear indication of the concrete and practical way out of the oil embargo and, possibly, sanctions as a whole. The political climate had changed to the point where the provision of such a list was possible for the first time. It had been constructed by UNSCOM on the basis of hard, objective information, and it relied on our willingness, in principle, to accept explanations from Iraq, if we were genuinely given the last pieces of information described in the road map. The Revolutionary Command Council's statement made no reference to any of this.

As we traveled toward Baghdad, it was clear that Iraq had not attempted to fulfill the terms of the special schedule for work during the preceding six weeks. I intended to have this out with Aziz and to try once more, in the time remaining before our next six-month report in October 1998, to make serious progress.

The question the Revolutionary Command Council statement raised, however, was far deeper and more disturbing. Was it possible that Iraq had refused to provide the information sought in the special schedule for work precisely because UNSCOM was cutting too close to the bone? When the talks opened on August 3 in Baghdad, it became clear, quickly, that this was indeed the case.

10

THE FIVE-DOLLAR BET

THE TALKS THAT BEGAN in Baghdad on August 3, 1998, proved to be terminal.

The avowed purpose of this round of discussions was to assess our progress over the previous two months in following the disarmament "road map." That had been deficient, but I hoped to reach an agreement with the Iraqis on further work before my next biannual report to the Security Council, due in October 1998. I was still trying to find a way to get the disarmament job finished and then turn our work over to long-term monitoring.

The meetings began with Aziz inviting me to provide our view of recent developments. I reported that UNSCOM had carried out all of the tasks assigned to it under the schedule for work. Unfortunately, Iraq had not provided all of the new information and documents we had requested, which would have greatly assisted in bringing the disarmament issues toward closure. I then went on to assess what had been achieved in each weapons area.

In all three areas, I reported, there remained significant holes in the information we needed to close the relevant files. For example, in the missile area, there was the issue of SCUD propellant; in chemical weapons, VX; and in the biological area, the declarations made by Iraq remained implausible, almost useless. I concluded by noting that the issue of concealment still needed to be addressed.

Aziz began his response in his usual terse, confrontational style: "I am not surprised at all to hear what I hear from you. I am not surprised. I was expecting that." UNSCOM, he said, persisted in its frivolous demands for documentation because it was focused on minor issues. It was imperative to distinguish between issues of major importance, which were needed to meet the disarmament requirements of the Security Council, and issues of minor importance, which could be pursued in the monitoring phase of UNSCOM operations.

According to Aziz, UNSCOM had deliberately created an artificial confusion between these major and minor issues in order to delay the lifting of sanctions. Aziz placed the blame squarely on my shoulders: "You promised me that the scheduled work on the outstanding disarmament issues would be done honestly and quickly, so that you could make a report in October different from the previous reports. That means a good report, a positive report, that would enable the Council to consider the implementation of paragraph 22. This did not happen. The work on the side of the teams you sent was neither honest nor quick."

As the meeting progressed and Aziz grew more agitated, he did not even try to mask his contempt for UNSCOM and its verification requirements. At one point, he lifted his teacup and spoon and mockingly said, "You need to verify, verify, and verify whatever we tell you. 'This is a cup of tea.' 'Yes, it looks like a cup of tea, but we are going to verify it.' 'This is a spoon.' 'Yes, it looks like a spoon, but we are going to verify it.'" He spat out the words contemptuously. That he was indeed holding a cup of tea was self evident and unlike so many Iraqi declarations, didn't require verification.

Aziz argued that my team and I needed to answer only two questions in order to recommend the lifting of sanctions to the Security Council: Did Iraq retain any weapons of mass destruction? And did Iraq retain capabilities for the production of these weapons? The answer to both questions, he said, was obviously "No." This was the blackest lie, especially with respect to Iraq's clearly established knowledge and capabilities.

Aziz was sure, for instance, that a "chemical" explanation could be found by Iraqi experts for the traces of VX that had shown up in the missile-warhead remnants. And he added that the VX issue was not even worth considering because Iraq had already declared that it had put more deadly substances into its warheads: "If Iraq filled warheads with VX, why should Iraq not say that to UNSCOM? What's the reason? We declared that we filled warheads with anthrax. Anthrax, according to the experts, is more lethal than VX. So as we admitted that we filled warheads with anthrax, why should we not admit that we filled them with VX, if that was the case?"

Bear in mind that a few moments earlier, Aziz was proclaiming that Iraq had none of these capabilities!

He did not want to discuss this matter further. He accused UNSCOM of working to maintain sanctions so as to please the United States and United Kingdom. Furthermore, UNSCOM was using a verification model based on Western standards inappropriate for a developing country like Iraq, and its inspectors were also creating a "sinister atmosphere" in which they "brainwashed" the international experts who examined Iraq's biological weapons program. Iraq would present its case on VX directly to the international community.

This last remark alluded to the propaganda campaign on VX that Aziz himself headed and that was well under way. His closing comments, in fact, seemed to be more like sound bites for public consumption than serious responses to UNSCOM's concerns, and, again, all of this was being videotaped.

He then declared: "Mr. Butler, it is your obligation to report the truth to the Security Council. The truth is that Iraq has no proscribed weapons or capabilities in any of the areas within the mandate of the Special Commission. You must not be swayed by UNSCOM's so-called experts. They are not objective. Your duty is to take the direct political responsibility and report the truth."

In response, I rejected Aziz's reference to the concept of major and minor issues. The Security Council had never had in mind some notional distinction between what was major and minor. It had stated clearly that Iraq must declare all of its proscribed weapons and programs so that UNSCOM could verify them and supervise their disposal. Iraq had failed to do so. And I utterly rejected his attack upon the integrity of UNSCOM.

At the end of the morning session, Aziz indicated that when we met again in the evening he would present the formal reply of the government of the Republic of Iraq. Whenever Aziz insisted on using the full title of the regime he served, it was a signal that he would be acting on political instructions directly from Saddam Hussein later that day.

We left the Foreign Ministry's conference room and headed back to the BMVC for lunch. Charles Duelfer shared my car, and we used the opportunity to compare notes on the situation, which we agreed was serious. I said, "I have a feeling that, before the day is out, we'll be ejected from Iraq."

"Do you really think so?" Duelfer replied.

"I'm sure of it," I answered. "In fact, I'll bet you five dollars on it."

"It's a bet," Duelfer agreed.

The UNSCOM team spent the afternoon discussing the circumstances we were facing and how we might counter various approaches Iraq might take during the evening session. Our plans proved to be unnecessary.

At 8:00 P.M., we reconvened around the table in the Iraqi Foreign Ministry. Tariq Aziz spoke. "Mr. Butler," he declared, "I want to convey to you and your colleagues the decision of the government of the Republic of Iraq." He then made a gesture toward technical discussion by briefly mentioning some of the outstanding issues in each weapons area, but this was basically filler. "All of the requirements set by the Security Council have been satisfied," he remarked. "There is no further work to be done, nor is there any additional information for Iraq to provide concerning its past programs of weapons of mass destruction."

Then, his grand move: "Mr. Chairman," Aziz announced, "it is clear that you have one single duty to perform: to return to New York, declare that Iraq is disarmed, and recommend that the Security Council proceed with the necessary steps to lift sanctions.

"What I ask you is fair," he added. "Go, and report to the Security Council that you have finished the job. If you fail to do this, let it be on your conscience. You must have the courage and determination to speak the truth."

My response was as straightforward as possible: "I will not do what you ask because I cannot. You have refused to give us the evidence required to support your claim. I cannot wave a magic wand over your weapons to make them disappear."

Aziz interrupted me angrily. "UNSCOM cannot prove to me that Iraq is not disarmed!" he said.

"You misstate the matter, Mr. Deputy Prime Minister," I replied. "Our job is to verify your claim. It is not to prove a case to you. We are not prosecutors or inquisitors. The council established a three-step system, and you know it very well: Iraq declares, UNSCOM verifies, and together we destroy, remove, or render harmless. That's what the law says. It says nothing about proving any case to you or to your government."

Shifting ground, Aziz reiterated his claim and his demand. "Iraq does not possess any more weapons of mass destruction. This is the fact. You have no physical evidence contrary to the Iraqi declarations, and you know this is true. Go back to the council, say this, and relieve your conscience."

"Please have no concerns about my conscience," I replied quietly. "I assure you, I expect to sleep easily in my bed tonight. As for what you have asked, I must say again that I will not do it because I cannot do it."

As so often before in our negotiations, we'd struck a brick wall. This time, the impasse had an air of finality.

"It's clear," Aziz said, "that there is no point in continuing our talks, or indeed any conversation or work with UNSCOM. If you are not prepared to report immediately that Iraq is in compliance with the Security Council's resolutions, I have no reason to believe that you will do so in October. So further discussion is useless."

I wondered aloud about the talks scheduled for the next day. Aziz stated that they would be pointless unless I was prepared to change my mind. I said I doubted that would be the case, but I said we might talk on the telephone. On that note, the meeting ended. His comments about not continuing were clear in their implication: It was over.

Back at the hotel, Charles Duelfer ruefully handed me a five-dollar bill. I asked him to date and sign it, which he did. I still have it in my possession. I then set in motion the process of summoning our aircraft to Baghdad for the next morning and advising the secretary-general, the president of the Security Council, and those permanent members I could find of the grave circumstances in which we found ourselves.

Two DAYS LATER, on August 5, 1998, Aziz notified the Security Council that Saddam, through the Revolutionary Command Council and the Iraqi Regional Command of the Arab Baath Socialist Party, had decided to suspend UNSCOM's disarmament work. Iraq also advised the International Atomic Energy Agency that it was no longer prepared to cooperate with it. Iraq was now seeking to place nuclear weapons in the same category as the other weapons of mass destruction—free of international monitoring and control.

Aziz's letter maintained that "the Special Commission had refused to inform the Security Council of the essential facts of the situation." According to him, UNSCOM was needlessly focused on

details of no value with respect to the requirements of section C of resolution 687 (1991). It had also continued with its methods of obfuscation and misinformation by referring to marginal issues, and misleading the Council and world public opinion into thinking that those issues were of some importance with respect to the requirements of disarmament. In addition, it had attempted to conjure up the crises and provocations which characterized the work of [UNSCOM] throughout the past seven years. The purpose of this was entirely clear, namely to perpetuate the embargo in accordance with the policy of the United States of America.

The letter also included the formal statement issued by the Revolutionary Command Council and the Arab Baath Socialist Party. Baghdad was not merely halting UNSCOM's work but also demanding specific changes in its makeup and administration. These conditions would require the Security Council to:

Create a new executive bureau to lead and direct all the activities and functions of the Special Commission. It should be composed of an equal number of members who represent the nations that are permanent members of the Security Council. The chairmanship of the bureau should be on rotation basis. Iraq should participate as an observer in the bureau's work. . . .

Restructure the Commission's administrative units at its main office in New York and at its offices in both Bahrain and Baghdad according to the same principle. . . .

Remove the Commission's main office from New York to the United Nations Headquarters in either Geneva or Vienna so as to insulate it from direct influence of the United States of America.

I wrote to the Security Council on August 12 pointing out that UNSCOM, under Baghdad's suspension of disarmament activities, could no longer determine whether Iraq was violating its disarmament obligations. I pointed out that

inspections planned in the chemical, biological and missile fields will be delayed pending resolution of the current situation. These discussions and inspections were aimed at bringing to closure outstanding disarmament issues which need to be resolved if the Commission is to be in a position to report that Iraq is in compliance with its disarmament obligations, as established by the Council.

The Security Council spent some days considering my statement. The best it could agree to do was to authorize the president of the Security Council to write me a private letter in response, indicating that the council considered Iraq's announcement totally unacceptable.

Meanwhile, a new attempt at a solution was being floated. Discussions had already started, in both the Security Council and the Office of the Secretary-General, concerning a concept called "comprehensive review." Security Council Resolution 1194 (September 9, 1998) demanded that Iraq rescind its decision of August 5 while expressing the council's readiness to consider a "comprehensive review" of Iraq's compliance with all relevant resolutions. This signaled that Security Council members would now become directly involved in dealing with issues for which UNSCOM, the IAEA, and the Iraq-Kuwait Compensation Commission, to name just three, had formerly been responsible. The purpose was to find a political solution to the Iraqi issue. No one wanted to sit through further Iraq episodes every six months.

Hence the phrase "light at the end of the tunnel," which the proponents of comprehensive review frequently used. These friends of Iraq argued that, in all human sympathy, we had to understand why Iraq was losing its patience with UNSCOM and the Security Council—especially since Iraq was naturally skeptical as to whether sanctions would ultimately be lifted, even if it did comply with the disarmament resolutions. This was highly specious, ex post facto reasoning. Having decided to cheat on the system from day one, Iraq's fundamental purpose had always been to mask and obfuscate. It wasn't a matter of "losing patience" at all. Iraq's patience was endless. It would resist and wait the Security Council out.

Having conceded, reluctantly, that Iraq had indeed broken the agreement made during his visit to Baghdad in February, Secretary-General Annan and his staff shifted their focus to another means of solving the Iraq problem. His office now became one of the main proponents of comprehensive review, thereby seeking to relieve Iraq of the burden of sanctions, somewhat irrespective of its disarmament status.

The secretary-general's office drew up the principles that would govern the conduct of a comprehensive review, and Kofi Annan himself presented them to the Security Council. The draft document, circulated on October 5, 1998, was brief but very revealing. It proposed "two main phases, the first phase being devoted to Iraq's compliance with Section C of resolution 687 (1991)—disarmament—and the second phase being concerned with Iraq's compliance with all other requirements arising out of the relevant resolutions."

Annan's proposal was remarkably similar to one previously prepared by the Russian mission to the United Nations. Both documents included the following objectives:

- [to] clearly determine if Iraq still possesses weapons of mass destruction or any equipment for its production;
- clarify if Iraq is still undertaking attempts to restart the proscribed military programs or production of any kind of proscribed weapons;
- confirm on the basis of evidence the validity of any allegations of non-compliance by Iraq with regard to section C of resolution 687;
- establish a reasonable timetable for investigation of all remaining issues of the Iraqi proscribed military programs; and
- answer the question whether Iraq still constitutes a military threat for the region.

These goals seemed unobjectionable, but my colleagues in UNSCOM and I were concerned about the third point, because it shifted the onus of proof from Iraq to others. A statement by UNSCOM—for example, that it either could not verify or did not find an Iraqi declaration credible—now became an active allegation against poor Iraq that *we* had to prove! In this context, the Russians were lobbying for a softened approach, saying that any assessment "should take into account the tremendous humanitarian cost of sanctions and the political changes which occurred in the region since 1991." They also urged that "the Security Council should acknowledge that a certain degree of incertitude is acceptable."

Annan's proposal also departed substantially from past Security Council resolutions by summarizing the principal question to be determined as whether Iraq "constitutes a military threat for the region" rather than whether it continued to hold prohibited weapons. It also sought to set a precise timetable under which such a determination could be made, virtually promising Iraq in advance that, regardless of the circumstances, there would be a date certain for its release from sanctions.

Finally, Annan's proposal went a long way toward establishing a kind of moral equivalence between UNSCOM and Iraq by inviting Iraq to provide its own separate account of how it had complied with the requirements of disarmament and allowing it to table evidence to substantiate its claims whenever it considered that to be appropriate. Iraq had, of course, repeatedly offered extensive statements about the process, mostly false and unverifiable. The implication now was that those statements would be given at least equal status with UNSCOM reports.

While reflecting the thinking of the secretary-general's senior staff, it was apparent that this proposal had largely been significantly influenced by Russia—and, even further behind the scenes—by Iraq.

I SENT MY REQUIRED six-month report to the Security Council on October 6, 1998. It made clear that the disarmament phase of UNSCOM's work was, in many respects, near its end, but not yet completed. Iraq had prevented it from being completed and was now moving to obstruct UNSCOM's monitoring work. I also addressed the concept of comprehensive review, saying that UNSCOM would cooperate with such a review if the Security Council chose to proceed in that way.

Meanwhile, two other developments took place that would play crucial roles in the final unwinding of UNSCOM.

I'd received analyses from French and Swiss laboratories of missile-warhead samples from the same site where VX traces had been found. As I reported to the Security Council on October 26, no traces of VX were found by the Swiss laboratory, while the French laboratory reported somewhat ambiguous outcomes that might have been consistent with the presence of VX.

I'd also asked a group of international experts to examine all the laboratory findings and offer their best suggestions as to how we should use the results. This group, some fifteen experts, included those from U.S., French, and Swiss labs. In their findings, they recommended that UNSCOM ask Iraq first to recount the origin and history of the warhead fragments and then to explain the presence of nerve-agent degradation products. They also suggested that Iraq be invited to explain the presence of a compound known as VX stabilizer and its degradation product.

The report's findings weren't surprising. The missile fragments analyzed in each of the laboratories were from the same destruction pit but were not from the same warheads. It was therefore always possible that there would be different outcomes. Thus, the conclusions asking Iraq for further explanation for the phenomena identified were sound.

What happened next, however, was one of the sorrier episodes in the history of the Security Council's dealings with Iraq. First, Iraq mounted a massive propaganda campaign, as Aziz had said it would. It claimed that the findings from the Swiss and French laboratories showed that VX had not been present. Of course, this ignored the findings of the U.S. lab, which none of the experts from any country doubted. Still, Iraq played this card enthusiastically, with a fair degree of success.

Accordingly, the revelation that Iraq had lied about its weaponization of VX became marginalized politically. Of course, the weaponization of VX was actually only part of the larger VX-production issue. But the fact that Iraq had never given UNSCOM an unambiguous or clear statement with respect to its VX production was utterly lost.

The confusion thus sown was compounded some nine months later when, as one of my last actions as executive chairman, I expressed concerns about the status of the chemical laboratory in our Baghdad office. As a result of Iraq's last expulsion of UNSCOM staff, it had been unattended for too long, and the Iraqi summer was nearing, with its potential electrical failures. I proposed having UNSCOM scientists visit the laboratory for the purpose of shutting it down.

Iraq proceeded, with help from Russia and then France, to squeeze every last drop out of this propaganda lemon. Russian Ambassador Lavrov charged, before the Security Council, that UNSCOM had endangered the lives of millions of Iraqis by storing VX and other deadly substances in its laboratory. Lavrov went even farther, alleging that we'd imported VX into the laboratory in order to contaminate the destroyed missile-warhead remnants that had been the subject of analysis a year earlier. Both were blatant lies, and the Russians knew this well.

T HE SECOND KEY development was Scott Ritter's August 1998 resignation from UNSCOM. He had led our Concealment Unit and served often, with great distinction, as a chief inspector in the field. Ritter's subsequent actions—public statements, writings, TV interviews, briefing of journalists (including revealing the contents of documents), and briefings on Capitol Hill in Washington—attracted great attention. His actions and their impact deserve some analysis.

First, the resignation, tendered in a letter to me. In the letter Ritter stated his view that UNSCOM's task had become impossible and that illusory disarmament action was worse than none.

In my reply I commended the great work he had done, thanked him and his wife for the sacrifices they had made, and indicated, echoing Voltaire, that while I may not agree with his views I would defend his right to express them (as indeed I had in the context of Iqbal Riza's earlier complaints to me about a CNN program called "The Inspectors' Story").

Second, his allegations. Essentially, there were two, although with many variations: I had taken direction from the U.S. government; and UNSCOM had allowed itself to be a conduit for U.S. intelligence collection in Iraq.

On the first of these, Ritter repeatedly called his opinions and impressions hard facts. They were rarely accurate. For example, Ritter was aware that on one occasion, early in 1998, I had spoken with Madeleine Albright from Bahrain via telephone. Ritter subsequently stated that I had met her in Bahrain. I never did. He has since written that my pointing out this inaccuracy was to split hairs. I strenuously disagree. Imagine the visibility of such a meeting and how much more pressure could be brought to bear, face to face, if that is what was intended. The difference is substantial. He wrote and spoke of high-level conversations between me and a variety of senior U.S. officials as if he had been present, when in fact he had not. It was by means such as these that he turned his impressions into purported fact.

During my term as executive chairman I held many meetings in New York and in many other capitals with ministers and senior officials of interested governments. This was a very important part of my job. Of course, my interlocutors made their views clear, commented on mine, and stated preferred courses of action. Our meetings were professional, not social. They dealt with common, serious concerns about Iraq and UNSCOM's work. Ritter specifically charged that I took direction from the United States. This never happened. Senior U.S. officials never crossed the clear line between saying what they thought would be best, on the one hand and seeking to give me directions, on the other. They accepted my sole responsibility as the chief executive of UNSCOM for its directions, policy decisions, and actions. They made clear that they would accept my exercise of that responsibility, and they recognized that my independence of action was crucial. This was tested in practice during the numerous occasions on which I took decisions that were not exactly to their liking. And they passed that test, accepting those decisions.

I cannot know with certainty why Ritter asserted that I accepted undue influence from the United States especially as he occasionally heard me criticize U.S. thinking. I do know that he disagreed with some of my decisions on the nature and scheduling of inspections he had proposed and might lead. When I took those decisions I told him my reasons. They had to do with protecting the mission of UNSCOM, as well as my assessment of what actions were or were not appropriate.

It is true that I did not always run UNSCOM exactly as Ritter would have preferred. His allegation that this was the result of outside influence is false. In this context, I felt that Ritter sometimes seemed to think that he and his work for UNSCOM was virtually the whole show. It certainly was not.

My decisions on UNSCOM field operations rested on a multiplicity of sources of information: our archive; reports from our staff in Baghdad; information given by UN member states; defector information; our own scientific and technical analysis (to which Ritter made only the slightest contribution). Having studied such materials and after discussion with UNSCOM's senior technical experts—in missiles, chemistry, and biology—I would then consider what inspections, interviews, or document searches should be conducted provided any given action was consistent with UNSCOM's basic mandate, laid down by the Security Council. This was a complex process, carried out meticulously. Ritter's lurid public accounts of the decisionmaking process ignored all of this.

UNSCOM was an international team of men and women representing some thirty nationalities; many had the highest levels of scientific and technical skills, and all showed extraordinary courage and perseverance. I consider it to be one of the greatest privileges of my life to have worked with the UNSCOM team. A lot of the work was grinding, tough, repetitive, and often without the swashbuckling character that seemed to be associated with the concealment-related work Ritter carried out.

These women and men were, justifiably, deeply hurt by Ritter's actions after his resignation. They didn't recognize themselves in his subsequent characterizations of the work of UNSCOM. They were right. Indeed, not one of them has ever stepped forward to support Ritter's assertions.

Ritter's allegations on UNSCOM's use of intelligence assistance provided by UN member states was the more damaging of his claims. It needs to be placed clearly in the correct context.

First, the resolutions of the Security Council called on all UN member states to give UNSCOM all possible assistance. Such was the law. Some forty states did assist us, by providing intelligence materials and equipment for gathering information relevant to our work. Significantly, some states who could have helped us declined to do so, or did so only halfheartedly.

Second, as I've explained, from the first days of UNSCOM Iraq sought to conceal its weapons programs and cheat on the disarmament process. Consequently, Rolf Ekeus decided to try to breach the Iraqi wall of deceit, a task I willingly took over when I became executive chairman. In pursuit of this mission, I accepted help from the intelligence branches of some UN member states, who provided it in the same way they supported other UNSCOM efforts.

Naturally, UNSCOM made use of a variety of intelligence sources. Our own people would sometimes travel to question Iraqi defectors about Saddam's weapons programs. In other cases, governments forwarded information relevant to our work. Particularly, some governments also supplied sensor equipment, including, for example, such basic tools as ground-piercing X-ray machines. The U-2 provided by the United States for photographing weapons-related facilities is another example.

Because of Iraq's aggressive concealment program, UNSCOM was forced to become increasingly investigative in its methods, as well as protective of its own plans and activities. We used simple counterintelligence devices to shield our conversations and brought in listening devices—uncomplicated electronic gadgets one could buy at any Radio Shack. We sometimes used these devices while driving toward the site of a no-notice inspection in an effort to determine whether the Iraqis were exchanging radio messages about hiding and secreting materials. They were moderately effective but never played any major role in our efforts.

Toward the end of my time at UNSCOM, we asked the U.S. to provide a more elaborate method for monitoring Iraqi messages. It was designed to help us know when Iraq was hurriedly removing materials as an inspection team approached and possibly to learn where the material was going. This was an interesting possibility because Iraq had repeatedly acted in precisely this way. An initial installation was done of this technology; we quickly found that it didn't work well, and I ordered it removed. I decided not to reinstall it. In retrospect, I think it may have been better not to have approved even the initial test of the technology because it *could* have been used to collect information having nothing to do with disarmament. Any step that could support an accusation that UNSCOM was engaged in spying—even if untrue—would have harmed us. The brief deployment of this monitoring equipment is the closest we came to making such a mistake.

Is it possible that some member state could have somehow taken advantage of UNSCOM personnel or facilities for its own intelligence-gathering purposes? I can't know for certain. It is conceivable that a supplier country could have hidden some intelligence-gathering capability into equipment it had supplied us. If that happened, however, it was without my knowledge or approval.

Yet it is likely that individuals working for UNSCOM debriefed their governments about information learned on the job. In virtually every UN agency, it's an unspoken fact of life that individual staffers provide governments with information on their work. In this light, any Russian or French complaint about UNSCOM's gathering of intelligence information is hypocrisy. Both governments had officers within UNSCOM who came from intelligence backgrounds within their own governments, and they surely kept Moscow and Paris informed.

In considering whether to authorize any given mission, I made it clear to all staff that any proposal put before me must have a definite basis in the UNSCOM disarmament mandate handed down by the Security Council. If that basis wasn't clear, I'd insist on an explanation, and we wouldn't proceed until I received a satisfactory answer.

Furthermore, I made it clear to every person in UNSCOM that I viewed every paper I signed as one that I might someday choose—or be required—to "table" (i.e., to present publicly) before the Security Council. My Australian background, where strict governmental accountability, including accountability to the parliament, is a living tradition helped shape my by-the-book attitude on this. I never approved any inspection plan without seeing a defensible summary of the evidence—maps, U-2 photos, documents—showing why this particular site was relevant. Every plan, every document I approved needed to be one that, at least in principle, I'd be willing to table at and defend before the member nations of the Security Council. This was a rather high hurdle for the UNSCOM staff to surmount, but I'm convinced it was a necessary one.

Ironically, Scott Ritter was the officer whom I had to caution most repeatedly on the need to restrict activities to disarmament purposes. In his zeal to uncover the mechanisms by which Saddam had concealed his weapons programs, Ritter often focused his inspection plans on the Republican Guard and the office of the Special Security Organization, both of which had helped to develop and run the concealment effort. Ritter, I believe, wanted to send a signal to these people by showing up at their offices, thereby proving that we knew who and where they were. This wasn't a completely pointless idea, and we did in fact occasionally target the SSO. But I often had to rein him in.

One of the UNSCOM documents Ritter improperly showed to a journalist, after he resigned, was just such a submission from him to me. I had thought it wrong and unconvincing and to make the point had, somewhat economically, written in the margin of its opening paragraph "bullshit." I discussed this submission with Ritter later explaining my reasons for this reaction, which he said he accepted. I've sometimes wondered why he chose to leak that particular paper!

Ritter was an outstanding field officer: tough, determined, able. I was impressed by the extent of his knowledge about Iraq and the concealment mechanism. But when he proposed field operations that were excessively complex and seemed as much focused on defeating the "bad guys" (i.e., the Republican Guard and the SSO) as on finding the weapons, I objected. His colorful style used to land him on Iraqi TV—of course, in the unenviable propaganda role of the "Ugly American." Iraqi television viewers would see Ritter towering over one of our Iraqi minders, gritting his teeth and chopping the air with his hand and spitting out demands: "We have a right to inspect this building! Now will you let us go through!" I used to joke: "Promise me, Scott, you won't chop the air any more—I don't want to see you chopping on TV again!"

Forced by the Iraqi concealment effort to use intelligence in pursuit of our disarmament mission, UNSCOM was vilified for it. We were accused of giving information to the United States to help it plan U.S. bombing campaigns, even of trying to use radio signals to pinpoint Saddam Hussein's location to guide U.S. efforts to assassinate him. These accusations were without foundation, and not a shred of credible evidence has ever come to light suggesting otherwise.

As for me, I was always happily a light-year distant from U.S. military planning. When I was asked, sometimes in private, sometimes in public, about whether I thought military action against Iraq was appropriate, I always replied, "You're asking the wrong person. I'm the disarmament man, not a military man." And I was consistent about this.

Is it possible that some UNSCOM data, without my knowledge, made its way into the vast hopper of information used in U.S. military targeting? Maybe. Perhaps, some U.S. nationals on our staff received telephone calls from military planners in Washington: "We're interested in bombing such and such a laboratory in Baghdad. Do they do the arms work in the east wing or the west wing there?" Such conversations aren't inconceivable.

But consider the weaponry the U.S. military boasts, in evidence during the Operation Desert Fox bombing of Iraq as well as the Kosovo conflict: laser-guided missiles, targeted by satellites, capable of hitting a specific truck within a convoy or the wall of a building, leaving the rest intact. U.S. intelligence capabilities are equally advanced (although not infallible, as the accidental bombing of the Chinese embassy in Belgrade demonstrated). U.S. spy satellites can practically read auto license plates from fifty miles up; they can take heat-sensitive photos that show, as if by magic, whether a factory is in operation or not. Anyone who thinks that a military with tools like these would rely on information from an operation like UNSCOM, equipped with a thirty-five-year-old U-2 and a fleet of thirty-year-old helicopters rattling around the countryside of Iraq, is not dealing with reality. If anything, we at UNSCOM coveted the highly advanced intelligence data the Americans owned, which could have been very useful to our disarmament mission. But that information is so secret, so precious, so zealously guarded that there was never any chance it would be made available to UNSCOM.

Iraq's claim that UNSCOM was being used for spying in support of U.S. interests was propaganda, meaningless except for the fact that many people who should have known better believed it.

Two fundamental points remain in the sorry episode of Ritter's resignation and subsequent accusations. First, they obscured the enormous difference in size between the massive Iraqi attempt to cheat on and avoid their disarmament obligations and the modest attempt by UNSCOM to defend against this. This crucial sense of *proportion* was lost. Second, Ritter's allegations were manna from heaven for the Iraqis, as they came precisely when Iraq had taken a central, strategic decision to shift attention to UNSCOM: Iraq was not the problem, UNSCOM was. Ritter poured petrol on this fire, and Iraq gratefully warmed its hands over it.

T HE SECURITY COUNCIL wound up its consideration of the proposed comprehensive review toward the end of October 1998. By then, the main focus of its negotiations had become an October 30 letter drawn up by the president of the Security Council, Ambassador Sir Jeremy Greenstock of the United Kingdom. It established terms of reference for such a review that were rather different from those floated a month earlier by the secretary-general. In particular, it omitted the guarantee that Iraq would be released from sanctions on a certain date. Ambassador Greenstock was to the point: "Council members cannot prejudge the outcome of the review in advance of their consideration of these reports." The letter also restored somewhat the onus of proof on Iraq, which the secretary-general's proposal had sought to shift to UNSCOM.

Uneasy about the British draft, the friends of Iraq forced some changes in it, but the letter ultimately won acceptance in the Security Council.

On October 31, 1998, Iraq announced its reaction. At a meeting with representatives from UNSCOM's Baghdad office, Hossam Amin, the director of Iraq's NMD, declared that the Revolutionary Command Council and the Baath Party had essentially extended their August 5 decision to shut down all of UNSCOM's disarmament work by shutting down all of its monitoring work as well. A statement issued by Baghdad asserted that there would be absolutely no cooperation with UNSCOM until the Security Council lifted sanctions, restructured UNSCOM, and removed me as executive chairman.

This was the full-breakout decision. As far as Iraq was concerned, UNSCOM was dead. Thus, Iraq commenced the end run that would produce a military crisis, UNSCOM's banishment, and the opening of one of the deepest rifts in the Security Council since the end of the Cold War.

In response to Iraq's decisions, the United States and the United Kingdom immediately moved to increase their armed forces in the Persian Gulf.

11

THE FINAL DECEPTION

As Iraq sought to put an end to UNSCOM's disarmament and monitoring work, the atmosphere of crisis deepened at UN headquarters. The Security Council met continuously, and individual members conferred informally in the corridors, looking for ways to stabilize a rapidly deteriorating situation. Meanwhile, the military buildup in the Gulf continued.

The Security Council asked me to prepare a report on the current status of UNSCOM. On November 4, 1998, I informed the council that UNSCOM was in no position to provide any level of assurance regarding Iraq's compliance because the Iraqi decisions of August 5 and October 31 had made it impossible for us to carry out our disarmament and monitoring responsibilities. I had decided, nevertheless, to maintain a full UNSCOM staff presence in Iraq so we could resume work without delay should the situation change.

Baghdad was now attempting to draw a distinction between UNSCOM and the International Atomic Energy Agency, whose monitoring work it was prepared to allow to continue. However, the IAEA's director-general, Mohamed El Baradei, reported to the Security Council that IAEA could not function adequately without UNSCOM's technical services and facilities, thus making Iraq's gesture to IAEA a hollow one.

Following several days of discussion, the Security Council adopted Resolution 1205 on November 5, 1998. It condemned Iraq's decision to cease cooperation with UNSCOM as a "flagrant violation" of its obligations and demanded that Iraq rescind, immediately and unconditionally, its decisions of October 31 and August 5. However, the Security Council reaffirmed "its readiness to consider, in a comprehensive review, Iraq's compliance with its obligations under all relevant resolutions" once Iraq had resumed full cooperation with UNSCOM and IAEA.

Notably absent from this text was any threat to use force in carrying out the resolution, even though it had been adopted under Chapter VII of the UN Charter, which invests the Security Council with enforcement powers. It also addressed the question of the duration of the prohibitions from Resolution 687 using the now somewhat bowdlerized "light at the end of the tunnel" language. The intent was to signal Iraq that, if Iraq complied with its disarmament obligations, the oil export sanctions would be removed forthwith. No individual member of the Security Council, including the United States, would renege on that undertaking. The attempt at reassurance was well-meaning, and Resolution 1205 was adopted unanimously. It was then robustly ignored by Iraq.

On November 10, 1998, I received a call from the acting permanent U.S. representative to the UN, Ambassador Peter Burleigh, who, by chance of the calendar, was also president of the Security Council for the month of November. I visited him in his office across the street from the UN headquarters building at about 7:00 P.M. Burleigh explained that he was meeting with me in his capacity as U.S. ambassador, not as president of the Security Council, on instructions from the highest levels in Washington.

He put to me the same message he would later send to the UN secretary-general and to the IAEA's director-general. Considering the crisis Iraq had provoked and its refusal to obey the requirements of the Security Council, the United States had decided to draw down the staff in its embassies throughout the region. The U.S. government therefore advised me, as executive head of UNSCOM, to consider evacuating UNSCOM staff from Iraq. Burleigh emphasized that he was not providing me with advance notice of any decision to take military action against Iraq, merely a suggestion that such an evacuation, given the paramount importance of the safety of staff, would be prudent.

I told Burleigh that I would immediately order an evacuation and would advise Secretary-General Annan of my decision. He agreed that was the right decision. I then said it would be normal for me to advise the president of the Security Council of this decision and ask him to convey it to the other members. How should I do that? Switching roles, Burleigh said that I had just done so. I accepted this procedure.

Back at UN headquarters, I called together a small team comprising Charles Duelfer, Colonel Danny Rouse, our chief of operations, and Ewen Buchanan, our policy and public-affairs adviser. I placed a call to Secretary-General Annan while listing on a whiteboard behind the door of my office the key steps needed to execute a safe evacuation, which we would check off as the night went on.

The evacuation of our staff from Baghdad proceeded on the evening of November 11. Our core team at headquarters in New York tracked every step carefully: the flight of our L-100 from Bahrain to the Habbaniyah air base, the rounding-up of all our Baghdad staff under the pretext of an early-morning meeting, and the bus ride to the airport, where they were quickly loaded onto the plane with a few personal possessions and flown to Bahrain. At every stage, we feared Iraq might seek to impede their progress or take them hostage. That didn't happen.

Kofi Annan, who was on an official visit to North Africa, issued a press statement from Marrakech on November 11 to express his concern over the escalating crisis. "I am saddened and burdened," he said, "by the Iraqi decision of 5 August and 31 October not to cooperate with UNSCOM." He urged Saddam Hussein to rescind these decisions and resume cooperation with UNSCOM and IAEA. Extolling the virtues of comprehensive review, Annan promoted it as means to "map out the remaining steps, provided Iraq cooperates, thus allowing Iraq to see light at the end of the tunnel."

Two days later, Annan wrote directly to Saddam to repeat the terms expressed in his press statement. However, if Annan's letter was intended to convince Saddam that Iraq was obliged to abide by Security Council resolutions, its language was certainly less than compelling. Annan's words depicted the Security Council as a supplicant rather than an enforcer of international law:

> I can report to you that without exception, all the members of the Security Council expressed preference for a diplomatic solution of the crisis. . . . The Security Council also unanimously endorsed the press statement . . . in which I addressed a personal appeal to you, Mr. President, to take the necessary steps for a diplomatic solution to become possible.

With U.S. and British aircraft carriers, bombers, and troops massing in the region, a new Gulf conflict seemed inevitable. Then, as if judging that it had for the moment extracted the maximum possible concessions from the world community, Iraq backed down.

On November 14, Tariq Aziz replied to Annan's letter following a joint meeting of the Revolutionary Command Council and the National Command of the Arab Baath Socialist Party presided over by Saddam Hussein. Iraq, Aziz stated, had decided to "resume working with [UNSCOM] and the IAEA and to allow them to perform their normal duties in accordance with the relevant resolutions of the Security Council." Weirdly, he went on to say that "Iraq's intention was not to sever the relationship with [UNSCOM and IAEA] or to halt implementation of its obligations under section C of Security Council resolution 687." He claimed, instead, that their sole purpose had been to have sanctions removed in order to end the suffering of the Iraqi people.

Aziz rejected any suggestion that Iraq was capitulating out of fear of a U.S. assault. Iraq's newfound flexibility, he said, was principally due to appeals from the UN secretary-general and Iraq's supporters on the Security Council, namely, China, France, and Russia.

Perhaps emboldened by the tone of Annan's letter, Aziz used the opportunity to put forth Iraq's version of "comprehensive review." He listed nine points that had already been discussed with China, France, and Russia and that he said would have to be adopted in order for the comprehensive review to be "serious, impartial, and productive."

This list of nine points was vintage Iraqi reasoning, ignoring the technical and disarmament aspects of comprehensive review in favor of Iraq's political requirements. According to the Iraqis, the comprehensive review would have to take place immediately, last a very short time, and lead inevitably to the lifting of the oil embargo. One curious sentence also sought to restrict the interpretations of international law that could be made by members of the Security Council "in respect of all matters pertaining to Iraq." The meaning of this purported requirement was never made clear, but it seemed to suggest that only Iraq's interpretation of the relevant Security Council resolutions would be the authoritative one.

The Iraqis also specifically referred to my leadership of UNSCOM as an issue that needed to be resolved: "The question of Butler and the composition of the Special Commission and its practices is extremely important. The Security Council should give it serious consideration in order to ensure future good relations." In this context, Kofi Annan told me, subsequently, that the Russians had been pressuring him to fire me. So the "question of Butler" was part of the Iraqi and Russian agendas.

In short, this Iraqi declaration was something of an ultimatum. Iraq's demands would have to be fulfilled for it to consider further cooperation with the Security Council. If there were any doubt about the highly selective and demanding nature of Iraq's declaration, such doubts were removed by the last of the document's nine points. In requiring that "these assurances be communicated directly to the leadership in Baghdad either by the Secretary-General or by a Security Council delegation," Iraq was stipulating that assurances from the council would be welcome only if delivered by parties acceptable to it.

O N THE AFTERNOON of Saturday, November 14, an emergency session of the Security Council was scheduled. As UNSCOM's policy team assembled in my office to prepare for the meeting, we didn't know whether a decision had been taken in Washington and London to attack Iraq. But Charles Duelfer had spoken on the telephone with a contact in Washington who'd said, "It's pretty clear what's going to happen, Charles. All I have to do is look out my window." It seems that the Pentagon parking lot was far fuller than usual for a Saturday afternoon, and everyone in and around the Pentagon was dressed not in the weekend casual attire of open-necked shirts and blue jeans but in full uniform. This was an unambiguous signal. The Pentagon does not go to war in blue jeans.

In an effort to forestall the impending military strike, the Kofi Annan circulated to council members his letter of November 13 to Saddam Hussein together with Aziz's reply, calling it "a positive response" to his appeal. But when the Security Council meeting opened, it became immediately apparent, particularly after comments by the American and British ambassadors, that the secretary-general's characterization of the Iraqi response as "positive" was not shared by everyone. After all, the Security Council had previously decided the nature and scope of a comprehensive review and conveyed this decision to Iraq on October 30. Iraq's response had been to shut down UNSCOM's operations on the next day. Now Iraq sought to impose a list of demands about the comprehensive review before it would consider renewing its cooperation with UNSCOM.

A confusing disjunction soon emerged between what was stated in Aziz's letter and the list of demands actually conveyed in its annex. Russian Ambassador Sergey Lavrov characterized the letter as indicating Iraq's intent to back down and resume cooperation. He argued that the nine-point annex was simply a statement of its preferred position with respect to comprehensive review.

At the same time, Sandy Berger, President Clinton's national security adviser, spoke publicly from the White House in uncompromising terms about the tendentious nature of Iraq's various assurances: "The Iraqi letter sent today to Secretary-General Annan is neither unequivocal nor unconditional. It is unacceptable. . . . Unfortunately, the letter shows unmistakably that Iraq has no intention of complying with the Security Council resolutions. . . . We will be consulting with our friends and allies about next steps."

The conflicting interpretations of Iraq's letter led to the need for further clarification—and to one of the more farcical episodes in recent Security Council history. With the council adjourned, I witnessed a Russian diplomat and his Iraqi colleague drafting Iraq's official response in the corridor outside the chambers. Late in the afternoon of November 14, that joint effort produced a second letter signed by Iraqi Ambassador Nizar Hamdoon. He characterized Aziz's letter as constituting a "decree of the Iraqi leadership regarding the resumption of cooperation with [UNSCOM and IAEA]. The two bodies will be permitted to carry out their regular duties."

This was an amazing statement. Aziz's letter had given no assurance of resumed cooperation, but we were told by Ambassador Hamdoon that it should be read as precisely such an assurance. It was then argued in the Security Council, principally by Ambassador Lavrov, that the matter was answered and closed.

This development, however, left the Iraqi demands for comprehensive review in something of a suspended state. Another adjournment was called, and the Russians and Iraqis drafted a third letter of assurance. Now Ambassador Hamdoon stated that the "appendix containing the views and preferences of the Iraqi government with regard to the substance of the comprehensive review . . . are not linked to the clear and unconditional decision of the Iraqi government to resume cooperation with [UNSCOM and IAEA]."

Hamdoon went on to say that the Iraqi decision rendered void the earlier decisions to suspend cooperation with UNSCOM and IAEA.

This latter point was important, because Security Council Resolution 1205 had required Iraq to formally rescind those decisions. In fact, it was diplomatic shadow play—declarations voiding earlier decisions that had affirmed earlier suspensions of promises later to be rescinded through subsequent declarations, and on and on and on.

The Security Council met into the night of Saturday, November 14. The meeting ended with the U.S. representative saying that he would need to refer these events and the letters of assurance to his government for consideration. We left the chamber not knowing what the outcome would be.

The next morning, I appeared on NBC's *Meet the Press* to discuss the situation. I'd previously heard from Ambassador Burleigh that there was likely to be a statement by President Clinton at around the same time, so I prerecorded the interview with anchor Tim Russert, then traveled to Burleigh's residence, at his invitation, to listen to the statement from the Oval Office.

Clinton's appearance and his statement were both remarkable. Clearly tense and angry, the president asserted that Saddam Hussein had backed down at the last possible second only because U.S. bombers were on their way to the Gulf. Having given thorough consideration to Iraq's assurances, and in consultation with British Prime Minister Tony Blair, Clinton had instructed the military to call off its attack. He then issued a warning: If Iraq went back on its promise to cooperate in full with UNSCOM and IAEA, there would be an immediate U.S. military response, with no further discussion or warning.

Following his statement, President Clinton agreed to take some questions from the media. The first one was obviously painful to him. The reporter, Sam Donaldson of ABC, pointed out that Clinton's national security adviser, on the preceding afternoon, had likened Iraq's assurances to a Swiss cheese—filled with holes. What had changed in the past few hours? Why was the president now prepared to accept those assurances?

Rather than answer directly, President Clinton reiterated the seriousness of his threat. This was Iraq's last chance. Either it would keep its word and cooperate fully, or there would be immediate military action without further discussion.

Peter Burleigh and I learned subsequently that the onset of attack had been only an hour or so away at the moment of Clinton's decision.

The Security Council met on the afternoon of Sunday, November 15, to consider the position it would now adopt to bring the latest crisis to a conclusion. Having taken note of Iraq's various statements and letters, the Security Council agreed to accept them as a rescinding of the decisions of August 5 and October 31. UNSCOM could resume its work on "an immediate, unconditional, and unrestricted basis."

The most important passage of this press statement, however, implied a certain wariness about Iraq's behavior. It stated that the confidence of Security Council members in Iraq's intentions needed to be established "by unconditional and sustained cooperation with [UNSCOM and IAEA] in exercising the full range of their activities." Moreover, the Security Council had authorized its president to state that the comprehensive review would proceed only when "the Secretary-General has confirmed on the basis of reports from [UNSCOM and IAEA] that Iraq has returned to full cooperation."

I had no doubt of the position in which this statement put me. I had to test the earnestness of the promises made by Iraq. This test had also to be seen against the background of the unequivocal statement made by the U.S. president to the effect that if Iraq broke its word there would be no further discussion, only military action.

L ATER THAT DAY, I set two actions in motion.
First, I decided to immediately return all of our staff from Bahrain to Baghdad so they could resume their work. This was carried out during the course of Tuesday, November 17.

Second, I wrote a letter to Aziz in which I discussed the substantive work that needed to be done in each of the main disarmament areas. I set forth precisely what materials and information we needed in order to be able to bring to a close the disarmament phase of UNSCOM's work with Iraq. I essentially sought to clear away as many outstanding issues as possible prior to comprehensive review.

Emphasizing my desire to work constructively with Iraqi authorities, I stated in this letter that I continued "to believe that, with Iraq's full cooperation, [UNSCOM] can proceed to bring the respective disarmament areas to account, expeditiously." I told Aziz, plainly, in subsequent letters of November 18 and 19 that UNSCOM was determined "to resolve outstanding disarmament issues as quickly as possible" but this would only be possible if his government were to provide full information.

While Baghdad considered my requests for information, I worked with UNSCOM's technical leaders to design the necessary fieldwork for our mission. We identified five key areas in which we needed to restart our work, including the obvious three—missile, chemical, biological—as well as import-export controls and personal interviews with individuals previously involved in Iraq's illegal weapons-manufacturing programs.

In assembling the UNSCOM inspection teams and drawing up the mission plans, I decided to use a graduated approach that would lead toward the conduct of no-notice inspections of concealment-related areas. I intended to reach that point within three to four weeks from the date of the claimed resumption of full cooperation. I wasn't sure how long it would be before I could report to the Security Council, but I hoped it might be within four to six weeks.

UNSCOM was under intense pressure to work fast. Kofi Annan, for one, asked me to be as efficient as possible, seemingly edging again toward confusing superficial cooperation with substantive compliance. The Russian and French representatives at the UN were also agitating for speed. Ambassador Lavrov seemed to imply that Iraq's assurances and our staff's return to Iraq were in and of themselves enough to certify that Iraq had resumed cooperation with UNSCOM, irrespective of the outcome of the work.

I didn't agree. I still believed that the issue was compliance with the law *leading* to substantive disarmament outcomes. I would not buy into some diplomatic exercise—a tour of obviously sanitized Iraqi sites that added nothing to our understanding of their weapons-of-mass-destruction programs. These were not popguns we were talking about; they were hugely powerful and utterly terrifying weapons.

Within three days of my letters to Aziz, I received replies that were as dismissive as they were obfuscatory.

First, Iraq signaled that relations with UNSCOM had been downgraded. Aziz himself would not respond to my requests; they would be directed to a lower level, while he dealt directly with the Security Council only.

Second, Iraq continued to attack UNSCOM as an organization. Dr. Riyadh al-Qaysi, Iraq's undersecretary for foreign affairs, replied to my first letter of November 17 by characterizing my request for information as running "counter to the prevailing trend approved by the Security Council." He concluded by expressing his hope that UNSCOM would "discard this unprofessional approach which would unjustifiably lead to the prolongation of work, and thereby maintaining the inequitable embargo on the people of Iraq." In the weeks that followed, the Iraqis reinforced this stance by insisting, again, that Iraq was disarmed and would not give UNSCOM any further materials or information.

On November 20, I wrote to the president of the Security Council, providing a first look at the replies I had received from Iraq, which advanced the view that the comprehensive review process had already commenced. This idea essentially reversed the relationship the Security Council had envisioned. According to the council, if I reported that Iraq had resumed its cooperation with UNSCOM and was complying with the Security Council resolutions, then a comprehensive review might be conducted. Yet the Iraqis repeatedly refused to provide answers to my questions on the ground that all would be revealed in the comprehensive review, preparations for which, they argued falsely, were already well advanced.

Iraq's foot-dragging peaked in the most difficult weapons area—biological weapons. Dr. al-Qaysi argued that there was no need to provide any further information on Iraq's biological weapons program because the comprehensive review would "determine whether the disarmament phase has been completed, or whether steps in the biological file need to be taken to fulfill the requirement of the disarmament phase."

In truth, there had never been any serious disarmament phase in the biological area. In the preceding eighteen months, international experts had repeatedly concluded unanimously that Iraq's disclosure statement in the biological area was deeply deficient and provided no basis for any credible level of verification. Iraq was still refusing to throw any light on this dark area. I had asked Aziz for access to important documentation, particularly that held in the archives of the Military Industrialization Corporation, which had primary responsibility for the manufacture of Iraq's illegal weapons. Iraq refused, claiming that my request was "provocative rather than professional." Iraq took the same approach to questions in all of the weapons fields, quibbling about the existence of documents or the need for them. For instance, when I reminded the Iraqis to supply us with a copy of the document Dr. Kraatz-Wadsack had discovered in July 1998 at the air force headquarters, which the Security Council had ordered to be handed over, I was told quite simply that this would not happen.

During the last two weeks of November 1998, Iraq bombarded UNSCOM and the Security Council with papers offering their version of the disposition of the proscribed weapons, claiming that these weapons had variously been used, destroyed, lost, perished, or become useless. None of this information was new. Indeed, some of it sought to alter and make more benign declarations previously made by Iraq. All in all, this was another step backward.

Iraq obviously believed that the Security Council did not have the will or stomach to enforce the law. They'd concluded, rightly, that at least some members of the Security Council would simply be overwhelmed by the weight of the materials and the arguments they'd provided. Neither the diplomats nor their capitals would consider it a useful investment of time to try to analyze or unravel Iraq's voluminous, cleverly assembled but phony arguments.

Meanwhile, UNSCOM was reduced to appealing to Iraq to provide information to meet an increasingly stripped-down set of basic requirements. Without this information, the only rational conclusion to be drawn was that Iraq continued to retain illegal weapons capability.

The Security Council met again on November 24, 1998, to consider, informally, the progress that had taken place since its crucial meetings ten days earlier. In these consultations, the friends of Iraq insisted that Baghdad had already kept its promises by entering into discussions with UNSCOM, permitting some fairly routine inspections, and providing a small number of pieces of new material.

Russia and China also insisted on establishing a system of weekly progress reports by UNSCOM. This was illusory vigilance on their part and, more pertinently, it was a make-work requirement designed to keep UNSCOM on the defensive. I sent the first such report to the Security Council on December 3. It recorded that, on the whole, the resumed inspection and monitoring activities in the biological, missile, and chemical areas had been proceeding satisfactorily. There had, however, been negative incidents involving Iraq's refusal to provide access to a particular site and the discovery of undeclared biological equipment at another. This was in addition to Iraq's refusal to provide the information and documentation I had asked for.

The report also provided further details on the unsatisfactory exchange of correspondence between UNSCOM and Baghdad. It noted, in particular, that Iraq was now claiming that UNSCOM was to blame for the VX residues we'd found in a destroyed missile warhead—"a deliberate act of tampering," according to Dr. al-Qaysi.

Once again, a fair reading of Iraq's commitment of November 14 would have led to the conclusion that Iraq was failing to keep that promise, only two weeks into the process.

T HE PRESSURE to bring this period of testing to a close grew substantially as we entered December. According to Iraq's supporters in the Security Council, the game was over. Iraq had abundantly demonstrated its renewal of full-scale cooperation, while UNSCOM's concerns and complaints were mere carping. To support these claims, Iraq's supporters cited the tables of contrived statistics, provided by Baghdad, on the number of contacts between UNSCOM and Iraqi officials; visits made to sites; and sites under monitoring. Quantity, not quality, was the point here.

The Russians asked me repeatedly how much longer I would need. At the beginning of December, I said that the process would take just a few more weeks. UNSCOM needed to conduct tests in all five major fields of work before I could properly fulfill the requirement placed upon me on November 14. I wouldn't require an extensive test in each of the five fields—one random or representative test would suffice—but we were constrained by the time needed to assemble the expert teams required to carry out the inspection work.

In my mind, no-notice inspections at sites where illegal weapons components were likely stored would be the acid test. Many of us within UNSCOM believed that Iraq—if our information was right and we approached a site where illegal weapons were hidden—would prevent us from entering. Iraqi authorities so feared exposure that they would prefer to face the consequences of an outright inspection blockage.

All this time, we continued to receive defectors' and intelligence information on Iraq's continuing efforts, working through overseas front companies, to resupply its manufacturing capability for weapons of mass destruction. These facts put more pressure on us to make sure that our assessment was correct. We knew how high the stakes were. We also had to make certain that the intelligence we received was accurate. Iraq and its allies were eager to pounce on any UNSCOM mistakes. Had they shown we acted recklessly, it would be a huge propaganda victory. It could also damage wider international efforts to preserve the weapons-of-mass-destruction nonproliferation regimes and undermine the authority of the Security Council itself.

Now both the Russian and French ambassadors urged me to visit their capitals to discuss the progress on Iraqi compliance. Their interest was to get through this testing period as quickly as possible and conduct a comprehensive review. The Russians in particular pushed me for definitive time estimates. How much longer would it take to test Iraq's cooperation? How much time would we need for a comprehensive review? When I said that such a review would take a few weeks to be done properly, they were unhappy, believing, incredibly, that a comprehensive review of little more than a few hours—a couple of Security Council sessions—should suffice for the council to declare Iraq disarmed and lift the oil embargo.

I agreed to visit Moscow and Paris in early December. All the while, forces of the United States and the United Kingdom were being maintained in the Gulf with a high degree of readiness. The image of an angry, shaken, and thoroughly resolved President Clinton on the morning of Sunday, November 15, remained vivid.

12

DESERT FOX AND THE TWILIGHT OF UNSCOM

B Y THE BEGINNING of December 1998, I had devised plans for the conduct of the remaining inspections necessary to test Iraq's November 14 promises. These inspections were to include some sites where prohibited materials were most likely secreted.

The person I recruited to lead these inspection teams was a former Australian army officer, Colonel Roger Hill. He had already served as an UNSCOM inspector on many occasions, including the entries to presidential sites in March 1998, and he had worked as an assistant to Scott Ritter in the concealment area. Hill had two outstanding characteristics: an unsurpassed knowledge of Iraq's weapon programs and methodologies, and a character that was firm but uninfected by prejudice. Hill was keen to do the job, and he came to New York for briefings and discussions before setting off for Baghdad. I then departed for Moscow via Paris, accompanied by a small team that included the policy advisers provided to me by France and Russia.

My first meeting at the Quai d'Orsay, as France's Ministry of Foreign Affairs is known, was with Jean de Gliniasty, then the head of the division responsible for France's relations with the United Nations and an extraordinarily skilled and sophisticated diplomat with an outstanding policy mind.

De Gliniasty advanced a single French position: Of the choices available, it would be better to continue some arms-control monitoring in Iraq without sanctions rather than to retain sanctions with no monitoring.

This reflected a profound policy difference between France and the United States. Paris believed Washington's policy had two goals: the maintenance of sanctions and, ultimately, the removal of Saddam Hussein. On the former, France sought the removal of sanctions for economic reasons; on the latter, France doubted Saddam could be removed by other than natural means. Since these two elements of U.S. policy were connected—sanctions would remain in place as long as Saddam Hussein remained in power—U.S. policy looked dismal to France. France's view ignored the clarification the United States had given about implementation of sanctions removal, if Iraq was properly disarmed.

Without directly challenging France's proposition concerning sanctions and monitoring, I stressed the importance of ensuring that any monitoring system in Iraq was competent and comprehensive enough to do the job correctly. France, I feared, would have been content with a monitoring system that was less than robust. In fact, the government of Jacques Chirac was edging toward a position where it assessed Iraq as having been substantially disarmed and certainly posing no threat to France. They apparently believed that Iraq's capability of producing weapons of mass destruction was limited. Since it would take Iraq a fair amount of time to develop a truly threatening arms program, it might well be that, in the meantime, there would be political change in Baghdad.

France thus argued that a monitoring system that guaranteed some degree of continuing international vigilance over Iraq would be sufficient and that the benefits of removing sanctions and normalizing relations with Iraq would outweigh any deficiencies in the monitoring. De Gliniasty and I debated our different views without changing anyone's position.

I then had a working lunch with Loïc Hennekine, secretary-general of the French Foreign Ministry. Hennekine was a recent appointee to the Quai d'Orsay, having previously served as France's ambassador to Canada. Early in the luncheon, he made quite a fuss about declaring himself to be no mere diplomatist but a man who preferred frank, indeed brutally frank, expression of views. This seemed to signal that he was about to hit us with the French equivalent of a two-by-four to the forehead; our side of the table braced for the blow. What in fact occurred was something more like a slip of the tongue. In discussing Iraq's promises of November 14, Hennekine expressed the hope that we were now in a position where trust and confidence in Iraqi statements had been "restored."

Taking advantage of Hennekine's preference for frankness, I told him I was astonished at his implication that there had been a *prior* period in which Iraq had behaved in a trustworthy fashion. In fact, Iraq had lied to us from the beginning.

Hennekine did see this point and stepped back—well, at least half a step. He acknowledged the logic of my statement. This did not deter him, however, from moving on to his principal point: the need for UNSCOM's work to be ended without further delay, for sanctions to be lifted, and for Iraq to be returned to "normal" membership in the international community.

Taking courteous note of Hennekine's wishes, I expressed the hope that I would be able to report Iraqi compliance in order to move the situation forward. I emphasized that this outcome was largely in Iraq's hands and that whatever France could do to encourage Iraq to behave properly would be appreciated.

A RRIVING IN Moscow on December 4, we were taken to lunch with Deputy Foreign Minister Viktor Posuvalyuk, whom I'd met with during my previous visit to Moscow. At lunch, the groundwork was laid for the conversation I'd have later that day with Foreign Minister Igor Ivanov. Posuvalyuk repeated the now familiar Russian refrain about Iraq's new attitude and improved level of cooperation. From Moscow's perspective, military action against Iraq would certainly be a disaster. It would solve nothing and lead only to UNSCOM's destruction. Russia therefore hoped that our work in testing Iraq's position would end soon so that we could move on to a comprehensive review.

The real conversation took place in the Foreign Minister's conference room in the Russian Foreign Ministry headquarters at 6:45 P.M. on December 4, 1998.

Unlike his predecessor, Yevgeny Primakov, whose heaviness and pedantry were so redolent of the Soviet period, Igor Ivanov was warm, charming, and friendly. He began our two-hour talk by stating that it was important to move forward on the Iraq issue. Like Posuvalyuk, he emphasized that military action against Iraq would be fruitless: UNSCOM's achievements would be lost, the United States would be embroiled in Iraq for many years to come, and my own name would be linked to the catastrophe. Under these circumstances, he argued, a political solution was the only viable approach.

The foreign minister said he was by no means an advocate for Saddam or Iraq, simply a realist. Iraq was only one of many countries with weapons of mass destruction. Since the search for an unambiguous solution was probably futile, the main objective should be to minimize Iraq's threat to the region while making certain that other countries, such as Iran and Israel, did not represent a threat to the region.

Ivanov then warned me that whatever inspections I planned for the future should not provoke a new crisis. Russia was a loyal partner of UNSCOM and wanted to help, he claimed, but it was my personal responsibility to avoid a breakdown. Ivanov managed to maintain his charm through all this, but the element of threat was plain.

In my response, I pointed out that it was not UNSCOM's job to decide whether Iraq represented a threat to the region, a concept to which Ivanov had given great attention. Our job required us to disarm and monitor Iraq and to provide the Security Council with the facts that would allow it to make the correct political decisions.

I then told Ivanov that UNSCOM would soon conduct a series of disarmament-related inspections. They would be based on evidence at our disposal and would be consistent with our mandate. I expected to report to the Security Council on the results by December 14, 1998. If the government of Iraq was cooperative, I believed I could report in a way that would enable the Security Council to begin the comprehensive review just after Christmas or in early January 1999.

I made clear to Ivanov that I'd instructed UNSCOM's chief inspectors to avoid any action that might be seen as a provocation. Ivanov interjected to say that provocations did not necessarily have to be intentional. Perhaps revealing Russia's real stance, he implied that it was solely UNSCOM's responsibility to seek to avoid a crisis. If a problem arose, then finding the solution was my job.

The foreign minister then asked how long it would take, through a comprehensive review, before we could declare Iraq disarmed. Given the key remaining issues in the missile and chemical areas, I replied, we might have a satisfactory account of Iraq's weapons-of-mass-destruction program within six to eight weeks. But since this could be done only if Iraq gave us the information and materials we requested, I asked Ivanov to tell Aziz that Iraq needed to provide us with those materials promptly.

Ivanov remarked that Moscow was well aware of who made the decisions in Baghdad, and Aziz's own position in Saddam's regime was weak. Nevertheless, he added, Moscow sought to support Aziz because they thought he was among the more reasonable leaders in Baghdad.

Toward the end of our conversation, Ivanov returned to a slightly threatening attitude. He repeated that my report to the Security Council might determine whether or not there would be military action. Moreover, my actions might affect the course of Russian foreign policy: "You know," he remarked, "the Duma is on the verge of ratifying the START II Treaty [the Strategic Arms Reduction Treaty]. Prime Minister Primakov and I are very keen on having them do so. But if there is a military attack upon Iraq, the Duma will never approve the treaty. You should bear this in mind, Mr. Butler, as you write your report."

U PON MY RETURN to New York, I sent the Security Council my second weekly report on UNSCOM activities in Iraq. It covered the period December 3–9, 1998, and showed an increase in Iraqi attempts to prevent UNSCOM from carrying out its inspections.

On December 4, 1998, for example, Iraq prevented UNSCOM 261, a biological weapons team, from carrying out its very first inspection. The next day, Iraq impeded another biological weapons inspection by refusing to allow the inspectors to question personnel or to take audio or video records of their discussions. Iraqi officials also gave unbelievable accounts of the presence or absence of relevant personnel and the dates and purposes for which pieces of equipment had been moved in and out of the facility.

Inspections by UNSCOM in the chemical weapons area fared no better. During an inspection on December 5, 1998, Iraqi minders from the National Monitoring Directorate imposed conditions contrary to the rules, especially preventing the photographing of bombs. Nevertheless, we managed to locate some undeclared dual-use pieces of production equipment.

The Iraqis' blocking of UNSCOM 258's attempt to inspect a building connected to the Baath Party on December 9, 1998, aroused particular interest in my office. I'd ordered a concealment-related inspection there because we believed Iraq was storing materials related to its missile program—perhaps including missile parts and components—at this site.

The fact that we were denied access naturally suggested that our suspicions were correct.

Aziz responded with an elaborate complaint to the UN secretary-general on December 15, 1998, about UNSCOM's working methods. Aziz claimed that UNSCOM had tried to perform its inspection of the Baath Party building "in an intrusive and provocative manner." According to him, UNSCOM, not Iraq, had failed to abide by the terms of the Memorandum of Understanding. Our team, in Aziz's words, had "relied on false and misleading information meant to provoke the Iraqi side and in violation of UNSCOM commitments to respect Iraq's dignity, sovereignty and national security."

Remarkably, the influence of Iraqi propaganda had continued to grow as the months passed. The sheer persistence of the Iraqis, along with the deepening fatigue felt by all members of the Security Council over this issue, made it increasingly difficult for some council members to focus on the facts of Iraqi concealment. Instead, the idea that Iraq was being pursued by an overzealous posse of cowboys gradually spread.

At the same time, the actions of Scott Ritter were worsening the situation. With his numerous public statements accusing UNSCOM of having been "captured" by U.S. intelligence authorities, Ritter was stirring up a controversy that helped add to the atmosphere of confusion and doubt. Iraq, of course, seized on Ritter's charges with glee, treating them as a revelation, from within UNSCOM itself, that it had never been a valid representative of the UN but rather a mere puppet of U.S. foreign policy.

Kofi Annan's senior advisers took the allegations of spying seriously enough to prompt them to initiate an internal investigation. A former CIA operative was hired to compile a chronological history of UNSCOM. Although Annan's advisers tried to keep the investigation secret and even denied its existence, my staff and I quickly learned about it. Subsequently, I was passed a copy of the operative's written report by a friendly third party.

Of course, I'd explained to Annan why UNSCOM had been forced to take an investigative approach to its disarmament mandate, and I'd outlined in detail for him the use that Rolf Ekeus and I had made of intelligence assistance provided by UN member states. I'd also made clear to him the strict rules I'd insisted upon: that no UNSCOM activity should be undertaken that wasn't clearly related to our primary mission. In particular, I told him, I'd scrupulously avoided any entanglement that could make it appear that UNSCOM was working on behalf of any individual state rather than carrying out the work assigned to it by the Security Council.

I formed the impression that Annan accepted my assurances, and he said so publicly on at least one occasion; I can't say the same about his senior staff. It was known in the UN corridors that key members of Annan's senior staff regarded UNSCOM as illegitimate, an agency that did not conform to the proper UN culture. Simply put, they couldn't bear the unusual—and essential—degree of independence we enjoyed.

Ritter's allegations provided this clique with the weapon they needed, and they chose to believe the Iraqi propagandist interpretation of his claims because it suited their view of UNSCOM. What could be more illegitimate than a UN organization, flying the blue flag, working secretly on behalf of the CIA?

As it turned out, the report produced as a result of the UN-authorized investigation of UNSCOM turned out to be merely a chronology of main events since the end of the Gulf War. It was very accurate and, ironically, demonstrated that from the beginning Iraq had sought to cheat and disobey the disarmament requirements. It did not support Ritter's allegations.

T WO DECISIVE events took place in the second week of December 1998.

In Iraq, Roger Hill's inspections continued to hit the wall. He described being shown empty buildings, obviously sanitized for his visit, while the accompanying Iraqi authorities stood about laughing and saying, "What else did you expect? That we would show you anything serious?"

This was more than a nuisance and a waste of time. Continuing with such meaningless inspections would mean that the number of "successfully completed" inspections would continue to rise—at least in the eyes of Iraq's friends on the Security Council—even as the depth of Iraqi deception grew.

Under the circumstances, Hill recommended to me that we cancel an important inspection planned for the weekend of December 12–13. After some reflection and discussion with my colleagues, I agreed. This brought to a close Hill's inspection mission along with the overall period of testing Iraq's November promise. I then began consulting with all of UNSCOM's technical leaders to finalize the report I had decided to put together by Monday, December 14, 1998.

By now the chief inspector in each weapons area had returned from Iraq to our New York headquarters. In two major meetings, I asked them to review their experience of the past month and to state whether or not Iraq had provided the promised degree of cooperation. In every case, the answer was "No." Every inspector had had access blocked, documents withheld, facilities sanitized, and interviews forbidden.

So, once again, Iraq had failed to keep its promise. My problem was how to report this fact. Having reached this view by December 10, I signaled it to any ambassador on the Security Council who approached me with the exception of Sergey Lavrov. The Russian ambassador was clearly avoiding me. I thought this might present a problem in the deliberations of the Security Council, and I warned Secretary-General Annan that we might have a problem.

As I wrestled with how best to frame my report, U.S. National Security Adviser Sandy Berger invited me to an informal meeting at the U.S. mission to the UN in New York on December 11. I agreed, although I was concerned that I might find myself being pressured over my report (which never happened). In fact, Berger emphasized his desire not to interfere in my job and his awareness of the political dangers of such interference.

Berger simply asked me to describe the circumstances as I saw them. I recounted our experiences in the field and said that my report to the Security Council would record those facts. As things stood, I couldn't give the Security Council the assurances it required concerning Iraq's cooperation.

The ultimatum President Clinton had laid down on November 15 hung over our conversation, but Berger couldn't or wouldn't say what specific consequences would flow from my report. He said that no decision for military action had been taken.

At the end of our conversation, Berger reaffirmed how important it was for UNSCOM to carry out its work objectively. He was aware of the difficult situation in which I had been placed and thanked me for the way in which I'd handled it.

Many commentators and critics have said that I should have known that military action was inevitable, given the nature of the report I was preparing, but the concept of "inevitability" in such circumstances is specious, implying a degree of certainty not available in international relations or justified in the circumstances then surrounding the Clinton administration. In addition, Iraq had chosen to play a game of dice with the Security Council. It had done so many times previously and suffered little as a result. Now the United States and the United Kingdom were moving substantial forces into the Gulf and asserting that they had full right under the UN resolutions to use force against Iraq. There seemed to be a high degree of probability that force would be used—but there was no inevitability to it. Only the U.S. commander in chief, the president, could make that decision, and then only if the British prime minister agreed (which he had, not one month earlier, at the last moment). Besides, I was required by the Security Council to report the facts as UNSCOM had experienced them during the preceding month in Iraq. I had a choice about the words I would use but little leeway on the facts.

During the course of Monday, December 14, I worked on the final text of my report to the Security Council. I forwarded it to the secretary-general around 5:00 P.M. with the recommendation that he transmit it to the Security Council immediately. He did so, and it was released on Tuesday, December 15, 1998.

My report had four parts: a reminder to the Security Council of precisely what Iraq had promised and precisely what task the council had assigned me; contextual material by which the range of UNSCOM activities since November 17, 1998, could be judged; a summary of UNSCOM's experience in each category of work from November 17 to December 15; and my conclusions.

The first part of the report pointed out that Iraq had repeatedly promised sustained, full cooperation with UNSCOM, including under the terms established under the Memorandum of Understanding of February 23, 1998, and the commitment it had made to the Security Council on November 14, 1998.

The second part sought to remind the Security Council that UNSCOM had always had to deal with false disclosure statements, illegal unilateral destruction of relevant materials, and the practice of concealment. I wrote:

> This situation, created by Iraq, in particular through the inadequacy of its disclosures, has meant that the Commission has been obliged to undertake a kind and degree of forensic work which was never intended to be the case. The work of the verification of Iraq's

disclosures should have been far easier and been able to be under-taken far more quickly than has proven to be the case.

Third, over the preceding month, Iraq had failed to provide the complete cooperation it had promised and, indeed, had sought to impose new restrictions in some areas. Thus, having given deep thought to the meaning of my report, I concluded:

> In addition, during the period under review, Iraq initiated new forms of restrictions upon the Commission's work. Amongst the Commission's many concerns about this retrograde step is what such further restrictions might mean for the effectiveness of long-term monitoring activities.
>
> In spite of the opportunity presented by the circumstances of the last month, including the prospect of a comprehensive review, Iraq's conduct ensured that no progress was able to be made in either the fields of disarmament or accounting for its prohibited weapons programmes.
>
> Finally, in the light of this experience, that is, the absence of full cooperation by Iraq, it must regrettably be recorded again that the Commission is not able to conduct the substantive disarmament work mandated to it by the Security Council and, thus, to give the Council the assurances it requires with respect to Iraq's prohibited weapons programmes.

These conclusions stated the facts. As is evident, they focused only on arms control and disarmament in Iraq and Iraq's attempts to prevent it.

In forwarding my report to the Security Council, Kofi Annan chose to observe that our report included "material that relates to issues prior to 17 November 1998." It's not clear why he found it necessary to make such a remark, but apparently he sought to sideline that material by calling attention to it in this way. He also observed, "With regard to the period since then, the report presents a mixed picture and concludes that UNSCOM did not enjoy full cooperation from Iraq."

Annan then proposed three possible options to the Security Council: conclude that the experience since November did not provide a sufficient basis to move forward with a comprehensive review; decide that Iraq had not provided full cooperation but should be permitted additional time to demonstrate its commitment to do so; or proceed with comprehensive review in any case.

It is difficult to decide whether these options were shaped more by a relentless determination to help Iraq, whatever its behavior, or by discomfort with the facts. The second option—that Iraq be given more time—was particularly fatuous in light of the opportunities Iraq had squandered during its seven years by playing an elaborate shell game with UNSCOM.

Once my report had been circulated to members of the Security Council, I received a telephone call from U.S. Ambassador Peter Burleigh inviting me for a private conversation at the U.S. mission. As he had less than five weeks before, Burleigh informed me that on instructions from Washington it would be "prudent to take measures to ensure the safety and security of UNSCOM staff presently in Iraq." The United States had begun measures to reduce its staff levels in embassies throughout the region, and British authorities were doing the same. Repeating a familiar script, I told him that I would act on this advice and remove my staff from Iraq.

I went to my office and, with a small team of senior staff, commenced the implementation of what had become a detailed and familiar evacuation plan. On this occasion, however, we had to take care of some twenty staff out in the field some distance from Baghdad. They were a missile team conducting monitoring work northwest of Baghdad, halfway to the Jordanian border, a mixed group including nationals from three countries considered friendly to Iraq: Russia, France, and China. We'd decided beforehand that if evacuation became necessary, we would send eight vehicles from our office in Baghdad, pick them up in the field, and transport them straight across the border into Jordan.

In New York, we stayed up through the night until we were satisfied that the evacuation of the staff by air had been completed and that our staff leaving by ground to Amman had crossed the border safely into Jordan. Like the previous evacuations, this third—and final one—proceeded smoothly.

O N DECEMBER 16, 1998, the Security Council met to consider, as a matter of urgency, UNSCOM's latest report. This was to be the fateful day.

In introducing my report, I emphasized the Security Council's mandate to me to provide factual advice with respect to very specific promises made by Iraq one month earlier. The report was based on testing Iraq's cooperation and compliance in all areas of UNSCOM's work. It had been done quickly but thoroughly. In each of those areas, the chief inspectors had reported that Iraq failed to keep its promise. It was for these reasons that I had written the conclusions given in the report. They were unavoidable.

Lavrov, the Russian ambassador, rose to respond. He began by calling me a liar: "Either you lied during your recent visit to Moscow, or you've lied in this report—or both." It was a savage speech, in which Lavrov charged that I'd drastically curtailed the inspections and tailored the report to provide the United States with a justification for bombing Iraq. According to Lavrov, all of this was done while we were only weeks away from fully disarming Iraq.

Lavrov's accusations were based on two questions Foreign Minister Ivanov had raised during our meeting in Moscow. First, regarding the time it would take for UNSCOM to conclude its testing period, I'd made it plain that a further two weeks would be required, and I'd specifically mentioned December 14 as the date on which I believed I could sign off on my report. Lavrov now claimed that I had, in fact, intended to continue inspections for a longer period and then cut them short as a favor to my American friends.

Second, I'd told Ivanov that it could take UNSCOM as little as six weeks to finish the disarmament work with Iraq in the missile and chemical areas—if Iraq cooperated. The biological area would take longer. Lavrov now misrepresented these statements in the Security Council. He claimed that I'd said that all could be over within a matter of three or four weeks, although I never made any such statement.

My staff and I tried to speak with representatives of the Russian mission about these distortions but were turned away. We were later told through an intermediary that Lavrov knew that what he was saying was not true, but he intended to continue to say it. Lavrov also attacked UNSCOM's account of what had happened in the last month. He claimed that Iraq had offered us splendid cooperation in more than 400 encounters and that we had chosen to highlight the two or three instances of noncooperation.

As Lavrov was concluding his extraordinary remarks, a commotion was heard outside the Security Council meeting room. A messenger hastened to the secretary-general and whispered a message, which caused Annan to leave the room immediately. Other messengers soon appeared to inform us that the television set in the anteroom was broadcasting reports on the new U.S.-British bombing campaign against Iraq.

Operation Desert Fox had begun.

Lavrov seized this news. Declaring that all was now revealed, he argued that the news proved UNSCOM had helped facilitate U.S. military aggression. UNSCOM was dead, and there would be no point in discussing the report any further because it was not worth the paper it was written on. The council adjourned.

Some ninety minutes later the meeting resumed. I asked for the floor to reply to Ambassador Lavrov, who immediately left. I reviewed his remarks, seeking to rebut them in an objective way; the British ambassador also gave a reply, but there was clearly little interest in such a debate.

Secretary-General Annan issued a statement in which he characterized this as a "sad day," including for him personally. He emphasized the humanitarian needs of the Iraqi people and the wider region but failed to mention the need for compliance with the resolutions of the Security Council and never used the words "disarmament" or "arms control."

Subsequently, there was speculation—indeed, some accusation—that President Clinton's decision on Desert Fox had been to "wag the dog"—a decision designed to distract attention from the impeachment process then under way. Only one person knows the answer to that rather simplified thesis—President Clinton—but at least three very significant considerations make me doubt it.

For one thing, British Prime Minister Tony Blair was staunch on this occasion, as he was again a few months later in the NATO action against Slobodan Milosevic. It is not credible to think he would allow his government and armed forces to participate in a mere distraction. Second, although the U.S. president is commander in chief and the military chain of command is strictly observed, those who lead America's armed forces are not automatons. They are asked for, and give, their advice on the basis of the highest professional standards. Had they believed that the reasons in this case were specious, they would have raised their concerns with the president; given the way information leaks throughout Washington, we would have heard of this. The president would have taken an enormous political risk had he decided to put U.S. military personnel in harm's way for inadequate reasons or against their will.

Perhaps above all there were the basic facts at issue: Iraq's defiance of the Security Council, then its promise to void its decisions of October and to resume full cooperation with UNSCOM, followed by its breaking of that promise. A classic case of Iraq's cheat/retreat/cheat tactic. The belief that President Clinton's decision was taken for personal political reasons would tend to render these facts meaningless, where they clearly were not.

Almost a year earlier in Bahrain, my security guard, Dennis Grimm, had wondered aloud whether the president's travails would lead to "wag the dog," a phony war. My response had been to wonder whether the circumstances then unfolding in Washington might have the opposite effect—weaken the resolve by, or make it harder for, the United States to take an enforcement decision against Iraq, if that became necessary.

This is a complex issue not least because so much of politics today is fought out in public and on television, making public perceptions of policy and, additionally, anticipation of what those perceptions might be factors in decisionmaking itself. Grimm was thinking about a policy of public distraction. My concern had to do with a possible inhibition upon action. Theoretically, either could have been true, but the reasons I have cited above make it hard to believe that Desert Fox was decided upon for reasons of public distraction or the related concern to shape public perception that the president remained in command and resolute.

More important, both intrinsically and for an understanding of the December 1998 decision to use force against Iraq, are the questions, What did it achieve and what followed it?

Reports from the field indicated that Desert Fox did damage Iraq's weapons-of-mass-destruction capability, but perhaps because of its brevity (four days), it was not decisive. Paradoxically, it led to an extended absence from Iraq of any arms-control or disarmament work and then to the development of a new approach to that work, the effectiveness of which is questionable.

In these circumstances, it is hard not to see Desert Fox as a failure, particularly because of its brevity. This has led some commentators to argue, in retrospect, that it had indeed been a mere political ploy by the consummate politician. Such a conclusion would be less credible had the United States thereafter strongly resisted Russia's determination to seize the opportunity to declare UNSCOM dead, which it did with alacrity and success. If one uses the test of looking rationally at outcomes, without ascribing motives, it could be argued that the death of UNSCOM also became U.S. policy because that is what has happened.

Of course, policymakers in Washington may well protest: "How can you say that?! We continue to state that Iraq's arms must be controlled; we bomb them in the no-fly zones every other day; Congress has devoted money to getting rid of Saddam; and sanctions are still there (more or less)." Yes, yes, yes—but the weapons capability remains, and there is only a slim prospect that the proposed new control system will either be accepted by Iraq or will work.

This argument can become sterile quickly, and I certainly do not suggest that one and only one mechanism—the original UNSCOM—could do the job and that its demise was, thus, deeply wrong. A far more salient question is this: What will future U.S. policy be toward controlling Saddam's weapons capability? This should be an important issue in the campaign for the U.S. presidency in 2000. We will know well before November 2000 what Russian President Vladimir Putin's policy will be.

In the Conclusion of this book, I make a proposal for action to deal with the overall issue of controlling weapons of mass destruction. It begins with U.S. leadership, which might start with the current administration opening the issue with the new Russian president. Putin's inauguration and his desire to put Russia back on the world stage offer an opportunity to make a key decision on weapons of mass destruction, which the end of the Cold War has made possible. If the Clinton administration is seeking a historic legacy, this is it.

THE UNSCOM staff that had been evacuated to Bahrain and Amman were brought together in Bahrain, where I decided to maintain them in hope they might return to Iraq when military action was over. They still had much work in updating archives and records and designing ways to track down Iraq's remaining illegal weapons. They could do this in Bahrain.

At headquarters in New York, we commenced preparation for a comprehensive review. I felt strongly that there would be a need for a consolidated document setting forth the overall historic record as a baseline both for identifying what remained to be accounted for and profiling the

nature and scale of concealment. So we spent our time sifting information for this document while following the news accounts of Desert Fox.

The operation ceased after four days, with the onset of Ramadan, the
Muslim holy month. The bombing was relatively substantial and
seemed to be targeted at sites related to weapons of mass destruction and
the Iraqi military.

As people the world over debated what had gone wrong and how the
latest conflict might have been avoided, allegations against UNSCOM
multiplied, principally through articles published in the *Washington Post*.
Scott Ritter crisscrossed the airwaves promoting the idea that
UNSCOM had either knowingly or unwittingly been deployed by the
CIA to collect information to track, and perhaps eliminate, Saddam
Hussein.

The Office of the Secretary-General issued a statement on this subject on January 6, 1999: "We not only have no convincing evidence of
these allegations; we have no evidence of any kind. We have only
rumours. Neither the Secretary-General nor any member of his staff has
access to classified U.S. intelligence, although UNSCOM does." As an
aside, the first of these claims about access to classified U.S. intelligence
is not true; the second is—and entirely legal. The statement noted that I
had categorically denied allegations that we had assisted U.S. intelligence efforts in Iraq. Two days later, I issued my own public statement
denying the charges on behalf of UNSCOM.

The members of the Security Council continued to hold informal
discussions on possible action. Russia, France, and China—now joined
by Malaysia as a newly elected nonpermanent member—hardened their
positions in support of Iraq. In their belief, Iraq had been subjected to
misbehavior (including spying) by UNSCOM and to illegal aggression
by the United States and the United Kingdom.

In Moscow, Foreign Minister Ivanov had formerly been at pains to say
that Russia supported the implementation of the Security Council resolutions and UNSCOM's work in that regard. Now Ambassador Lavrov
was appearing on international television, proclaiming UNSCOM's
demise with undisguised satisfaction. UNSCOM, and especially
Richard Butler, deserved condemnation for their wicked misdeeds; the
death of UNSCOM merely brought Iraq one step closer to justice.

Canada had also been elected to a term on the Security Council. Now
Canadian Ambassador Robert Fowler stepped forward with a possible

solution to the impasse. Fowler suggested that the Security Council establish three expert panels to examine Iraq's compliance under the various resolutions, dealing with disarmament, arms control, and monitoring; humanitarian concerns; and compensation to Kuwait.

The panel concept, of course, was simply comprehensive review by another name. The Russian, French, and Chinese representatives staked out a predictable position in condemning Desert Fox. However, the United States and United Kingdom refused to back down from the reasons for which they had attacked Iraq. They argued that Iraq had to return to compliance with the law so that the work of UNSCOM and IAEA could be resumed.

After a fair amount of consideration, the Security Council decided to adopt a version of the Canadian proposal and to put the chairmanship of these panels in the hands of Brazilian Ambassador Celso Amorim, a former foreign minister of his nation. Amorim saw himself as something of a disarmament expert and seemed to relish the opportunity of becoming the man who might solve the Iraq problem.

Amorim was broadly sympathetic to Iraq, but, perhaps more important, he had a deep attachment to problem-solving as such. He'd said to me one day that he was well aware that Saddam Hussein was a homicidal dictator who had not been adequately disarmed and remained deeply attached to weapons of mass destruction. Then he asked, "But do we really need to have the Iraq problem on our table every six months?"

I was mildly stunned by the question. It implied a distinction between the substance of a problem and the need for its solution. To me, logic demands that the two be linked. When I pointed this out to Amorim, his response was purely diplomatic: "Substance is important," he agreed, "but we've all become very tired of the Iraq problem. Isn't there some way of getting rid of it, once and for all?"

"Certainly," I answered, "by disarming Saddam."

"Oh, well," he shrugged, "I'm afraid that's probably too much to ask."

This was the man the Security Council had just appointed to head the next phase of the disarmament effort.

Amorim consulted me about who should sit on the disarmament panel. He'd decided that the panel should include some twenty people drawn from various parts of the world, including a number of experts from UNSCOM. However, my participation was out of the question, having been firmly vetoed by Lavrov.

This Russian veto didn't much bother me. I thought the panel should work substantially at a technical level, and I was more concerned with having UNSCOM's technical leadership included. Nonetheless, I expected to attend when the recommendations of the panel were presented to the Security Council—in other words, I intended to be involved at the policy level.

UNSCOM staff worked diligently on a basic document that would serve as UNSCOM's main submission to the panel on disarmament. Despite the vast size of UNSCOM's archive on Iraq's weapons programs—several million pages of material—they managed to produce a document of just 280 pages that contained the basic overall record of what had been achieved and what remained to be done.

This document could be circulated only after it was formally accepted as a document of the Security Council. In defiance of the UN principles of truth and transparency, the Russians and others sought to suppress the document on the ground that it had been prepared by UNSCOM. Ambassador Lavrov even stated that he would refuse to read it. (Nonetheless, he sent members of his staff to UNSCOM's office to pick up a computer disk containing the document for ease of transmission to Moscow.) The formal acceptance of the report was brought about through the good offices of Ambassador Danilo Türk of Slovenia and Ambassador Peter van Walsum of the Netherlands, who exercised their right to call for the document to be formally tabled and circulated. After this, Lavrov did not protest the proposal to translate the document into the official UN languages. It's cheaper for the Russians to get Russian-language documents through the UN translation service rather than to pay for the translation themselves.

Having conducted an extended series of hearings in the disarmament panel, Ambassador Amorim submitted his report to the Security Council in early March 1999. Its most noteworthy features were a list of priority outstanding issues in disarmament and a lengthy discussion of the need to build an adequate long-term monitoring system that would both take care of issues that had not been finally accounted for in the disarmament phase and ensure that Iraq did not reconstitute weapons of mass destruction in the future.

However, the bottom line of Amorim's report was the same as UNSCOM's. Despite all the diplomatic machinations since the crisis of late 1997, as well as the extraordinary indulgence shown to Iraq by at least three permanent members of the Security Council and the Office of the Secretary-General, this disarmament panel, which was hardly stacked against Iraq, concluded that Iraq had never fully met its disarmament obligations under the resolutions of the Security Council.

It was for this reason, and because of the passage of events in November and December—Iraqi promises made then thoroughly broken—that another attempt at enforcement was made: Operation Desert Fox.

Months earlier, Tariq Aziz had said to me, with extreme bombast, "Let them bomb us, ten, twenty, a hundred missiles—it will make no difference. Tell the Security Council." I did and it didn't make a difference. Indeed, Iraqi defiance was subsequently rewarded, or at least appeased, by a version of comprehensive review!

Iraq's main triumph was the removal of all disarmament inspections and the shutdown of all monitoring systems. As the results of these efforts demonstrated repeatedly, they both worked. They had discovered Iraqi weapons and capabilities, mainly when Iraq's attempts to block them failed. Iraq's hostility to inspections is itself a testament to their potential effectiveness. The absence from Iraq of such work should be a source of grave concern.

Yet many people do not seem concerned. Why is this still so? I am indeed conscious of the fact that for most observers—interested members of the public—the story of UNSCOM and Iraq, of inspections and the recurrent crises, has been complex, with acronyms, technical jargon, the stiffness of diplomacy, and, of course, the difficulties of fathoming how a dictatorship operates. So perhaps it is necessary to attempt to answer, briefly, some of the main questions.

Is Iraq as dangerous as it was a decade ago? Elementally, yes. Although a good portion of the arms Iraq had acquired were removed, Saddam still satisfies the three criteria usually advanced in judging whether or not a crime was committed: motive, means, and opportunity. He clearly continues to have the motive and means to threaten great danger, and now the opportunity for renewed weapons development, given the extended absence of international arms control in Iraq.

Does the world community have an obligation to remove a person with a track record like that of Saddam? That is a difficult question legally and even more difficult politically. But there are laws under which he could be indicted for crimes against humanity. Serb leaders have been indicted, but their cases illustrate an important difficulty: the unwillingness of states to apprehend those who have been formally indicted. What is far clearer is the need and ability of the community of nations to stop the illegal actions of a leader such as Saddam. This was done for almost a decade. It seems the will for such action has now largely evaporated (see the Conclusion of this book).

What of UNSCOM? Did it behave badly, become a bunch of cowboys, allow itself to be captured by Western intelligence agencies? Would it have done better during 1997–1998 if it had been led by a more flexible, more compromising person than I? Not surprisingly, my answer to each of these questions is a firm "No."

Each issue encapsulated in these questions has been the subject of an intense propaganda campaign mounted by Iraq and, increasingly, by its supporters. It is said that the first victim of war is truth. Such was the case with respect to Iraq's strategic decision, taken late in 1997, to spare no effort in shifting the focus away from its refusal to carry out its obligations, to UNSCOM as an institution, and then to Richard Butler as UNSCOM's leader. The motive for this was to preserve their weapons-of-mass-destruction capability, which—they realized shortly after meeting me—I was determined to prevent. The truth of UNSCOM and its leadership was the prime target and first victim of this propaganda war.

In the vast majority of the countless inspections UNSCOM conducted, the inspectors behaved with scrupulous courtesy and professional integrity. While executive chairman, in the two or three instances where the behavior of an inspector was questionable, I removed that person from Iraq immediately.

As for UNSCOM providing intelligence assistance, I have answered those issues earlier in this book. I must concede, however, that the propaganda campaign was successful. The business of arms control is serious, and if it is to succeed it will always rely on intelligence materials—as it should. The prospect of using intelligence legally should bother no state that is in compliance with the law; it deeply disturbs those that are not. Outlaws hate to be caught and therefore decry the system which pursues them—in this case the use of intelligence. Iraq's citing of national sovereignty and dignity as its main concerns had resonance in a world of sovereign states. That world would do well to remember these facts if it retains an interest in a secure future.

As for my personal style—recorded in this book—the Iraqis had a brief look and asked themselves a question in 1997: Will this new man let us off the hook? Can we do a deal that will allow us to keep our weapons capability? Within a few months, they determined neither would occur. As subsequent months went by, their assessment was affirmed by the clarity I imposed on their disarmament requirements. These were not exaggerated, just very clear. The offer I made on a new "top-down" approach on biological weapons was an example. It was new and creative in an area that had been marked by extreme deceit—the "black hole." This offer was never responded to precisely because it retained, at its core, determination to find the weapons.

I believe that any other leader of UNSCOM who had the same determination—whether European aristocrat or reflective Buddhist from Southeast Asia, as opposed to an Australian who, because of his cultural and intellectual background, spoke straighter than is customary in those other cultures—would have had the same experience, because it has always been about the weapons and Iraq's determination to keep them.

Incidentally, the implied idea that Iraqi leaders are sensitive flowers who would respond positively to sweet talk is simply a joke. They regularly indulged in abuse, during our discussions, at a level that was simply extreme. I almost never responded. It was a game I refused to play.

Personalization of disagreements is a key Iraqi tactic; after all, it is consistent with a culture of intimidation. They followed this tactic with both Rolf Ekeus and me. Its basic principle is *shoot the messenger*.

During 1997–1998, Iraq's stance and interests were increasingly supported by Russia, France, and China even though it was defying the law they had made in the Security Council and for which, as permanent members, they had a particular responsibility. This phenomenon has revealed the real contours of the post–Cold War world in which these three key states have clearly defined, separate interests in addition to their obviously shared concerns about a unipolar world (see Chapter 13).

The period since the collapse of the Soviet Union has seen Russia absorbed by two fundamental concerns: the building of a new national political and economic system; and the loss of its influence in the world (indeed, the loss of its superpower status). Russia's Iraq policy has been built in this context, and it has addressed those two concerns, which are, of course, interconnected. The relative absence of U.S. influence in, and its difficulties with, Iraq has given Russia possibly its only opportunity since the end of the Cold War to act as a major power, coequal to the United

States. This is intrinsically attractive, plays well at home politically, and could help economically through Iraqi-Russian cooperation, especially in the oil sector. The U.S. actions on Serbia and in response to Russian actions in Chechnya have increased Russian determination to play its Iraq cards.

France has no comparable superpower aspirations, but it does have deep antipathy toward a unipolar and largely Anglophone world. It, too, sees U.S. difficulties over Iraq as providing it with an opportunity to advance its interests against such a world. And like Russia, it has identified potentially great economic benefits in its relationship with Iraq.

China sees important international issues through the prism of state sovereignty and integrity, particularly its claim to Taiwan and its incorporation of Tibet. The constant Chinese mantra in the Security Council asserts the fundamental importance of state sovereignty, nonuse of force, and nonintervention. Above all, China has an allergy toward any successful multilateral intervention in the name of international law (which it sees as cutting across state sovereignty), because it fears that such successes could, ultimately, build a case in favor of independence for Taiwan and Tibet. There is, of course, also the historic Chinese xenophobia—no small matter. These factors are so large that they almost seem to call into question China's willingness to carry out its wider responsibilities as a permanent member of the Security Council, although it would be patently absurd for the largest nation on earth not to hold that seat, as long as those seats exist in their current form.

This necessarily brief, and doubtlessly incomplete, analysis suggests that a way must be found for these states to exercise their great power in favor of the control of weapons of mass destruction without fueling their anxieties about a unipolar world—U.S. power—that have been reflected is their policy toward Iraq.

In conclusion, what emerged from the UNSCOM period, from years of extraordinarily expensive, time-consuming, dangerous, and unnecessary diplomatic and military maneuvers on several continents, was an anticlimactic denouement, which left still unresolved the challenge of Saddam Hussein and the threat he posed, and a revelation of the real shape of the post–Cold War world.

13

SON OF UNSCOM

A s I WRITE, there has been no disarmament effort or monitoring in Iraq for a year and a half. In December 1999, the Security Council adopted a resolution creating a successor agency to UNSCOM, the United Nations Monitoring, Verification, and Inspection Commission (UNMOVIC). To understand what this may mean for the future of arms control in Iraq and around the world, it's important to review the political maneuvering that brought us to this point.

While the Security Council debated various draft resolutions regarding the resumption of disarmament, UNSCOM remained in operation, though at drastically reduced levels of activity. We maintained a skeleton staff in Bahrain and a small team in New York but no field operations in Baghdad, where the UNSCOM offices and warehouses were shut down and sealed. As the months passed, the contracts of many staff members ran out and were not renewed. However, we kept about a third of our core technical staff, who spent most of their time in New York improving and completing our database on Iraq's weapons programs. This database still exists today at UN headquarters. It is a unique resource of extraordinary volume and significance. It is also dangerous—in the wrong hands. What will happen to it in the future is, therefore, a critical question.

During the spring of 1999, we hoped that a resolution defining a new disarmament mandate might be passed within a few weeks. That was not to be. First, the conflict with Serbia in Kosovo erupted, diverting the attention of the Security Council for three months and making it almost impossible for any other subject to be addressed. Work wasn't resumed on the draft resolutions until July, just days before the UN's traditional summer break. Then, from September until early December, there were repeated breakdowns and postponements in the negotiations.

At midyear 1999, my own status changed: On June 30, my initial contract as UNSCOM's executive chairman would end. I'd long known what that would mean. In January, after the very public and strident Russian attacks on me, supported by France and China, I'd realized that those three members of the permanent five would never agree to a renewal of my contract. I also felt strongly that the job I had been hired to do had changed in ways I could not support.

Accordingly, I made a public statement that it was not my intention to renew my contract with UNSCOM. I said I hoped that this last contribution to the disarmament of Iraq might prove to be my best. I had in mind plagiarizing the saying, "Nothing became him so well in his job as his leaving it." On this prospect and Russian and Iraqi propaganda, I said: "If anyone thinks my departure will induce Iraq to say, 'Oh, now that Butler's gone, we'll happily give up our weapons,' they're not living on the same planet I live on. Saddam's interest in weapons of mass destruction has nothing to do with me or my presence at UNSCOM."

I N THE SECURITY Council, the United States immediately made it clear that a proposed Russian resolution on Iraq—a resolution that closely reflected Iraqi preferences—was unacceptable. By September, the United States was prepared to support a British approach, which was by then cosponsored by the Netherlands. This proposal acknowledged that there were remaining disarmament issues that should be addressed without delay, after which an effective monitoring system ought to be established. Under the British plan, if Iraq cooperated with these two efforts, sanctions would be suspended for a limited time (ranging, in various versions of the resolution, from thirty to 120 days), with renewal if Iraq continued to cooperate. The actual elimination of sanctions would take place, as provided in the original resolutions, when complete disarmament had been achieved. The negotiations in October through December focused on the British-Netherlands resolution, and the U.S. and British representatives held several rounds of meetings in the capitals of the Security Council member states, seeking consensus.

The number of countries supporting this resolution gradually increased until, by November, the necessary majority of nine out of fifteen Security Council members had been identified, with eleven within reach. However, mere passage of the resolution wasn't enough. The United States and United Kingdom were eager to send a message of international unity to Saddam and, therefore, were hoping to win affirmative votes from as many as fourteen council members (China being the possible holdout).

In an effort to convert the Russians and the French, the United States and United Kingdom began making concessions—small ones at first, then larger ones. In November, the Netherlands dropped off as cosponsor of the resolution. Their ambassador, Peter van Walsum, is a distinguished diplomat I've known since 1970, when we were both junior officers at the UN. He takes disarmament issues very seriously, as does his government. They had a very clear sight of the politics that were being played out among the permanent five. The Netherlands decided to leave it to them.

As the resolution reached its final form, it continued to retain some of the crucial elements needed to produce meaningful disarmament. It specified that the new agency would be given, essentially, the same substantive mandate as UNSCOM's. It would also acquire the property, equipment, archives, rights, and principles of operation formerly enjoyed by UNSCOM. Iraq would still be obligated to fulfill the requirements set forth in all relevant Security Council resolutions. The outstanding disarmament tasks identified by the Security Council panel would then need to be carried out, and an effective monitoring system would be established. So far, so good. But the resolution also contained a series of worrisome provisions.

UNMOVIC would be under the direction of the UN secretary-general, which was never true of UNSCOM. Its executive head would be appointed by the secretary-general in consultation with, and *by the approval of,* the Security Council; such a formal requirement was not the case with respect to UNSCOM's executive chairman. He would be surrounded by a college of commissioners, to which he'd have to submit any major policy decision for advice and consent. By contrast, my board of commissioners were advisory only and had no policy authority. Furthermore, the UNMOVIC commissioners would not be technical experts but rather diplomats appointed by governments and representing the national point of view—in short, political commissars.

Whereas I was able to recruit staff directly to UNSCOM purely on the basis of their skills, UNMOVIC staff would be recruited under UN rules and would be, to the greatest extent possible, UN civil servants. Thus, under the new regime, the staff would not necessarily be experts; they could be replaced by bureaucrats. The resolution also specified that UNMOVIC staff must be given "cultural training" to ensure that they would be "sensitive" to Iraqi feelings—a provision that would make an ideal hook for a *Saturday Night Live* sketch.

Next, UNMOVIC was directed to draw up a list of final Iraqi disarmament requirements and inform Iraq as to what it must do to meet those requirements. This seemingly logical directive in fact sets up the possibility of serious error. Only one entity in the world can name the weapons Iraq has—namely, the Iraqi government. Now, in effect, UNMOVIC would be required to tell Iraq what weapons it has, and if Iraq was willing to say, "Fine, here they are," Iraq would be declared disarmed. A hotly disputed item such as the SCUD propellant would likely never show up on UNMOVIC's list, because the political commissars wouldn't allow it to happen. This provision in the resolution is the core of the political fix it represents.

The resolution provided that the cap on oil exports under the Oil for Food program would immediately be lifted. Other sanctions would be suspended for 120 days as soon as the new executive chairman reported that he was at work and receiving Iraqi cooperation. Every time he submitted another favorable report, the suspension would be extended for 120 days.

Finally, if Iraq was still cooperating after one year's time—three 120-day periods—and if some (unspecified) form of arms monitoring was then in place, the resolution implies that sanctions would then be completely abolished, irrespective of the state of disarmament.

These were serious concessions and would significantly impair the ability of UNMOVIC to credibly uncover and eliminate Iraq's prohibited arsenals. Were the flaws in the resolution serious enough to warrant its rejection? It's a delicate question. Many would argue that some UN presence in Iraq is better than none. This may have been the point of view of the Netherlands: It was apparently concerned that the concessions were excessive, but in the end it voted for the resolution. Others contend that a fig leaf of inspections giving respectability to Iraq while producing no true movement toward disarmament is worse than nothing at all, indeed, positively dangerous. Perhaps the true answer will emerge only over the next year or two, as the efforts of UNMOVIC encounter failure or success.

In the formal Security Council debate about the resolution, the Russians crowed about the fact that the final resolution didn't require "full cooperation" by Iraq but rather "cooperation in all respects." Understandably puzzled, a television reporter asked me to explain the difference. My response: "I have no idea. There's clearly no *real* distinction, but apparently an important political one."

In his speech on the occasion of the adoption of the resolution, Russian Ambassador Sergey Lavrov confirmed my suspicion. He explained that he found the word "full" offensively redolent of the past. It was the word I had supposedly used to justify military attacks against Iraq. And I'd highlighted the same word in my report to the Security Council, since "full cooperation" was what Iraq had promised and failed to deliver. Ambassador Lavrov evidently remembered this and so chose to substitute a synonym with apparently different political connotations. This diplomatic word-splitting will serve Saddam well.

A vote on adoption of the resolution was scheduled for the week of December 13, 1999. However, like most matters pertaining to Iraq, this vote did not go smoothly. The week before, Tariq Aziz had visited Moscow to urge that the resolution be rejected—despite the many concessions it contained. (As I so frequently experienced as head of UNSCOM, it's typical of the Iraqi leaders, when offered concessions, to pocket them as their due and immediately press for more.)

Russia had finally settled on a strategy of abstention. This would signal its support of its Iraqi clients while permitting the resolution to go into effect, giving Russia the appearance of being "responsible" on the international scene.

When Russia's decision became known, France asked that the vote be delayed for further consultations. It was a move inspired by French panic. France had planned to approve the resolution. But it was crucial, in its view, to leave no daylight between France and Russia on any question related to Iraq. To do otherwise could have jeopardized French business interests in Iraq. Thus France played (and continues to play) both sides of the street, happily accepting every benefit from its place in the Western alliance while never feeling seriously restrained in pursuing narrower national interests. They know that, after a period of agitation, their allies will always forgive and excuse them: "Oh, well, you know how the French are." They suffer no losses from this game, and so they go on playing it. The major French oil companies, Elf Aquitaine and Total, had signed massive contracts with the Iraqi oil industry; in addition, only two weeks earlier articles in the Iraqi government press had threatened to void those contracts if France didn't support the proposed resolution.

Thus, the French couldn't afford to let the Russians posture as Iraq's only true friend on the Security Council. They used the timeout to try to convince the Russians to vote in favor of the resolution and thereby preserve France's pro-Iraq position in the West. However, Russia decided not to budge, so France made its choice and went along with Russia (and Iraq). Of course, the West will forgive them.

The resolution creating UNMOVIC (resolution 1284) was finally passed with eleven affirmative votes on December 17, 1999. Russia, France, China, and Malaysia abstained. The hoped-for unity among the permanent five, which the United States and United Kingdom had so desperately sought and for which they'd paid the price of significant concessions in the final resolution, had failed to materialize. This was a serious failure in Security Council politics. The signal sent to Saddam was an unfortunate one: If even this compromise resolution couldn't be passed unanimously, what hope was there that the Security Council might be resolute in the face of the next challenge from Iraq?

Utterly predictably, given Security Council disunity, Iraq immediately stated it would have nothing to do with the new resolution and UNMOVIC.

Despite Iraq's stated (illegal) position, the resolution had been adopted, so the secretary-general, Kofi Annan, was bound to implement it. His first required step was to appoint an executive chairman of UNMOVIC within thirty days.

As the process advanced, Secretary-General Annan considered and discussed with the Security Council some twenty-five candidates. There was no agreement. On the due date, he courageously put forward his choice—Rolf Ekeus. This was vetoed by Russia and then France. Outside the council chamber, that is, on the record, the Russian ambassador said in public that Russia had blocked the Ekeus nomination because Iraq didn't want him! So Russia had delivered Saddam's veto. Lest there be any doubt about this, Ambassador Lavrov went on, promising that

UNMOVIC's program of work and staff appointments would be treated in the same way: Iraq would have to approve. As for the waning authority of the Security Council that this episode demonstrates, one can be forgiven for remarking "How the mighty have fallen!"

A few days later another candidate was put forward: Dr. Hans Blix, the seventy-one-year-old former head of the International Atomic Energy Agency. This was agreed to, although the Iraqis again reiterated that they have no intention of working with UNMOVIC.

Blix's first task will be to draw up a work plan for UNMOVIC, which he must submit to the Security Council for approval. There will also be action by Secretary-General Annan and Blix to recruit staff.

A week before Blix arrived to take his post, Charles Duelfer submitted his resignation to the secretary-general, stating "the original task remains incomplete . . . the body which created UNSCOM [the Security Council] now abolishes it without recognition of its work"; and "sustained commitment to credible monitoring and disarmament is difficult, if not impossible . . . in a political, multilateral environment with shifting objectives and priorities."

There is speculation that Iraq's declared policy of noncooperation with UNMOVIC is not firm but rather a negotiating position. The truth, at the time of this writing, is not clear. What is clear, however, is that Russia can be expected to block agreement on any aspect of UNMOVIC's role of which Iraq does not approve. Russia, which did not vote for the resolution, finding it politic not to veto it, will now deliver its veto by other means: preventing the resolution from carrying any real force.

But Russia is, of course, not alone on the Security Council. The extent to which it can have its way is proscribed, in part, by the policies of other members. If the United States, for example, fails to insist that the resolution be implemented honestly, if it allows Russia and others to traduce it, then we will know that the real purpose of Resolution 1284 was not to re-establish serious disarmament and arms control in Iraq but to solve the problem of Iraq's recalcitrance by political agreement—to declare victory and go home.

W E CAN NOW reflect on the history of UN attempts to disarm Saddam Hussein and begin to tally the extraordinary costs incurred by Iraq's unremitting policy of concealment and resistance.

They include the maintenance of economic sanctions, causing untold suffering on the part of ordinary Iraqis; the thousands of hours and hundreds of millions of dollars expended by UNSCOM on inspections that should have been unnecessary; recurrent cycles of military conflict resulting in needless death and destruction; the loss of authority suffered by the Security Council; the heightening of tension among the world's Great Powers; and, not least, the erosion of respect for the UN and for the nonproliferation treaties concerning weapons of mass destruction.

There have been other, less obvious, costs. The oil Iraq never pumped deprived its people of money that could have been applied to development. The ongoing crisis has also contributed to political and military anxiety in the Middle East, with an immeasurable impact on the larger peace process.

And, I feel bound to record, on a more modest but very human scale—there was the heavy price paid by the men and women of UNSCOM and their families.

Once, during one of our meetings, Tariq Aziz referred derisively to UNSCOM's Chilean helicopter pilots. I said, "It's interesting you should mention them. I just came from a meeting we held to say farewell to some of those pilots, who are on their way home at the end of their tour of duty. You know, they've done their work at great cost. One of them was wearing a little badge he'd made from a photo of his wife. He's a newlywed who left his young wife for three months to serve this mission. I think he deserves our respect, don't you?"

Aziz snapped back, "It was probably a picture of his mistress." That was Aziz—a foul mind and petty imagination. The pilot had had tears in his eyes when he'd showed me the badge. It was his most important medal.

All these costs, in dollars and in human suffering, may be traced to a single cause: Saddam's refusal to obey the law and give up his weapons of mass destruction. Yet Saddam managed not only to evade his responsibilities but to shift the focus of debate to the "wickedness" of UNSCOM and the suffering caused by sanctions. One moral is this: When a determined criminal flouts international law under cover of the principle of state sovereignty, the world system, as currently constituted, appears unable or unwilling to stop him.

If this message spreads, especially with regard to weapons of mass destruction, civilization will be dealt a double blow. First, when a rogue succeeds in facing down the authority of a legitimate lawgiver, the willingness or ability of the lawgiver to enforce the law is brought into doubt. Second, if Saddam gets away with his weapons program, other states—even those that are reluctant to harbor weapons of mass destruction—will feel obliged to obtain them as a deterrent against their less-principled neighbors.

The modern arms-control movement, launched in 1946 and given momentum on December 8, 1953, with President Dwight Eisenhower's historic "Atoms for Peace" speech, has played an important, often under-recognized role in maintaining global security over a half-century. The treaties against weapons of mass destruction—providing rules, standards, and methods of verification to prevent the proliferation of such weapons—were crafted with great difficulty throughout that period. The confidence they gave to the peoples of the world has been one of the great accomplishments of our time—one that has been damaged, hopefully not irreparably, by the behavior of Iraq.

THE EXISTENCE of weapons of mass destruction in the hands of such a regime is, in itself, cause for plenty of sleepless nights. This restlessness applies not only to those in the Middle East whom Saddam has sworn to eliminate; it also includes policymakers in the world's capitals. For them, the danger of being sucked into a regional crisis heightened by weapons of mass destruction is a serious one. But in a larger context, the greatest threat—the theme of this book—extends far beyond Saddam Hussein, Iraq, and the Middle East.

The fact that the Russians have adopted an advocacy role representing the interests of Iraq at the UN, as well as on the world stage, is deeply worrying. Russia continues to hold, but possibly not securely, thousands of nuclear weapons and substantial quantities of weapons-grade fissile material, the ingredient for more weapons. These dangerous materials can be classified in three ways.

First, there are nuclear weapons that are part of Russia's central strategic system, targeted principally at the United States. These include, for example, warheads for intercontinental ballistic missiles or other missiles that might be delivered by strategic bombers. These weapons are under the control of the Russian military and could be used, it is assumed, only with the authorization of the Russian president.

Second, there are shorter range nuclear weapons for battlefield and tactical use, including artillery shells and small missiles, some portable enough to be fired from the shoulder or by a small cannon. These weapons raise serious questions of control because of their portability and because they are widely dispersed throughout the country. Could a regional commander fire them without presidential authorization? How securely are they stored? No one knows for certain, but there have been reports that some are kept in tin sheds secured with a single padlock. Some of these weapons could fit into a large briefcase or a small trunk, which could then be picked up and carried away by an Iraqi or other terrorist. One shell could wipe out an attacking phalanx of troops and tanks; a barrage might be the equivalent of a Hiroshima-type bomb.

The third category of dangerous materials includes weapons-grade fissionable material, mainly plutonium produced as a consequence of nuclear fission in a reactor. Russia has manufactured vast amounts of plutonium in both its civilian-energy and military programs. Unfortunately, no one knows *how much*—a fundamental accounting problem that makes the theft and sale of nuclear material possibly untraceable. The former Soviet command economy worsened the problem. Factories would simply produce to capacity, whether or not the need for the product was real. And because of the employment they generated and the political connections of their managers, many factories producing unneeded materials never shut down. For example, the famous Russian T-34 tank used during World War II was produced for many years after its design had been superseded. Eventually, parts of the Russian woods were filled with needless T-34s, never to be used.

The overflow of unneeded plutonium stores is a similar phenomenon. Plutonium is stored in small pieces—rods cut into segments placed in separate, lead-lined boxes. This storage procedure is necessary because once an amount equivalent to some eighteen kilograms is put together, it forms a critical mass that could begin to fission spontaneously. And because of the accounting problem, it is possible that storage facilities in Russia contain quantities of plutonium that are different from the official records. Such discrepancies are ideal for the support of a black market.

Russia's economic troubles make the problem still graver. Of course, soldiers, scientists, and engineers who are poorly paid, if paid at all, are easy targets for bribery and the temptation of black-market profits. And the same national economic crisis has had other serious effects.

During an exercise in the fall of 1999, the Russians, for the first time in almost ten years, flew strategic bombers capable of carrying nuclear weapons over Norway. NATO forces went on alert, and planes were sent aloft to track the Russian jets. Afterward, the Russian defense minister admitted that the nation's economic troubles were forcing the Russian military to rely more heavily on their relatively inexpensive nuclear forces, rather than on relatively costly conventional soldiers and weaponry.

The general's statement has since been promulgated as official doctrine and reaffirmed by President Vladimir Putin, immediately after his election in March 2000. What this means for further progress in nuclear arms control, as well as the ongoing efforts to contain Russia's "loose nukes," is deeply disturbing. The closeness of the Russian regime to that of Saddam Hussein compounds the problem in a frightening fashion.

14

CONCLUSION: THE PRINCIPLE OF THE EXCEPTION

THE OPENING STATEMENT of the August 1996 report of the Canberra Commission on the Elimination of Nuclear Weapons, although it addressed nuclear weapons specifically, also applies, in virtually equal measure, to chemical and biological weapons:

> The destructiveness of nuclear weapons is immense. Any use would be catastrophic.
>
> Nuclear weapons pose an intolerable threat to all humanity and its habitat, yet tens of thousands remain in arsenals built up at an extraordinary time of deep antagonism. That time has passed, yet assertions of their utility continue.
>
> These facts are obvious but their implications have been blurred. There is no doubt that, if the peoples of the world were more fully aware of the inherent danger of nuclear weapons and the consequences of their use, they would reject them, and not permit their continued possession or acquisition on their behalf by their governments, even for an alleged need for self-defence.
>
> Nuclear weapons are held by a handful of states which insist that these weapons provide unique security benefits, and yet reserve uniquely to themselves the right to own them. This situation is highly discriminatory and thus unstable; it cannot be sustained. The possession of nuclear weapons by any state is a constant stimulus to other states to acquire them.
>
> The world faces threats of nuclear proliferation and nuclear terrorism. These threats are growing. They must be removed.

During the last fifty years, the international community created a collection of treaties designed to prevent the proliferation of weapons of mass destruction. These treaties cover nuclear, chemical, and biological weapons, as well as aspects of the missile technologies to deliver those weapons. The formulation of these treaties rested on three considerations. The first was a moral consensus to the effect that such weapons were inadmissible in civilized society and constituted an unacceptable threat to peace and security. Second was a political commitment made by states to give effect to this moral consensus by drawing up the relevant treaties, which were then opened for accession by all states. Third was the creation of international organizations charged with the task of verifying compliance of states that had signed the treaties.

This tripod served the international community and the objectives of the treaties well, although, of course, not flawlessly. The greatest impediment to complete success has been the decision by some states not to join the agreements and abide by their terms. But, the deepest anxiety faced by such states is that the treaties could be cheated on *from within* and that the means of verification would neither deter nor detect such cheating.

Saddam Hussein's dubious gift to this world has been to constitute the outstanding case for the possibility of cheating from within; in particular, having joined the Nuclear Non-Proliferation Treaty, he then proceeded to create atomic weapons clandestinely. This makes him very different from states such as Israel, which has created an atomic weapons capability but did not cheat from within, having never entered any of the treaties in the first place.

The other major question raised in the minds of states by the treaty-based approach to arms control is this: What would happen in the event of proven cheating? Would there be enforcement?

The anticipated answer has been that enforcement action would be taken through the political system of the United Nations, specifically through the UN Security Council. A number of the treaties make specific reference to the role of the council to this effect. For example, in the case of the Nuclear Non-Proliferation Treaty, all parties must enter a nuclear safeguards agreement with the United Nations agency having responsibility for nuclear weapons, namely, the International Atomic Energy Agency. Under that agreement, if the agency detects suspicious activity or what is defined specifically as "diversion" of peaceful nuclear activity to "any military purpose," such an instance is considered by the governing body of the agency—the Board of Governors. If the Board of Governors agrees that an infraction or suspicious activity is taking place, it must report this fact to the Security Council, which is expected to take appropriate political action, including enforcement of the treaty obligations, if necessary.

A few years ago, this mechanism was triggered when IAEA inspectors detected possible diversion being undertaken by North Korea in conjunction with one of its nuclear reactors. The established procedure was followed, leading to a report by the Board of Governors to the Security Council. But the Security Council refused to act because one permanent member, China, indicated that it would veto any such action on the basis of its close relationship with North Korea.

In other words, the system broke down. It happened not because there was any particular doubt about the substance of the report made by the Board of Governors or about the need for concern over North Korea's suspicious activities. The breakdown occurred because of the features of the Security Council system—specifically, the ability of any one of the permanent five to stop action in its tracks by using or threatening the veto.

This is the fundamental flaw in the treaty system: the unreliability of the enforcement mechanism. And if the worst nightmare of actual and potential treaty partners is cheating from within, then a close second (and, regrettably, a widely held anxiety) is that even if an infraction is detected it is not clear that anything concrete will be done to remedy it.

This gets to the heart of the political and security system created in San Francisco at the conference on the UN Charter at the end of World War II.

At that conference, it was considered essential to avoid the mistakes that had been made at the Versailles conference at the end of World War I that established the League of Nations. The main means to do this, established at San Francisco, was to place five permanent members within the Security Council and assign each the power to veto any matter of substance.

The Security Council was given responsibility in the UN Charter for the "maintenance of international peace and security." It was recognized that actions to maintain peace and security might include military enforcement. This was spelled out in Chapter VII of the Charter. But there was concern that the major-power victors of World War II might be reluctant to join the new organization, as the United States had failed to join the League of Nations, if they believed that this very enforcement power could be turned against them. Thus, they were given the veto to ensure immunity from potential actions against them.

In the years that followed, the exercise of vetoes went vastly beyond what was originally intended. The veto became the hallmark of the Cold War period, being cast some 270 times, mostly by the Soviet Union and the United States in defense of their interests and those of client states. The veto was also threatened on innumerable other occasions, with great political effect.

It has often been argued that even though the veto went beyond what was intended, in many respects it served as an important tool in managing the Cold War and possibly saved it from becoming a hot war. But over the years, the abuse of the veto has been and remains a matter of concern within the community of nations. Its use in defense of a state violating a treaty against weapons of mass destruction is, in my view, a disaster.

A more sophisticated way of viewing the post–San Francisco system—with the role of the Security Council and the veto at its heart—is to see it in the context of the perennial conflict that exists in international relations between power and principle.

Realists such as the great scholar Hans Morgenthau, and more recent distinguished practitioners such as Henry Kissinger, have argued that there are, in fact, no true principles in international politics, only interests, and that politics is fundamentally about the distribution and use of power in pursuit of those interests. This view is resonant of the balance-of-power approach that characterized Europe in the eighteenth and nineteenth centuries.

The other side of this argument is represented by the idealist approach. This school of thought recognizes, of course, that states have interests and may indeed be selfish about them. But it also recognizes that a politics based solely on self-interest will inevitably lead to conflict.

Therefore, it is argued, principles of behavior need to be developed to improve the role of law and civility in international relations, to mitigate conflict, and to permit the peoples of the world to use politics in pursuit of worthwhile goals that go beyond narrowly defined self-interests—goals such as peace, democracy, and human rights. When the pursuit of these wider goals conflicts with a nation's self-interest, reasonable means to resolve the resulting conflict need to be found, rather than choosing to abandon the principles of law.

Both pragmatists and idealists recognize and deplore the evils committed on the world stage, whether in Chechnya, Afghanistan, Rwanda, Kosovo, Iraq, or anywhere else. But their interpretation of these evils differ.

The pragmatists tend to regard such crimes as proof that the principles, such as those enunciated in the UN Charter—nonuse of force, human rights, and so on—are mere aspirations that are set aside whenever they are challenged by real power. For the pragmatist, international law carries no real or intrinsic weight, except to the extent that those in power are willing, for their own reasons, to submit to it. Under this reasoning, in effect, law becomes a mask for self-interest—the only true reality.

The idealist approach, which I confess to prefer, recognizes the challenge to the rule of law that is posed by, for example, Saddam, Milosevic, and, more recently, the Russians in Chechnya. If we accept the notion that the existence of such challenges invalidates the very concept of law or principles, then we are guaranteeing that the exercise of sufficient power will *always* overrule the law. The violations of international law we have witnessed repeatedly are inexcusable, but they do not render the law intrinsically meaningless any more than the persistence of homicides in civil society makes the law against murder meaningless. On the contrary, the laws and principles laid down at San Francisco and then developed, extended, and codified through numerous treaties, rulings, and international undertakings remain crucial to the future of civilization.

The laws that the international community developed during the past fifty years have been, and will continue to be, violated, and those countries with more power than their neighbors will always be tempted to seize advantage, even if it includes breaking the rules. But this only increases the need for an agreed system for resolving conflicts and for restraining those who would use force to violate the rights of others.

Irrespective of what one might conclude about this now ancient argument between power and principle, or with respect to the effectiveness of international law, I am persuaded that there are some concrete issues in international life of such gravity that they compel exceptional action and agreement. The need to control the proliferation of weapons of mass destruction, and to ultimately eliminate them, is the outstanding exception.

If we are to save ourselves from the inevitable use of weapons of mass destruction, either by accident or design, then we must provide the missing fourth leg: absolutely assured enforcement of the obligations under the treaties. That certainty of enforcement can be achieved if the following steps are taken: First, the permanent members of the Security Council must agree and solemnly declare to the world that they will always act together to remedy any situation identified by a credible report on the violation of any of the specified treaties. Second, this must mean that they will undertake never to use or to threaten to use their veto in such circumstances.

By these actions, they will make clear that they have given effect to what I suggest is the principle of the exception, namely, that weapons of mass destruction are fundamentally different from other threats to peace. They cannot be the subject of *politics as usual* because of their capacity to destroy everything. They constitute both the greatest threat and the great exception. This should be recognized and acted upon.

Had weapons of mass destruction existed in 1945 in the form they do today, it is possible that the UN Charter may have made special reference to them or, indeed, may have made them an exception. But they were not so known and therefore this was not done.

Since the end of the Cold War, there has been no global conference comparable to the San Francisco conference at the end of World War II. Had there been such a conference—and perhaps it is not too late—surely it is reasonable to think that one of the key questions at issue would be the main source of danger, indeed, the potential catastrophe, during the Cold War—the nuclear arms race. Another would have been chemical and biological weapons.

The permanent members of the Security Council should take the step I propose without delay. This would not be contrary to their powers or interests. It would not contradict the realist notion of the centrality of power; it would not signal uncritical support for an idealist approach to simply make an exception of weapons of mass destruction because of their special character. Indeed, success in this venture would enhance *their* security as well as that of all other states.

The permanent members would, of course, need to recognize that this action would have direct implications for them and their weapons systems. But in that context, they have already solemnly pledged to divest themselves of their own weapons of mass destruction through balanced negotiations. They must now reinvigorate that work.

In implementing such a nonveto agreement, there could be occasions where the only effective means of enforcement would be military action or the plausible threat of it. If, however, the Great Powers are firm in their commitment, this would be welcomed and joined by states around the world. As the norm of behavior outlawing weapons of mass destruction deepened its roots, the occasions on which military enforcement of that commitment become necessary, would be rare.

It might prove necessary to build a new international organization to carry out the work involved in maintaining the principles and treaties against weapons of mass destruction. Theoretically, a United Nations Council on Weapons of Mass Destruction could be established with the mandate to receive progress reports under the treaties, especially reports on infractions, and to take decisions on the kind of enforcement action needed to be taken, within which there would be no veto power. Clearly, this body would have a strong link to the Security Council because of the latter's overarching mandate for the "maintenance of international peace and security."

In this effort, the United States has an absolutely crucial role to play.

The key outcome of the end of the Cold War has been the emergence of a unipolar world with the United States at its center. But it must be recognized that the behavior of the United States since its accession to this incomparable power has received a mixed reception. During the past decade, we've seen the United States turning increasingly toward a unilateral approach to world problems. The traditional—and largely healthy—American debate between isolationism and engagement is being replaced by a rush, on all sides, toward unilateralism and engagement with the world only on terms dictated by the United States. This trend has caused anxiety.

Admittedly, the one remaining pole—the United States—is breathtakingly strong in military and economic terms. It is also one of the more benign superpowers in world history—committed to democracy and not imperialism, more peaceful than the Great Powers that briefly dominated the world in past eras. Nonetheless, the other nations of the world are increasingly asking some important questions: Do we want to live in a world dominated by one power, however benign? Should a multipolar world be sought in which several centers of military, political, economic, and cultural power could check and balance one another, much like the competing forces foreseen in the U.S. Constitution?

And doubts about the wisdom of specific U.S. foreign policy decisions only sharpen the question. U.S. decisions, such as the failure to ratify the Comprehensive Test Ban Treaty, add to the world's hesitancy to accept unipolarity. When American politicians promise, while reaching for high office, that if elected they will deliver *more* unilateralism and a *greater* emphasis on U.S. self-interest, it exacerbates the problem.

The American people and their leaders need to recapture the key insight of the post–World War II era: to define ideals and goals for international relations and then act on them is, in truth, eminently practical, not simply visionary.

At the end of World War II, the United States had the wisdom and courage to take the lead in shaping a new world order rooted in a principled view of international relations. The United States also acted with astonishing generosity to rebuild Europe and Japan. Generous America is needed again in the post–Cold War world.

There is another sensitive international political task for which the United States is uniquely positioned. The nations of the world that possess *undeclared* arsenals of weapons of mass destruction have an especially important place in the search for a new, more effective arms-control and disarmament regime. These weapons must be brought to the surface and included in the efforts to regulate and eventually eliminate them.

The undeclared nuclear arsenal of Israel, estimated by most experts as around 200 weapons, is a crucial challenge. Israel's motivation in creating such a stockpile is obvious: As a small nation surrounded by sworn enemies, Israel faces a compelling security challenge (India says the same of its situation with respect to China). Many in Israel view nuclear weapons as the guarantor of their national existence. Yet Israel's possession of such weapons in the heart of the volatile Middle East complicates the peace process, provides Arab nations (including Iraq) with a plausible excuse for their own weapons programs, and undermines the ability of the United States to stand unambiguously for arms control and disarmament. "After all," America's adversaries can claim, "the United States ignores the nuclear weapons held by its client state, Israel. Why should other nations enforce arms-control treaties against *their* client states— Iraq, North Korea, Pakistan?"

Action must be taken to reinvigorate nuclear disarmament negotiation and to bring *all* the world's nuclear weapons states into that work. This is actually envisaged in the relevant treaties. When that happens, one pivotal role for the United States will be to bring Israel into the fold. This effort relies on an overall Middle East peace agreement that includes guaranteed security for Israel. And an Israel without weapons of mass destruction must be able to depend on reliable international guarantees that its neighbors will never be allowed to build their own weapons of mass destruction. Building such a world is no overnight process. But it *must* come to pass one day if the greatest threat is to be truly controlled. As Israel's strongest and staunchest friend in the world, the United States must undertake to make this happen.

Similar action is required for chemical and biological weapons, for which the existing treaties, reliably enforced, would suffice.

I⊤ IS TEMPTING for any superpower to use its might in pursuit of purely national goals. In the early years of the twenty-first century, this temptation is especially strong for the people of the United States. International prosperity, the excitement of new technologies, burgeoning world trade, the spread of American free-market ideals and democratic values around the globe—all of these might make it easy for Americans to regard their nation's status as the last superpower as a virtual license to pursue pure self-interest at every turn.

Instead, Americans should regard it as they viewed their similar status in the aftermath of World War II—as a challenge to leadership. By leading the global community in the effort of reducing and then eliminating the unique danger posed by weapons of mass destruction, the United States can assure itself the highest and most justly honored place among nations in the annals of world history.

The greatest threat can be defeated by seeing it for what it is and excepting it from politics as usual.

Whatever approach is taken—in organizational terms—is of secondary importance. More important is to recognize and act on the certain knowledge that weapons of mass destruction threaten all humanity; that as long as they exist anywhere, others will seek to acquire them—the axiom of proliferation.

Realists can be expected to argue that this proposal is too idealistic, indeed, possibly utopian. I strenuously disagree. I am not capable of embracing the idea that a proposal meant to deploy the power of states against such weapons, the use of which could have consequences from which humanity would never recover, is fairly described as idealistic. On the contrary, this proposal is rooted in the ultimate realism. Its implementation requires the great powers to reorganize their priorities, their interests.

Finally, given my personal experience with Iraq, I find it irresistible to note how exquisitely appropriate it would prove to be if the consequence of the community of nations' failure in the closing years of the twentieth century to deal adequately with Saddam Hussein—and his addiction to weapons of mass destruction—led to a comprehensive solution to controlling those weapons.

By thus leaping right over Saddam to the larger problem, we could also take a quantum leap in our understanding of the relationship between power and principle in the twenty-first century. And it could not happen too soon. Right now, as I write this, UNSCOM has been out of Iraq for well over a year. No one is watching Saddam Hussein. You can be certain that he is not waiting idly for the UN to suddenly realize its failure. He is building—building weapons, as are other rogue states.

If a single missile loaded with nerve gas was to hit Tel Aviv, the world will never be the same. If a single canister of VX was released into the New York City subway system, the world will never be the same. If a single nuclear explosion hollowed out central London, the world will never be the same.

To conclude this book, I recall its opening epigraph, that is, the quote from Edmund Burke: "The only thing necessary for the triumph of evil is for good men to do nothing." Now consider these questions: What would Burke conclude about the challenge to all humanity posed by weapons of mass destruction? Would it meet the test of the triumph of evil if we did nothing?

Absolutely.

NOTES ON SOURCES

The source materials listed below are in chronological order in each of their categories. The chapter to which they are most relevant is indicated.

DOCUMENTS

"Report of the Secretary-General on the Activities of the Special Commission Established by the Secretary-General Pursuant to Paragraph 9 (b) (i) of Resolution 687 (1991)," S/1997/774, United Nations, 6 October 1997 (Chapter 6).

"Report on the Visit to Baghdad by the Executive Chairman of the Special Commission Established under Paragraph 9 (b) (i) of Security Council Resolution 687 (1991): 12 to 16 December 1997," S/1997/987, United Nations, 17 December 1997 (Chapter 8).

"Letter Dated 13 January 1998 from the Permanent Representative of Iraq to the United Nations Addressed to the President of the Security Council," S/1998/28, United Nations, 13 January 1998 (Chapter 8).

"Letter Dated 25 February 1998 from the Secretary-General Addressed to the President of the Security Council," S/1998/166, United Nations, 27 February 1998 (Chapter 9).

"Letter Dated 5 March 1998 from the Secretary-General Addressed to the President of the Security Council," S/1998/213, United Nations, 9 March 1998 (Chapter 9).

"Letter Dated 7 March 1998 from the Permanent Representative of Iraq to the United Nations Addressed to the Secretary-General," S/1998/207, United Nations, 8 March 1998 (Chapter 9).

"Letter Dated 9 March 1998 from the Secretary-General Addressed to the President of the Security Council," S/1998/208, United Nations, 9 March 1998 (Chapter 9).

"Report of the Executive Chairman on the Activities of the Special Commission Established by the Secretary-General Pursuant to Paragraph 9 (b) (i) of Resolution 687 (1991)," S/1998/332, United Nations, 16 April 1998 (Chapter 9).

"Letter Dated 22 April 1998 from the Permanent Representative of Iraq to the United Nations Addressed to the President of the Security Council," S/1998/342, United Nations, 22 April 1998 (Chapter 9).

"Letter Dated 16 June 1998 from the Executive Chairman of the Special Commission Established by the Secretary-General Pursuant to Paragraph 9 (b) (i) of Security Council Resolution 687 (1991) Addressed to the President of the Security Council," S/1998/529, United Nations, 17 June 1998 (Chapter 10).

"Letter Dated 20 June 1998 from the Permanent Representative of Iraq to the United Nations Security Council," S/1998/545, United Nations, 21 June 1998 (Chapter 10).

"Letter Dated 30 July 1998 from the Permanent Representative of Iraq to the United Nations Security Council," S/1998/703, United Nations, 30 July 1998 (Chapter 10).

"Letter Dated 5 August 1998 from the Chargé d'Affaires A.I. of the Permanent Mission of Iraq to the United Nations Addressed to the President of the Security Council," S/1998/718, United Nations, 5 August 1998 (Chapter 11).

"Letter Dated 5 August 1998 from the Executive Chairman of the Special Commission Established by the Secretary-General Pursuant to Paragraph 9 (b) (i) of Security Council Resolution 687 (1991) Addressed to the President of the Security Council," S/1998/719, United Nations, 5 August 1998 (Chapter 11).

"Letter Dated 7 August 1998 from the Chargé d'Affaires A.I. of the Permanent Mission of Iraq to the United Nations Addressed to the Secretary-General and the President of the Security Council," S/1998/726, United Nations, 7 August 1998 (Chapter 11).

"Letter Dated 10 August 1998 from the Chargé d'Affaires A.I. of the Permanent Mission of Iraq to the United Nations Addressed to the President of the Security Council," S/1998/739, United Nations, 11 August 1998 (Chapter 11).

"Letter Dated 26 October 1998 from the Executive Chairman of the Special Commission Established by the Secretary-General Pursuant to Paragraph 9 (b) (i) of Security Council Resolution 687 (1991) Addressed to the President of the Security Council," S/1998/995, United Nations, 26 October 1998 (Chapter 11).

"Letter Dated 2 November 1998 from the Executive Chairman of the Special Commission Established by the Secretary-General Pursuant to Paragraph 9 (b) (i) of Security Council Resolution 687 (1991) Addressed to the President of the Security Council," S/1998/1032, United Nations, 4 November 1998 (Chapter 12).

"Letter Dated 11 November 1998 from the Executive Chairman of the Special Commission Established by the Secretary-General Pursuant to Paragraph 9 (b) (i) of Security Council Resolution 687 (1991) Addressed to the President of the Security Council," S/1998/1059, United Nations, 11 November 1998 (Chapter 12).

"Letter Dated 14 November 1998 from the Secretary-General Addressed to the President of the Security Council," S/1998/1077, United Nations, 14 November 1998 (Chapter 12).

"Letter Dated 14 November 1998 from the Permanent Representative of Iraq to the United Nations Addressed to the Secretary-General," S/1998/1078, United Nations, 14 November 1998 (Chapter 12).

"Letter Dated 14 November 1998 from the Permanent Representative of Iraq to the United Nations Addressed to the President of the Security Council," S/1998/1079, United Nations, 14 November 1998 (Chapter 12).

"Letter Dated 26 November 1998 from the Permanent Representative of Iraq to the United Nations Addressed to the President of the Security Council," S/1998/1125, United Nations, 27 November 1998 (Chapter 12).

"Letter Dated 15 December 1998 from the Secretary-General Addressed to the President of the Security Council," S/1998/1172, United Nations, 15 December 1998 (Chapter 13).

"Letter Dated 15 December 1998 from the Secretary-General Addressed to the President of the Security Council," S/1998/1173, United Nations, 15 December 1998 (Chapter 13).

OFFICIAL CORRESPONDENCE

Letter from Richard Butler, Executive Chairman, UNSCOM, to Ambassador Bill Richardson, President of the Security Council, 16 September 1997 (Chapter 6).

Letter from Richard Butler, Executive Chairman, UNSCOM, to Tariq Aziz, Deputy Prime Minister of Iraq, 16 September 1997 (Chapter 6).

Letter from Richard Butler, Executive Chairman, UNSCOM, to Tariq Aziz, Deputy Prime Minister of Iraq, 1 October 1997 (Chapter 6).

Letter from Tariq Aziz, Deputy Prime Minister of Iraq, to Ambassador Juan Somavia, President of the Security Council, 29 October 1997 (Chapter 6).

Letter from Ambassador Nizar Hamdoon, Permanent Representative of Iraq to the United Nations, to Richard Butler, Executive Chairman, UNSCOM, 2 November 1997 (Chapter 7).

Letter from Kofi Annan, UN Secretary-General, to Saddam Hussein, President of the Republic of Iraq, 3 November 1997 (Chapter 7).

Letter from Richard Butler, Executive Chairman, UNSCOM, to Ambassador Qin Huasun, President of the Security Council, 5 November 1997 (Chapter 7).

Letter from Saeed H. Hasan, Chargé d'Affaires of the Iraqi Mission to the UN, to Richard Butler, Executive Chairman, UNSCOM, 6 November 1997 (Chapter 7).

Letter from Tariq Aziz, Deputy Prime Minister of Iraq, to Kofi Annan, UN Secretary-General, 6 November 1997 (Chapter 7).

Letter from Mohammed Said Al-Sahaf, Minister of Foreign Affairs of Iraq, to Ambassador Qin Huasun, President of the Security Council, 6 November 1997 (Chapter 7).

Letter from Adnan Malik, Head of the Department of International Organizations and Conferences, Ministry of Foreign Affairs, to Nils Carlstrom, Director of Baghdad Monitoring and Verification Center/UNSCOM, 13 November 1997 (Chapter 7).

Letter from Tariq Aziz, Deputy Prime Minister of Iraq, to Richard Butler, Executive Chairman, UNSCOM, 2 December 1997 (Chapter 8).

Letter from Richard Butler, Executive Chairman, UNSCOM, to Tariq Aziz, Deputy Prime Minister of Iraq, 3 December 1997 (Chapter 8).

Letter from Yevgeny Primakov, Minister of Foreign Affairs of the Russian Federation, to Madeleine Albright, Secretary of State, 4 February 1998 (Chapter 9).

Letter from Richard Butler, Executive Chairman, UNSCOM, to Kofi Annan, UN Secretary-General, and Permanent Members of the Security Council, 17 February 1998 (Chapter 9).

Letter from Ambassador Sergey Lavrov, Permanent Representative of the Russian Federation to the United Nations, to Richard Butler, Executive Chairman, UNSCOM, 18 February 1998 (Chapter 9).

Letter from Tariq Aziz, Deputy Prime Minister of Iraq, to Kofi Annan, UN Secretary-General, 23 February 1998 (Chapter 9).

E-mail from UN Secretary-General Kofi Annan to UN staff, 26 February 1998 (Chapter 9).

Letter from Kofi Annan, UN Secretary-General, to Tariq Aziz, Deputy Prime Minister of Iraq, 26 February 1998 (Chapter 9).

Letter from Richard Butler, Executive Chairman, UNSCOM, to Tariq Aziz, Deputy Prime Minister of Iraq, 6 March 1998 (Chapter 9).

Letter from Richard Butler, Executive Chairman, UNSCOM, to Ambassador Sergey Lavrov, President of the Security Council, 22 July 1998 (Chapter 10).

Letter from Tariq Aziz, Deputy Prime Minister of Iraq, to Richard Butler, Executive Chairman, UNSCOM, 23 July 1998 (Chapter 10).

Letter from Richard Butler, Executive Chairman, UNSCOM, to Tariq Aziz, Deputy Prime Minister of Iraq, 24 July 1998 (Chapter 10).

Letter from Tariq Aziz, Deputy Prime Minister of Iraq, to Richard Butler, Executive Chairman, UNSCOM, 25 July 1998 (Chapter 10).

Letter from Richard Butler, Executive Chairman, UNSCOM, to Ambassador Danilo Turk, President of the Security Council, 12 August 1998 (Chapter 11).

Letter from Kofi Annan, UN Secretary-General, to Ambassador Sir Jeremy Greenstock, President of the Security Council, 5 October 1998 (Chapter 11).

Letter from Mohamed El Baradei, Director-General of the International Atomic Energy Agency, Vienna, to Ambassador Peter Burleigh, President of the Security Council, 3 November 1998 (Chapter 12).

Letter from Richard Butler, Executive Chairman, UNSCOM, to Tariq Aziz, Deputy Prime Minister of Iraq, 17 November 1998 (Chapter 12).

Letter from Riyadh al-Qaysi, Under Secretary of Foreign Affairs, to Richard Butler, Executive Chairman, UNSCOM, 19 November 1998 (Chapter 12).

Letter from Richard Butler, Executive Chairman, UNSCOM, to Tariq Aziz, Deputy Prime Minister of Iraq, 19 November 1998 (Chapter 12).

Letter from Richard Butler, Executive Chairman, UNSCOM, to Tariq Aziz, Deputy Prime Minister of Iraq, 20 November 1998 (Chapter 12).

Letter from Richard Butler, Executive Chairman, UNSCOM, to Ambassador Jassim Mohammed Buallay, President of the Security Council, 9 December 1998 (Chapter 13).

Letter from Charles Duelfer, Acting Executive Chairman, UNSCOM, to Kofi Annan, UN Secretary-General, 24 February 2000 (Chapter 14).

SECURITY COUNCIL RESOLUTIONS

S/Res/687 of April 3, 1991 Cease-fire and establishment and mandate of UNSCOM.

S/Res/699 of June 17, 1991 Iraq to be liable for all costs associated with UNSCOM's work.

S/Res/707 of August 15, 1991 Iraq's compliance; inspection flights; Iraq to provide disclosures.

S/Res/715 of October 11, 1991 Approval of ongoing monitoring and verification plan.

S/Res/1051 of March 27, 1996 Approval of export /import monitoring mechanism for Iraq.

S/Res/1060 of June 12, 1996 Condemnation of Iraq's refusal to grant inspection access.

S/Res/1115 of June 21, 1997 Condemnation of Iraq's refusal to grant access and interviews.

S/Res/1134 of October 23, 1997 Condemnation of Iraq's behavior, further sanctions threatened.

S/Res/1137 of November 12, 1997 Condemnation of Iraq's behavior, imposition of travel ban.

S/1998/1194 of September 9, 1998 Condemnation of break of cooperation, suspends sanctions reviews.

S/Res/1205 of November 5, 1998 Condemnation of Iraq's decision to halt monitoring.

S/Res/1284 of December 17, 1999 Replacement of UNSCOM by UNMOVIC.

MEMORANDA AND NOTES

Notes from the talking points of UN Secretary-General Kofi Annan's briefing to the Security Council, 2 February 1998 (Chapter 9).

Memorandum from Richard Butler, Executive Chairman, UNSCOM, to Kofi Annan, UN Secretary-General, 9 February 1998 (Chapter 9).

Note from Richard Butler, Executive Chairman, UNSCOM, to Kofi Annan, UN Secretary-General, on Iraq's cartographic capabilities, 11 February 1998 (Chapter 9).

Memorandum from Richard Butler, Executive Chairman, UNSCOM, to Iqbal Riza, Chief of Staff, 18 February 1998 (Chapter 9).

Memorandum from Richard Butler, Executive Chairman, UNSCOM, to Iqbal Riza, Chief of Staff, 11 March 1998 (Chapter 9).

Unofficial transcript of presentation made by the delegation of the Republic of Iraq before an informal meeting of the members of the Security Council, 2 June 1998 (Chapter 10).

Note circulated by the Mission of the Russian Federation to the United Nations, "Proposals by Russian Federation for the Comprehensive Review of Section 'C' of Resolution 687 of the Security Council in Accordance with Resolution 1194," 28 September 1998 (Chapter 11).

OTHER OFFICIAL STATEMENTS

"Statement by the President of the Security Council," S/PRST/1997/54, United Nations, 3 December 1997 (Chapter 8).

United Nations Special Commission, "Necessary Conditions for Resolution of Priority Disarmament Issues," 4 June 1998 (Chapter 10).

Statement of Prakash Shah, Special Envoy of the Secretary-General in Baghdad, before the United Nations Security Council, 24 June 1998 (Chapter 10).

Statements made by Richard Butler, Executive Chairman, during the meeting held at the Iraqi Foreign Ministry, Baghdad, 3 August 1998, videocassette (Chapter 11).

Statements made by Tariq Aziz, Deputy Prime Minister of Iraq, during the meeting held at the Iraqi Foreign Ministry, Baghdad, 3 August 1998, videocassette (Chapter 11).

Press Statement by UN Secretary-General Kofi Annan, New York, 11 November 1998 (Chapter 12).

Samuel R. Berger, Assistant to the President for National Security Affairs, "Statement on Iraq," The White House, 14 November 1998 (Chapter 12).

Statement to the media by Richard Butler, Executive Chairman, UNSCOM, 8 January 1999 (Chapter 13).

PRESS RELEASES

"Security Council Expresses Intention of Restricting Iraqi Officials' Travel If Iraq Prevents Access to Sites and Individuals by UN Special Commission," Press Release, SC/6432/Rev.1, United Nations, 23 October 1997 (Chapter 6).

"Security Council Notes Agreement of Iraq to Rescind Earlier Decisions, Allow Resumption of UNSCOM and IAEA Activities," Press Release, SC/6596, United Nations, 15 November 1998 (Chapter 12).

OTHER SOURCES

Carr, Edward Hallett. *The Twenty Years' Crisis, 1919–1939: An Introduction to the Study of International Relations*. London: Macmillan, 1946 (Conclusion—arguments between realist and idealist approaches to international relations).

Morgenthau, Hans J. *Politics Among Nations: The Struggle for Power and Peace*. New York: A. A. Knopf, 1948 (Conclusion—arguments between realist and idealist approaches to international relations).

See also the writings of Henry Kissinger, both analytic and historical.

INDEX

Iraq's restrictions on size of entry
teams, 84–85, 115
return to Iraq following Russian-Iraqi
declaration, 107
Special Group composition, 147
Special Group established by
Memorandum of Understanding,
142, 144
threats to personal safety, 85–86, 88,
121
International Atomic Energy Agency
(IAEA)
Butler's posting as Australian
representative to, 13
and comprehensive review concept,
175
and Iraqi attempts to exclude
Americans from UNSCOM, 95
and Memorandum of Understanding,
141–142
role in disarmament of Iraq, 41, 78
and suspension of UNSCOM's
disarmament work, 187
and UN's failure to enforce treaties,
235–236
International law, 19
binding nature of, 34–35
idealist vs. pragmatic view, 237–238
implications of Iraq's noncompliance,
230–231
UN Charter provisions for
enforcement of, 34–35, 42–44, 163,
188
See also Iraqi noncompliance with
disarmament requirements;
Sanctions; Treaties and conventions;
UN Security Council
Iran, 23–24, 118
Iran-Iraq War, 18–20, 118
Iraq
Air force headquarters, 163–164, 196
cartographic capability, 131
Gulf War, 34–54
and Nuclear Nonproliferation Treaty,
23–24
payoffs to Primakov, 106–107
potential danger of, 218
relations with China, 165–166, 221. *See
also* China
relations with France, 221, 227–228.
See also France
relations with Russia, 104–109,
220–221. *See also* Russia

Russian-Iraqi declaration, 107–108
Iraqi leadership, 53. *See also* Aziz, Tariq;
Hussein, Saddam; Negotiating style
of Iraqi leadership
Iraqi noncompliance with disarmament
requirements
Amorim's comprehensive review
findings on (March 1999), 216–218
attempts to change terms of
Memorandum of Understanding,
140, 144–145
attempts to expel Americans from
UNSCOM, 91–92, 95–102,
119–120
blocked inspections. *See* Inspections,
blocked
CNN report on, 148–149
comprehensive review process used as
excuse for noncooperation with
UNSCOM, 196
concealment of weapons and
production systems. *See*
Concealment of weapons and
production systems
continued noncompliance following
crisis of November 1998, 194–199,
204–213
continued noncompliance following
Memorandum of Understanding
(February 1998), 150–151,
continued noncompliance following
"road map" proposal (June-July
1998), 160–165, 167–168
continued noncompliance following
UNMOVIC resolution (December
1999), 228–229
diversionary tactics, 130–132, 152–153
documents withheld, 50–52, 80, 120,
164, 169, 196, 207
false declarations on weapons and
equipment, 8–10, 50–52, 80–82,
159–160, 169, 178, 208, 220
illegal conversion of Volga and Al-
Samoud missiles, 162
implications of, 230–231
interference with aerial photography,
85–86, 150
interference with monitoring, 51,
99–100
landing rights denied to UNSCOM
aircraft, 73, 116
noncompliance subordinated to
UNSCOM's behavior, 109–110, 230

PUBLICAFFAIRS is a new nonfiction publishing house and a tribute to the standards, values, and flair of three persons who have served as mentors to countless reporters, writers, editors, and book people of all kinds, including me.

I.F. STONE, proprietor of *I. F. Stone's Weekly*, combined a commitment to the First Amendment with entrepreneurial zeal and reporting skill and became one of the great independent journalists in American history. At the age of eighty, Izzy published *The Trial of Socrates*, which was a national bestseller. He wrote the book after he taught himself ancient Greek.

BENJAMIN C. BRADLEE was for nearly thirty years the charismatic editorial leader of *The Washington Post*. It was Ben who gave the *Post* the range and courage to pursue such historic issues as Watergate. He supported his reporters with a tenacity that made them fearless, and it is no accident that so many became authors of influential, best-selling books.

ROBERT L. BERNSTEIN, the chief executive of Random House for more than a quarter century, guided one of the nation's premier publishing houses. Bob was personally responsible for many books of political dissent and argument that challenged tyranny around the globe. He is also the founder and was the longtime chair of Human Rights Watch, one of the most respected human rights organizations in the world.

. . .

For fifty years, the banner of Public Affairs Press was carried by its owner Morris B. Schnapper, who published Gandhi, Nasser, Toynbee, Truman, and about 1,500 other authors. In 1983 Schnapper was described by *The Washington Post* as "a redoubtable gadfly." His legacy will endure in the books to come.

Peter Osnos, *Publisher*